NIGEL HAWORTH'S
OBSESSION

DEFINITION:

"THE DOMINATION OF ONE'S THOUGHTS
OR FEELINGS BY A PERSISTENT IDEA,
IMAGE, DESIRE, ETC."

HOW A CHEF'S OBSESSION LED TO A DECADE OF FOOD FESTIVALS, ICONIC CHEFS AND CELEBRATED CUISINE AT NORTHCOTE

During his 25 years behind the stove at Northcote, Nigel Haworth has done many things. Among them are winning the hotel its Michelin star in 1996; putting Lancashire produce on the map with his appearances on the 'Great British Menu'; and keeping customers coming through the dining room doors for a quarter of a century with his innovative, accomplished British cooking. As one of the country's best-loved chefs, we've come to expect these achievements from him, but few would have predicted the way that Northcote – which sits 30 minutes outside Preston in rural Lancashire – would, once a year, become an epicentre for nationally and internationally celebrated chefs and food personalities coming together to cook.

Throughout the Obsession food festival, which has been held every January at the hotel for the past 11 years, this is exactly what it becomes. The festival has positioned itself firmly as one of the gems of the foodie calendar – hosting the likes of Phil Howard, Raymond Blanc, Pierre Koffmann, Angela Hartnett and Dieter Koschina among many others in its kitchens, and serving up refined, and often forward-looking, food to diners over the years. But while Obsession has gained momentum and culinary clout each year since its inception, it started rather more modestly, as an idea on a flight home from California, as Nigel Haworth explains.

"I went over to the festival of Food and Wine at The Highlands Inn in Carmel, California, off the back of a recommendation from a friend, Ian Harkness (former Chairman of Shire Inns), who had worked there for a week. I wasn't one of the billed chefs, but I was just going over there to work with the chefs to see what it was like. I stayed with Tony Baker, a former colleague of Ian's and now a great friend, who runs the Monterey Grill in Monterey. It was pretty inspirational – I ended up working with Charlie Trotter, Thomas Keller and Alice Waters, who was the doyenne of American food at that point.

"On my last day, after meeting Thomas Keller, we'd organised to go up to his three Michelin-starred restaurant, The French Laundry, and have lunch – which was, in retrospect, perhaps not the wisest thing to do before a flight home. Of course, we had an incredible lunch and I ended up missing my flight back to England. When I finally flew home, the week I'd had was fresh in my head. I started thinking about the possibility of doing something similar at Northcote. I knew we didn't have the same amazing wine culture as the Napa Valley but we did have great produce and stunning countryside in Lancashire. I was sure we could do something that would be interesting for the customers and be exciting and new. It also struck me that it would fill that quiet and gloomy time in January when there's nothing really going on. And so the festival was born."

When the idea was still very much in its embryonic stages, Nigel was down in London judging The Pierre Taittinger competition, when he got talking to Phil Howard (the two-Michelin starred chef of London's The Square restaurant). "I thought I'd be a bit cheeky and say, 'if I did a food festival would you be interested in coming up and cooking?' and he said 'without hesitation yes' and so, at Westminster College it started to take momentum." Soon after, Nigel won the 2000 Wedgwood Chef Potter competition, and the prize was a working holiday at The Saint Geran in Mauritius. It was here that during the filming of a food programme for Channel Four, he met and cooked with Rick Stein, Nick Nairn and Brian Turner, and convinced Nick Nairn to come on board.

An avid Blackburn Rovers supporter, every year Nigel goes to watch the team play away in Newcastle: the stomping ground of friend and fellow chef Terry Laybourne – and it was at one such match that he managed to entice Terry for the festival too. Together the four chefs started the first ever Northcote food festival in the January of 2001. Fast forward 11 years and the Northcote festival has become a yearly routine for Nigel, who, over the years, has extended the bill to seven nights and seven chefs then to 10 nights in the tenth anniversary year of 2010. But the first year was nerve-wracking and extremely tiring, as Nigel recalls. "I cooked on the Saturday night, and then a Jazz Brunch for 100 featuring Kenny Davern, a great character and jazz musician, on the Sunday. I slept all day Monday after doing that – I was absolutely knackered, it was a really big strain."

With top chefs appearing year after year (Phil Howard accompanied Nigel on the bill every year between 2001 and 2010), it's not difficult to see how Northcote manages

to fill all of the nights comfortably each festival. Looking back on the first ever festival though, Nigel remembers his anxiety about getting bums on seats. "The reason we did it in January was because it's a quiet month and I also thought I'd be able to access the chefs better then. You've had Christmas and New Year, and so to have something exciting at the end of January is a real attraction for diners. We didn't know if it would work, and it wasn't easy to fill. We managed to fill it though, and we did 50-60 covers each night."

The formula for the festival is a simple one: chefs can cook what they want, it is really about them expressing themselves for one night on the plate. "It's also about them coming up, having fun and spending some time with their family," says Nigel. "There are no add-ons. I encourage them to use regional produce from Lancashire but don't insist. They can stay for the whole week if they want, which some do. We've had some very merry nights – and there are some nights you can't get to bed at all."

OBSESSION

WITH SPECIAL THANKS

OBSESSION

ANDONI LUIS ADURIZ

ANDREW FAIRLIE

ANDREW PERN

ANGELA HARTNETT MBE

ANTHONY FLINN

ATUL KOCHHAR

BRETT GRAHAM

BRIAN TURNER CBE

BRUCE POOLE

CHRIS GALVIN

CHRISTIAN OLSSON

CLAIRE CLARK

CLAUDE BOSI

DANIEL CLIFFORD

DANYEL COUET

DARINA ALLEN

DAVID THOMPSON

DIETER KOSCHINA

ERIC CHAVOT

FERGUS HENDERSON MBE

GERMAIN SCHWAB

GIORGIO LOCATELLI

GLYNN PURNELL

HESTON BLUMENTHAL OBE

HUGH FEARNLEY-WHITTINGSTALL

JACOB JAN BOERMA

JAMES MARTIN

JEFF GALVIN

JOHN CAMPBELL

KEN HOM OBE

KENNY ATKINSON

LISA ALLEN

MARK EDWARDS

MARK HIX

MARTIN BURGE

MARTIN WISHART

MATTHEW FORT

MICHAEL CAINES MBE

MICHEL ROUX JR

NATHAN OUTLAW

NEIL WIGGLESWORTH

NICK NAIRN

NIGEL HAWORTH

PAUL CUNNINGHAM

PAUL HEATHCOTE MBE

PETER GORDON

PHIL HOWARD

PIERRE KOFFMANN

RAYMOND BLANC OBE

RICHARD CORRIGAN

ROBBIE MILLAR

ROWLEY LEIGH

ROY BRETT

SAT BAINS

SHANE OSBORN

SHAUN RANKIN

SIMON ROGAN

TERRY LAYBOURNE MBE

THEO RANDALL

TOM KITCHIN

TOM PARKER BOWLES

VIVEK SINGH

OBSESSION – A PASSION FOR PERFECTION

I have been accused of being obsessed with food, but I've never quite seen it that way. It seems to me quite normal to wake up in the morning wanting to eat the best food my money can buy. It seems quite natural to talk about food when you're eating it, to start planning the next meal before you've finished the one you're eating. It seems no more than right and proper to consider the source of ingredients, their particular qualities, the best possible way of preparing them, to anticipate the pleasures that they will give you.

And what better way to whet your appetite for the pleasures of the plate than by musing through the recipes in this book. Even if you can't cook all of them, or even any of them, you will have filled your imagination with the creations that range from the carefully calculated complexities of Heston Blumenthal to the inspired Indian originality of Atul Kochhar, from the elegant French classicism of Eric Chavot to the earthy British honesty of Mark Hix, from Italian intensity of Giorgio Locatelli to the idiosyncrasy of Glyn Purnell, to name only a few. You will have chewed over the Obsessions of some of the finest and most original talents working in kitchens around the world (although there are a couple of chancers included; I'll leave it to you to work out who they are). The fact that they have all come and cooked and conquered at Northcote speaks volumes about the magic of the place, and of the respect with which Nigel Haworth and Craig Bancroft are held. They are two men with a passion for food, if ever there were.

But at what point does a passion become an Obsession? I've never quite known the answer to that. The great Carlo Petrini, founder and president of Slow Food, in answer to a question about why he was obsessed with food, replied, "If I wear a pair of Armani pants they do not become a part of Carlo Petrini. If I eat a slice of ham, it becomes a part of Carlo Petrini. That is why I am passionate about what I eat." Passion? Obsession? Does it matter? It's the food that counts. And the pleasure. And there's more than your fair share in these pages.

Matthew Fort

OBSESSION

The Obsession Chefs	4
Foreword by Matthew Fort	5
2 0 1 1	10
Kenny Atkinson	20
Martin Burge	22
Martin Wishart	26
Simon Rogan	28
Hugh Fearnley-Whittingstall	30
Claire Clark	32
Lisa Allen	36
James Martin	38
Sat Bains	40
Vivek Singh	42
Nigel Haworth	44
2 0 1 0	48
Tom Kitchin	56
Matthew Fort and Tom Parker Bowles	58
Theo Randall	60
Ken Hom	62
Angela Hartnett	64
Lisa Allen	66
Nathan Outlaw	70
Phil Howard	72
Jacob Jan Boerma	74
Andrew Fairlie	76
Nigel Haworth	78

2 0 0 9	82
Daniel Clifford	88
Shaun Rankin	90
Glynn Purnell	92
Brett Graham	94
Phil Howard	96
Atul Kochhar	100
Jason Atherton	102
Paul Heathcote	104
Nigel Haworth	106
2 0 0 8	110
Anthony Flinn	114
Mark Edwards	116
Pierre Koffmann	118
Angela Hartnett	120
Phil Howard	124
Shane Osborn	126
Nigel Haworth	128
2 0 0 7	130
Andrew Pern	136
Raymond Blanc	138
Michel Roux Jr	140
Paul Cunningham	142
Michael Caines	144
Phil Howard	146
Nigel Haworth	150

2 0 0 6	152
Claude Bosi	156
David Thompson	158
Fergus Henderson	160
Andoni Luis Aduriz	162
Mark Hix	166
Bruce Poole	168
Phil Howard	170
Nigel Haworth	174
2 0 0 5	178
Eric Chavot	182
Sat Bains	184
Dieter Koschina	186
Roy Brett	188
Phil Howard	190
Richard Corrigan	192
Nigel Haworth	194
2 0 0 4	198
Peter Gordon	202
John Campbell	204
Rowley Leigh	208
Darina Allen	210
Phil Howard	212
Giorgio Locatelli	214
Nigel Haworth	218

2 0 0 3	220
Chris Galvin	224
Jeff Galvin	228
Christian Olsson	230
Phil Howard	232
Heston Blumenthal	234
Neil Wigglesworth	238
Nigel Haworth	240
2 0 0 2	244
Germain Schwab	248
Phil Howard	252
Robbie Millar	254
Brian Turner	256
Danyel Couet	258
Nigel Haworth	260
2 0 0 1	264
Terry Laybourne	268
Nigel Haworth	270
Phil Howard	274
Nick Nairn	278
Wine Man	280
Hospitality Action	282
Obsession Recipes/Chefs' Restaurants Index	284
Sponsors	288

OBSESSION

OBSESSION

2nd Edition published in 2011

First published in 2010 by Buckingham Book Publishing Ltd

Network House, 28 Ballmoor, Celtic Court, Buckingham MK18 1RQ

www.chefmagazine.co.uk

© Buckingham Book Publishing Ltd, 2011

In association with:

Northcote, Northcote Road, Langho, Blackburn, Lancashire BB6 8BE
www.northcote.com

Printed by Craft Print International Ltd

ISBN 978-0-9562661-9-4

Printed in Singapore

Publisher:	Peter Marshall
Managing Editor:	Shirley Marshall
Editor:	Sue Christelow
Assistant Editor:	Hilary Mayes
Assistant Editor:	Katy Morris
Design Director:	Philip Donnelly
Photography:	Myburgh du Plessis, with the assistance of Alice Warren, except:

Keith Pollard – Andrew Fairlie, Andrew Pern, Anthony Flinn, Atul Kochhar,

Kenny Atkinson, Martin Wishart, Phil Howard, Roy Brett, Shaun Rankin, Simon Rogan, Terry Laybourne, Tom Kitchin.

Hugh Adams – Andoni Luis Aduriz, Angela Hartnett, Christian Olsson, Danyel Couet, Darina Allen, Dieter Koschina, Nathan Outlaw.

Hugh Fearnley-Whittingstall, Jacob Jan Boerma, Ken Hom and Raymond Blanc images supplied.

Contributor:	Rosie Birkett

Eleven years of Northcote's Food and Wine Festival – our Obsession. I suppose on reflection we can't believe in many ways that a small idea has become a major part of our annual calendar, an obsession that really can never be let go.

The evolution has been an incredible journey, the people we have met, the friends we have made, the respect that has been earned and the skills that have been shared. That's what the whole story is about, an obsession of food, flavour and friendship, like minds coming together in 10 days of brilliance in the wilds of Lancashire in the depths of a January winter.

This book, that we hope you will enjoy, is part of the eleven years of our Obsession; a celebration and testament to everyone who has taken part over the years in whatever way. The journey would not have been possible without the commitment of all the staff, both in the kitchen, front of house and behind the scenes. The administration and marketing have been huge and the organisation incredible, but each year we have made it unscathed so a big thanks must go to Kaye Mathew for the eleven years' work behind this Obsession and its development. My head chefs over the years have been fantastic, Warwick Dodds and, in particular, none have assisted more than the brilliant and dedicated Lisa Allen. Lisa over the 10 years she has worked for me and the six years she has been head chef has maintained outstanding standards.

Sponsors deserve an enormous thank you – there are too many to mention all individually, but without them we could have never financed and driven this Obsession. I would, however, like to thank Nick Green and all the team at Villeroy and Boch for their support throughout the whole journey. EBLEX has supported us brilliantly over the years as has The Mall Group and this year we add our thanks to Baxter Storey for their support as a main sponsor. Louis Roederer continue their support, supplying us all with some of the finest Champagne available. Huge thanks must go to all our guests, family and friends who have stood by us and supported us by dining at the festival to join in our Obsession as without their willingness to attend there would be no festival. Lastly, Craig and I would like to thank our long-suffering wives, Kath and Helen, for their immense understanding throughout the eleven years of Obsession and the development of The Northcote Group; without their support we wouldn't be able to have our Obsession!

So it is here – eleven glorious years of an incredible Obsession. We sincerely hope you enjoy the moment and continue to enjoy it for many years to come.

NIGEL AND CRAIG

OBSESSION

2011

2011

Who said we wouldn't do 10 nights again? Despite the fatigue, the sore feet and weary limbs of 2010's last moments and the bodies of all the team saying never again. However, once all the euphoria had died down it was agreed unanimously, there was no going back from 10 nights. To see 10 different styles of food, characters and service over 10 days was an experience never to be forgotten. The planning for Obsession 11 started straight away and it was not long before we had the lineup of chefs secured for our eleventh year.

The first evening brought the brilliant Kenny Atkinson of The Orangery at Rockcliffe Hall. The North East delegation arrived the day before and enjoyed an afternoon watching quality football at Ewood Park, the home of Blackburn Rovers FC, followed by dinner at Northcote. Kenny and his team of three, the equally hardworking Tony, Rob and Dan, set to work in bringing the tastes of The Orangery including his famous 2010 'Great British Menu (GBM)' dish of North Sea mackerel bread wrapped with gooseberry textures which was

fantastic, helped by the superb quality of the mackerel from Inshore Fisheries.

Kenny's main course of the braised pig's cheek with his interpretation of pease pudding was equally fantastic and great with the Pinotage. It was a display by the 'little people' of true Great British cookery using the best of ingredients to the pleasure of our packed house on the opening night. The night was a huge success with those canny lads enjoying the customary Obsession late night at the bar.

The team from Martin Burge arrived during Monday ahead of the boss himself who was having to stay back at base to execute a busy Burns night. Tim, Robin and Adam arrived in good time to get the preparation done to ensure the two Michelin stars of Whatley would shine bright on the Obsession stage. The Whatley team began early with much work to do and an urgent request for some butternut squash fondants to be ferried up the motorway from Whatley as they had been missed off the van – they were expensive butternut squash fondants!

Martin's menu was one of true panache and intricate detail, the opening dish of mushroom foam with truffle essence and parmesan bon bon made an immediate impression – truffle scent filled the room and the customer reaction was truly appreciative of how something so small and delicate could be so powerful. Each dish met with similar reaction with the highlight of a superb venison roasted with caramelised bacon with its own sausage, cabbage purée and a hint of chocolate – brilliant.

Martin Wishart's day was next with the advance party arriving on Tuesday. It was great to see one of our old boys, Michael Yates, in this team, a local lad who was at Northcote in 2007 ably assisted by an ex-member of

Martin's team now based in the Lakes, Ryan. The boys had a lot to do on Martin's behalf but well briefed they got stuck in to create a menu full of homage to the great Scottish larder. Although one major ingredient had not arrived as scheduled – those elusive Scottish langoustines were nowhere to be seen! The boys managed to grab a break with a short lunch at The Fishes. Up bright and early the next morning with an air of expectation, but where were those langoustines? Finally they arrived one minute in front of Martin Wishart – he had practically followed them down the M6!

Martin was this year's AA Chef of the Year voted by his peers and is someone who holds huge respect in the industry. We were all looking forward to his Obsession menu and we weren't to be disappointed. Loch Fyne crab with a veal tartare was an absolute sensation, subtle, interesting and different, Dom Ott Rose the perfect foil followed by great ceviche of Scrabster halibut and a superbly flavoured Galloway braised beef cheek that was melt in the mouth – intense flavours with a superb twist of difference in the pumpkin seed brittle.

This was the night that chefs descended on Northcote – Terry Laybourne, the Newcastle legend, Ed Wilson from Terroir in London, James Mackenzie from The Pipe and Glass, Peter Neville from The Pheasant at Harome as guests and the arrival of Simon Rogan's team Mark, Richard, Simon and Penny. A gastronomic gathering of chefs and friends.

All late to bed on Wednesday evening, a few sore heads were apparent in the morning. Alas the L'Enclume team had an early start; great to see Mark Birchall back in the Northcote kitchen working alongside Lisa after an absence of six years. Mark is now Simon's Head Chef at L'Enclume. Simon and his wife Penny have created a very special place in the beautiful village of Cartmel with a unique style of food – it was a pleasure to have him at Obsession delivering the Rogan approach.

Farm to Fork is very much at the heart of Simon's food especially with his keen interest in growing organic produce at Howbarrow Farm. The menu started with a fabulous cod yolk with crispy rice and smoked bacon, which set the tone of the menu – simple delicate flavours with that unique creativity. A garden of Jerusalem artichokes was next; simply brilliant, then langoustines and herbs abound with Lady's Smock and Red Russian kale, stunning skate and a shoulder of Martin Gott's

suckling pig with young leeks for a main course – great dish until I realised I had twelve shoulder-less suckling pigs to use up after, no worries it was well worth it.

The River Cottage team were with us on Thursday, looking forward to Simon's evening. Tim, Gill and Gideon arrived as the advance party preparing the ground for Hugh's arrival the next day. The great spirit that runs through River Cottage and all that it stands for was very much in evidence as the guys prepared for Friday. We treated them to a Fishes pub lunch that went down a storm (fish, chips, squid and scampi).

The menu was a real taste of the best ingredients in their most simple form, letting the ingredients do all the work. The boys prepped and were ready to roll as Hugh arrived from his hugely busy schedule with his current worthy campaign 'Fish Fight' hitting the headlines, which

quite rightly had everyone talking. Hugh cast his eye over the kitchen to check the dishes with the team and then entertained the guests all evening while Tim, Gill and Gideon produced a superb dinner. The tenderest of venison carpaccio served with herbs and oils with fantastic flavours, home-made mozzarella made on the day by Gideon from unpasteurised organic milk from Gazegill Farm at Rimmington, fresh from the cows that morning, served with River Cottage's own cured hams and butternut squash – utterly superb. To follow a cerviche of gurnard and scallops and then hearty smoked pig's cheeks followed by a rhubarb crumble to die for. Hugh toured the tables to the delight of our guests who enjoyed a genuine River Cottage evening of great food, relaxed and full of fun.

OBSESSION

Our long-term friend and incredible pastry chef Claire Clark agreed to join Lisa in the Northcote kitchen for ladies' night. Assisting Claire was David, one of the chefs from Harvey Nichols in London. True to her word she was up early at 6.00am in the kitchen with David to start the mise en place, time needed to prepare 15 different types of petit fours and a very intricate dessert, devil's food cake with baked caramel and marshmallow – a very posh s'mores – not to mention a velvety light cheese soufflé. Of course our guest chef Claire was one half of an incredible duo with our very own blonde, Lisa Allen, taking the savoury dishes of tartare of Dexter beef with cured tongue followed by scallops, so elegant and subtle with ginger and lime accompanied by a fresh seaweed

texture. Wonderful Scottish lobster scallops and pumpkin risotto were certainly luxurious and hit the spot. Those Goosnargh ducks had an outing again, carefully put together as a trio with pickled girolles, parsnips and apple purée; grilled Ogle Shield Cheese with a fabulous pairing of Artisan Beer from Bowland made in the Champagne method was superb. The finale, however, was the white chocolate and whisky croissant butter pudding with single malt ice cream – James says this is probably his signature dish and what a dessert, so rich and moreish with a mere 2000 calories a portion! A good night followed although James and Chris had an early start being due in Abu Dhabi for a banquet for 500 people two days later.

The following night saw the return of a veteran (to replace Phil Howard who retired after 10 incredible years of support for Obsession). Sat Bains was the chosen man; his last visit was in 2005.

A great friend and serious talent, he and his team decided that they could not make it the night before with the team returning from a cooking demo in Milan. Time was going to be a bit tight but that was no worry to Sat, he arrived with John, Alex, Adam and Nanna (The Forager). As it turned out John had broken the key in the restaurant door and Alex had overslept – no pressure chief – no lunch for them! Not only was he late he can't count either, eight courses on a Monday could be a bridge too far, but we have been wrong before. The menu started with cured mackerel and caviar, pork belly and a purée of piccalilli, an obvious but stunning combination. Next was organic salmon, and oyster miso and naked celeriac

bouillon. Reggie's corn-fed Goosnargh duck liquorice, chicory and salted nuts was an absolute 'wow' and matched perfectly with the Pinot from Bon Climat.

Sunday came after yet another late evening with James Martin arriving after 'Saturday Kitchen', zooming up in the Bentley just in time to take a quick bow in our thanks to the Claire and Lisa night. Nigel, having appeared on 'Saturday Kitchen' with James, had ensured that this was a night, the Lancashire-Yorkshire banter would be strong and no doubt good humoured. James was ably assisted by Chris Start, his Executive Chef, who did a fantastic job in preparing the kitchens in advance.

Ham hock ballontine slightly warm with a deep fried hen's egg was a rustic start packed with flavour and

with winter truffles sent shivers down your taste buds – superb in every way. The special course of a forager's salad named after his postcode and our postcode was NG7-BB6 – genius. Foraging from Nottingham and foraging from Northcote provided an interesting blend of natural edible herbs and plants all from our uncultivated garden areas. Braised mutton, so rich and soft to the palate with intense flavours, was memorable, followed by great chocolate and refreshing rhubarb to finish – fantastic. We were in for a good night after service. Sat was on top form, the bar was buzzing and the gin and tonics flowing like a dream – large Blackwoods 60 certainly set us all up for a belter. Late to bed yet again rounded off with a local curry in the early hours was perhaps not the best idea in hindsight but very welcome at the time.

Tuesday night was The Cinnamon Club evening and one we were really looking forward to. Vivek, Hari and Palash arrived on the Monday and really enjoyed the Sat Bains experience with his brigade the night before. The Cinnamon team were in bright and early and the house smelt of fragrances and spices not common in the Northcote kitchen. Having seen Sat's extensive menu Vivek decided to make his own canapés and add a course in for good measure. Hari and Palash worked calmly and precisely blending spices and refining the dishes for Vivek's approval. What a sensational evening was about to unfold with a range of dishes that challenged the wine team. The delicacy and skill of the spice work was brilliant, every dish had subtle heat starting with a presence and building with more purpose till the heat was more intense. Beautiful scallops and mussels, subtle sweet and delightful with a great Vouvray for a perfect match. The squab pigeon tandoori was just sublime, so tender with its green chilli, coriander and pesto, vibrant colours and beautifully presented, which met with serious approval from the Tuesday night crowd. Great sea bass followed and then the most superb Cumbrian lamb with a beignet of sweetbreads and kidney with hints of cumin and spinach, tender pink lamb, just a hint of smoke and a gentle heat that intensified, superb with the Rioja and a real joy. The whole evening was a masterclass in Indian cuisine, really well appreciated by the audience. We had a quieter night after everyone left with an enjoyable hour or three with Vivek and his team discussing the interest in Indian cuisine and all aspects of its interpretation. We seriously appreciated their visit north.

The last night was here, my night, always a bit of extra effort needed by our tired team who had done a brilliant job for nine days. This year was going to be a tad

harder without the valuable assistance of Lisa who was away at the 'GBM' heats for this year's competition. 'Lisa Moore' and 'Tommy P', my Sous Chefs, did a great job in pulling the team together and the tenth night ran like clockwork. The John Dory and sage with our favoured Portuguese ham from the wine estate of Julian Reynolds in Portugal came together brilliantly and ate really well. The traditional breed of Indian Game chicken from Bill in Tarleton with black peas made a great dish with medjool dates. Runny butternut squash risotto, a new dish for Obsession, went down well and set everyone up for the Belted Galloways, supplied from Robert Greaves and which were in tremendous condition, aged for twenty eight days, beautiful beets and a touch of orange marmalade. Roasted pineapples with Eccles cake ice cream, influenced by Matthew Fort, then to finish my version of Manchester tart. A great night which closed on a high.

The team in every department throughout the property did us proud. The service was smooth and effortless, the wines were matched brilliantly and the kitchen performed excellently. The guests had a superb 10 days with some guests coming four or five times, all credit to them. Huge thanks goes to all the sponsors without whom we cannot perform, so to everyone involved thank you so much, bring on Obsession 12.

MARTIN BURGE

"For me food is not just substance it is an experience to be enjoyed. I have not touched the surface of possibilities that food can give me and this is my obsession."

OBSESSION FESTIVAL

HUGH FEARNLEY-WHITTINGSTALL

"Teaching me to cook was my Mum's solution to 'restless small boy syndrome'. If it was raining outside I'd be following my Mum around the house pulling at her skirt saying, "What can I do Mum, I'm bored!". Eventually she stood me up on a chair at the kitchen table, opened a packet of icing sugar, separated an egg, got some green colouring and peppermint essence out, and showed me how to make peppermint creams. I've never looked back."

SIMON ROGAN

"I don't know why and there is no particular reason for the interest in food I had from an early age. Turning my back on university, I was seduced into a culinary career by money rather than the prospect of knowledge. Obviously, this was wrong and the realisation that this was not enough for me came quite rapidly. So, I got myself another culinary job with the prospect of knowledge but with no money. My reasoning was turned on its head but it was too late and I was well and truly smitten with what I was now doing. From those first moments right up to ty to go.

L'Enclume, its food and its surroundings are everything to me and it is my obsession to provide the experience and enjoyment through the knowledge he present day, there is always something to learn and I feel very privileged to be in the position that I am in now, although there is still some waI am fortunate to have gained in our magical place."

MARTIN WISHART

"For as long as I can remember I've loved being around food. Once you acquire the principles and techniques to handle food, they are impossible to let go and to do it any other way. I find it crucial to hold what I am trying to create and to imagine how the flavours will come together. But what is more important is to be free from the worry of how good the end result will taste and concentrate on the careful process of getting there. Nothing can be more absorbing!"

CLAIRE CLARK

"I am Obsessed about CHEESE. I love cheese, more than chocolate. I could (do) live on cheese. The smellier the better!

I am Obsessed about perfection. It's second nature to me. I love to see food looking perfectly prepared on the plate but I am obsessed about production and the way it is prepared before it gets to the plate. It amounts to one thing ... attention to detail."

OBSESSION FESTIVAL

"I am obsessed with food and cooking because it's my way to connect with nature, the earth, the seasons and all the subtle variations there are every single day. Even if you cook the same dish for two months when it's in season, the actual nature of the ingredient itself changes every day. It requires a very special connection to be able to recognise the subtle variations and adapt the dishes, recipes or their cooking. On several levels, I find this extremely fascinating. That combined with the joy, the instant gratification of seeing a meal being enjoyed, are two very good reasons to stay obsessed with food!"

VIVEK SINGH

"My obsession with food stems like most chefs from their childhood and learning from their parents. Mine was even more food related because I was brought up on a farm. It was there I learnt the understanding that great cooking starts and ends with great ingredients. Over the years it's been a passion dear to me and the use of local, seasonal ingredients should be at the forefront of every chef. We have such a diverse selection of some of the finest food in the UK and it's not difficult to find and produce some amazing dishes with it."

JAMES MARTIN

KENNY ATKINSON

"I fell in to professional cooking by chance as a young boy washing dishes, there I was introduced to the kitchen life, excited by the ingredients, the food and the daily buzz that busy kitchens bring — it was then that my career dreams changed. Since that age of 17 I have become obsessed with food, it has taken over my life, sitting up to 3am in the morning reading cookbooks, drawing pictures for new and exciting dishes for my customers to enjoy, for me this is my life, this is my obsession."

NORTH EAST LINE CAUGHT MACKEREL GOOSEBERRIES, LEMON AND MUSTARD

Serves 4

INGREDIENTS

Breaded mackerel
English mustard
4 Mackerel fillets, pin boned and trimmed
4 slices White bread
Maldon salt, to taste
Rapeseed oil
Unsalted butter

Gooseberry purée
250g Frozen gooseberries
50g Caster sugar
½ Lemon, juice only
15g Unsalted butter
15ml Double cream
Green food colouring

Lemon oil
150ml Rapeseed oil
2 Lemons, zest only
1 sprig Thyme

Pickled gooseberries
30ml Water
30ml Gooseberry wine
30ml Chardonnay white wine vinegar
30ml Rapeseed oil
60g Caster sugar
1 Lemon, zest and juice
½ tsp Mustard seeds
8 Black peppercorns
1 sprig Tarragon
100g Gooseberries

Gooseberry jelly
300ml Gooseberry wine
50g Caster sugar
1g Agar Agar to 100g liquid

Pickled lemon
1 Lemon, peeled and finely sliced
30g Water
50g Caster sugar
50g White wine vinegar

Garnish
Lemon oil
English mustard
Red mustard cress

METHOD

Breaded mackerel
Brush a thin layer of mustard on to the mackerel skin. Using a pasta machine, roll the bread out as thinly as possible. Place the fish mustard-side down on to the bread and season the fish with salt. Trim the bread to size so that you can fold it over the fish. Brush the bread with a little mustard and fold it over the mackerel to seal it. Just before serving pan fry until golden brown on all sides in a little oil and butter.

Gooseberry purée
Place the gooseberries, sugar, lemon juice and butter into a vac pac bag and sous vide tightly. Cook in a water bath at 70°C for 1 hour. Remove from the bath and place into a blender. Blitz to a purée and finish with the cream and a few drops of green food colouring. Pass through a fine sieve and place into a plastic bottle. This will keep in a fridge for 5 days.

Lemon oil
Place all the ingredients into a pan and bring to a simmer. Remove from the heat and leave in a warm area for 6 hours to infuse.

Pickled gooseberries

Bring all the ingredients except the gooseberries to the boil. Simmer for 5 minutes, then add the gooseberries and bring back to the boil. Remove from the heat and leave to cool.

Gooseberry jelly

Bring the wine and sugar to the boil. Simmer for 1 minute and leave to cool. When cool, whisk in the agar agar and bring back to a simmer, whisking all the time. Pour into moulds and chill.

Pickled lemon

Blanch the lemon slices in boiling water for 2 minutes, then drain and refresh in iced water. In a separate pan bring the water, sugar and vinegar to the boil and simmer for 5 minutes. Add the lemon zest to the syrup and cook for a further 5 minutes. Leave to cool.

TO SERVE

Warm the jelly in a low oven preheated to 70°C for 10-15 minutes.

Paint a neat line of mustard on to the centre of the plate. Pipe five small dots of purée to one side of the mustard and two neat dots to the other side. Remove the jelly from the moulds and place on top of the two dots. Spoon a few pickled gooseberries over and around the jelly along with four slices of pickled lemon as well as some red mustard cress. Place the golden brown mackerel on top of the mustard and finish with a little lemon oil.

Chicory Mousse Layered with Bitter Coffee, Mascarpone Cream and Chocolate Leaves

Serves 4

Chicory Mousse Layered with Bitter Coffee, Mascarpone Cream and Chocolate Leaves

Serves 4

INGREDIENTS

Chicory mousse
75g Chicory beans
75ml Full fat milk + extra as needed
75ml Whipping cream
2 Medium egg yolks
20g Sugar
15g Milk chocolate, melted
2.5g Gelatine
10ml + 100ml Whipping cream

Syrup for soaking the joconde sponge
75g Espresso coffee
20g Caster sugar
50g Kalhua
50g Pedro Ximenez sherry

Joconde sponge
187g Icing sugar
187g Ground almonds
3 Large eggs, lightly beaten
35g Unsalted butter, melted
50g Caster sugar
6 Medium egg whites
50g Plain flour, sieved
Dark chocolate, melted, for spreading

Mascarpone mousse
55g Caster sugar
10ml Water
2 Medium egg yolks
85g Mascarpone cheese
2g Gelatine leaf
5ml + 75ml Whipping cream

Chocolate spray gun mix
300g Cocoa butter
300g 70% dark chocolate

Assembly
25g Melted dark chocolate for brushing

Garnish
24 Tempered chocolate leaves (4cm x 3cm)
4 Pieces of gold leaf
5g Gold dust

METHOD

Chicory mousse
In a frying pan toast the chicory beans on a medium heat. Pour the milk and cream into a vac pac bag with the toasted chicory beans. Seal the bag and place in a water bath set at 75°C for 30 minutes. Remove the bag from the water bath and pass the mixture through a fine sieve or chinois. Weigh out the infusion and add enough milk to make up to 125g. Whisk together the egg yolks and sugar. Meanwhile bring the infusion to the boil then pour over the egg yolks and sugar. Return to the heat continuously stirring with a spatula or wooden spoon. The mixture will thicken to make an anglaise. Pass the chicory anglaise through a chinois or fine sieve. Add the milk chocolate and set aside until required.

Take a glass bowl and soften the gelatine in cold water for about 10 minutes. Squeeze the gelatine to remove excess water. In a pan add 10ml of cream and the gelatine, then heat the mixture up gently until the gelatine has dissolved. Take the gelatine cream off the heat, pour onto the chicory anglaise and whisk until well mixed. Whisk 100ml of the cream to form soft ribbons and then fold into the chicory anglaise. Mix well. Pour the mixture into half-sphere moulds and freeze.

Syrup for soaking the joconde sponge

Make an espresso coffee and dissolve the sugar into the coffee. Add the rest of the ingredients. Set aside until required.

Joconde sponge

Place into a food mixer the icing sugar, ground almonds and half of the eggs. Whisk on high speed for 8 minutes. Add the remainder of the eggs and whisk on high speed for another 10 minutes. Add the melted butter into the mix and set aside.

Line a tray 60cm x 40cm with silicone paper.

Meanwhile, make a meringue by whisking the caster sugar and the egg whites until soft peaks are formed. Fold the icing sugar, almonds, butter and egg mixture into the meringue. Fold the sieved flour into the mixture. With a palette knife spread the mixture gently and evenly over the tray. Bake at 220°C for 10 to 12 minutes, until firm to the touch. Leave to cool and then spread a thin layer of melted dark chocolate over the top. Cut the sponge into eight hexagons using a mould as a cutter. Set aside. Discard any remaining sponge.

Mascarpone mousse

Dissolve the sugar and water in a pan and boil to 118°C to make a sugar syrup.

Meanwhile, in a mixing bowl add the egg yolks then pour in the sugar syrup and whisk the mixture to form a sabayon. Set aside.

In a separate bowl whisk the mascarpone cheese until soft and smooth. Fold the sabayon into the mascarpone.

In a glass bowl soften the gelatine in cold water for about 10 minutes. Squeeze the gelatine to remove excess water. In a pan heat up the 5ml of cream and add the gelatine until dissolved. Take the melted gelatine off the heat and then pour into the mascarpone sabayon and whisk until combined. In a bowl whisk the 75ml of cream to form soft ribbons and then fold into the mascarpone sabayon.

Assembling the mascarpone mousse and joconde sponge

Place the joconde sponge on the bottom of the hexagonal mould and soak the sponge with a tablespoon of the coffee syrup. In the mould pipe the mascarpone mousse up to half way. Repeat the layering of the joconde sponge, coffee syrup and the mascarpone mousse. Leave to set in the fridge for 2 hours.

Chocolate spray gun mix

Set up a bain marie and melt the cocoa butter and chocolate together until it reaches 50-55°C. Pass the chocolate through a chinois into a spray gun.

Assembling the mousse

Remove the chicory mousse from the freezer. Turn the mousse out of the mould by heating the outside of the mould with a blow torch. Meanwhile, melt some dark chocolate over a bain marie. Brush the bottom of each mousse with the melted chocolate. Place the mousse back in the freezer for 10 minutes.

Set up the spray gun. The temperature of the chocolate must be about 50°C so that the gun works efficiently. Remove the frozen mousses from the freezer and spray all over except the base, making sure they remain frozen while spraying. Lay the sprayed mousse on a tray lined with silicone paper and place in the fridge to defrost naturally.

T O   S E R V E

Light the blow torch and heat the outside of the hexagonal mould to assist with removing the mousse from the mould. Place the chicory mousse carefully on top of the mascarpone mousse. Arrange the tempered chocolate leaves around the outside of the mascarpone mousse to form a hexagon. Then place the pieces of gold leaf on top of the dome and sprinkle with a light dusting of gold dust on the edge of the plate.

HALIBUT CEVICHE
Serves 6

INGREDIENTS

Tomato fondue
1 small Shallot, finely chopped
1 Garlic clove, finely chopped
200g Plum tomatoes flesh, seeds removed
1 Bouquet garni
50ml Olive oil

Halibut
420g Halibut
Maldon salt
45ml Lemon juice
15ml Gastric (see below)
15g Sugar
5g Salt
Juice of half a lime
10g Tomato fondue
Tequila (to taste)
1 Sprig of fresh coriander
1 Tomato (skinned, deseeded and diced)
30g Mango, diced
3 whole Passion fruits

METHOD

Tomato fondue
Sweat the shallot and garlic in the olive oil in a saucepan without colouring. Add the tomato flesh and bouquet garni, cover with a paper cartouche (parchment paper lid) and slowly cook on the stove for 45-55 minutes, so that the fondue sweetens in flavour and is almost dry. Discard the bouquet garni and allow to cool. Place in a blender and purée until smooth.

Halibut
Dice the halibut into 1cm squares. Season with the Maldon salt.

Whisk the lemon juice, gastric, sugar and salt together. Add to the halibut along with the lime juice, tomato fondue and the tequila.

Finely chiffonnade (cut into long thin strips) the coriander leaves and add to the mix with the tomato dice.

Divide the mix equally between six 6-7 cm stainless steel rings placed in suitable serving bowls (as illustrated in the image below). Place the diced mango on top of the halibut. Cut the passion fruit in half and scoop out the seeds and juice into a bowl. Whisk the pulp together to break up the passion fruit. Finish the ceviche with a tablespoon of passion fruit over the top. Alternatively, arrange everything attractively on a plate as pictured right.

Gastric
Put equal quantities of white wine vinegar and caster sugar in a pan and bring to the boil. Let it cool before you measure out the quantity required.

JERUSALEM ARTICHOKES, FLESH AND SKIN, SOFT MALT, GOAT'S CHEESE, CALAMINT, HOWBARROW SHOOTS

Serves 4-6

INGREDIENTS

Jerusalem artichoke barrels
18 Jerusalem artichokes
Thyme, as required
Bay leaf, as required
Rapeseed oil, as required
Maldon salt, as required

Jerusalem artichoke purée/skins
500g Jerusalem artichokes
3g Salt
Rapeseed oil, as required
50g Double cream
50g Butter

Soft malt
75g Ground almonds
90g Malt flour
85g Chestnut flour
75g Butter
25g Sugar
50g Hawkshead Brewery Brodie's Prime Ale

Goat's cheese mousse
250g Goat's cheese
125g Semi-skimmed milk
3.5g Agar agar

Calamint oil
100ml Grapeseed oil
6 large sprigs Calamint, stem removed
¼ tsp Sugar

To serve
Radish shoots
Red chard shoots
Leek shoots
Purple sprouting broccoli shoots
Maldon salt

METHOD

Jerusalem artichoke barrels
Peel the artichokes and stamp out barrel shapes lengthwise with a 15mm apple corer. Toss the barrels with thyme, bay leaf, rapeseed oil and salt and place in a vacuum pouch. Vacuum and cook in a water bath for 1 hour 10 minutes at 85°C. Refresh in iced water when cooked. As an alternative to vacuum packing and using a water bath you can simply cook the artichokes in boiling salted water with the juice of ½ lemon.

Jerusalem artichoke purée/skins
Preheat the oven to 185°C. Place the artichokes and salt on double-layered sheets of tin foil, splash with some rapeseed oil, wrap up tightly and bake in the oven for 2 hours. When cooked well and cool enough to handle, carefully scoop out the flesh into a blender, keeping the skins as whole as possible. Blend the flesh with the cream and butter until smooth, season and push through

a sieve to remove any lumps. Chill. Split the skins lengthwise, but not all the way, so that you can twist them to double their length. Dry in a dehydrator at 60°C (or dry overnight in a very low oven) until fully dry and then deep fry at 190°C until golden brown. Season with salt.

Soft malt
Mix together the almonds, flours, butter and sugar. Split the mix into two and add the ale to one half to

form a smooth paste. Freeze the paste until solid and then grate over a silpat and dry in a dehydrator at 60°C. Return the dry half to the wet half.

Goat's cheese mousse

Melt the goat's cheese into the milk with the agar agar and cook out for a couple of minutes. Set in a bowl. When set blend in a food processor until smooth and correct the seasoning.

Calamint oil

Liquidise all the ingredients together and leave to steep for 2 hours. Strain carefully through a supabag or muslin cloth.

TO SERVE

Create a mound of artichoke purée and goat's cheese mousse in the centre of the plate. Sprinkle the soft malt over to completely cover. Stand three artichoke barrels into the soft malt followed by three crispy artichoke skins. Place a selection of the shoots over the dish and finish by drizzling around some calamint oil and Maldon salt.

TASTY FISH SOUP WITH CHILLI ROUILLE
Serves 4

You buy an inexpensive fresh fish, such as gurnard or grey mullet (ask the fishmonger to fillet it for you if you do not wish to do it yourself), then use the head, skin and bones to make a flavourful stock. The broth is enhanced with a few herbs and vegetables, the fish flesh goes in at the end, and you can splash out on a bit of squid or a few scallops, if you like. The finishing touch is a swirl of garlicky, chilli-hot rouille, though I have to say, the soup is delicious even without it. And croutons, made from leftover bread, add crunch.

INGREDIENTS

1 medium firm-fleshed Fish, 750g–1kg, filleted and skinned, skin, head and bones saved for the stock

Fish stock
2 Celery stalks, chopped
1 Garlic clove, peeled
1 Onion, roughly chopped
1 large Carrot, sliced
1 sprig of Thyme
1 Bay leaf
Stalks from a bunch of parsley, leaves reserved for serving
A few black peppercorns
A splash of white wine

Soup
2 Garlic cloves
1 large Onion
2 Celery stalks
2 Leeks
500g floury Potatoes
2 tbsp Rapeseed or olive oil
½ tsp Fennel seeds, roughly crushed

Rouille (optional)
1 hot Red chilli
1 quantity of Garlic mayonnaise

To serve
100–200g cleaned squid or 4–8 scallops (optional)
Leaves from the parsley bunch, finely chopped
Sea salt & freshly ground black pepper
Wholemeal croutons, to serve

METHOD

Fish stock
Put the fish head, skin and bones in a saucepan with all the ingredients for the stock. Add 1 litre of cold water and bring to a gentle simmer. Cook very gently for half an hour; do not allow it to boil hard as this spoils the flavour. Strain the stock, discarding the fishy bits and vegetables.

Soup
Finely chop the garlic, onion, celery and leeks. Peel the potatoes and cut into 1cm cubes. Heat the oil in a large saucepan, add the fennel seeds, garlic, onion, celery and leeks, then cover and sweat for about 10 minutes, until soft. Add the potatoes and the stock and return to a gentle simmer. Cook for 15 minutes, or until the potatoes are tender.

Rouille
Chop the chilli very finely and mix it with the garlic mayonnaise; set aside.

TO SERVE

Slice the fish fillets into bite-sized pieces. If using squid, slice the pouches into rings; if using scallops, clean and slice horizontally in half. Add all the fish and any shellfish to the simmering broth. Cook for 2 minutes until the fish is just done, then remove from the heat. Add the parsley and season to taste. Serve the soup in warm bowls, topped with a few crisp croutons and a good blob of rouille, if you like.

Variation
When fennel is in season, in summer and autumn, try using it instead of the leeks.

Amedei Toscano Nut Brown and Mandarin Chocolate and Praline Mille-feuille

Serves 50

AMEDEI TOSCANO NUT BROWN AND MANDARIN CHOCOLATE AND PRALINE MILLE-FEUILLE
Serves 50

INGREDIENTS

Baked chocolate mousse
510g Amedei Toscano nut brown chocolate
160g Butter, melted
110g Hazelnut praline paste
55g Dark cocoa powder
715g Caster sugar
120g Hazelnuts, ground
15 Eggs
20ml Vanilla extract

Chocolate praline ganache
450ml Double cream
300g Amedei Toscano brown chocolate, chopped
2 drops Sweet orange oil

Feuilletine
250g Toscano brown chocolate
500g Crunchy praline paste
125g Feuilletine

Mandarin sorbet
150ml Water
200g Sugar
2 Lemons, juice only
1 litre Mandarin juice
3 Mandarins, zest only, blanched

Oreo crumbs
300g Caster sugar
500g Plain flour
162g Cocoa powder
3.5g Bicarbonate soda
6g Salt
325g Butter (soft)

Mandarin pearls
100ml Mandarin juice
1g Agar agar

Candied hazelnuts
250g hazelnuts
Simple syrup (boil equal quantities of caster sugar and water together)
Vegetable or canola oil for deep frying

Mandarin and white chocolate mousse
150g Fond neutral
150ml Mandarin juice
300g White chocolate, melted
700ml Semi-whipped cream
2 Mandarins, zest only, blanched

Garnish
Tempered milk chocolate shards
Tempered white chocolate shards
Micro tarragon
Dark chocolate sauce
Mandarin segments

METHOD

Baked chocolate mousse

Preheat the oven to 325°C.

Melt together the chocolate, butter and paste over a bain marie. Sieve together the cocoa powder, sugar and hazelnuts. Whisk in the eggs, vanilla and the melted ingredients. Once incorporated, pour onto a lined tray 60 x 40cm, spread evenly and bake in the oven for 15 minutes.

Chocolate praline ganache

Boil the cream and pour over the chocolate. Let the bowl sit for 1 minute before whisking gently to a smooth emulsion. Add the orange oil and mix to combine. Pour into a shallow tray/half sheet pan approximately 30 x 20cm lined with acetate. Place a sheet of acetate on top and freeze.

Feuilletine

Melt the chocolate and praline paste over a bain marie, then add the feuilletine. Mix well. Spread thinly in-between two sheets of silicone paper with a rolling pin. Chill until firm.

Mandarin sorbet

Boil the water and sugar together. Remove from the heat and add the lemon and mandarin juices. Pass through a chinoise (sieve) and add the mandarin zest. Turn into an ice cream machine, following the manufacturer's instructions.

Oreo crumbs

Preheat the oven to 160°C.

Combine all the ingredients in a Robot Coupe (food processor) until a dough is formed. Break up into lumps and place on a baking sheet. Bake in the oven for 20 minutes until crisp and firm. Cool completely. Blitz in a Robot Coupe (food processor) to form crumbs. Store in an airtight container. The crumbs will keep for 2 weeks.

Mandarin pearls

Boil the juice and whisk in the agar agar. Cool. Place in a dropper and drop into a bath of very cold oil to form spheres. Store in fresh mandarin juice in the fridge. The pearls will keep for 4 days.

Candied hazelnuts

Cook the hazelnuts in the simple syrup until they are lightly coated. Using a spider (a wide shallow wire-mesh basket with a long handle) lift the nuts into a pan of hot oil and fry for 1 minute until golden brown and caramelised. Cool on a silpat mat.

Mandarin and white chocolate mousse

Place the fond in a bowl and whisk in the mandarin juice until it is smooth. Add the warm melted white chocolate and fold in with a spatula. Fold in the semi-whipped cream and the zest.

TO SERVE

Spread some chocolate sauce across the plate as shown. Cut the baked chocolate mousse into a strip. Cut the feuilletine so that it fits exactly on top of the mousse. Place a shard of tempered milk chocolate on top of the feuilletine as pictured. Cut a thin slice of the ganache and place on the shard as shown. Pipe the mandarin mousse in small bulbs down the strip of ganache as shown and place a tempered white chocolate shard on top.

Decorate the plate as depicted with the mandarin segments, candied hazelnuts, mandarin pearls, the oreo crumbs and sorbet. Finish the plate with the micro tarragon.

West Coast Scallops Lime and Ginger Infused, Salsify and Apple

Serves 4

INGREDIENTS

Lime and ginger infusion
4 tsp Caster sugar
10g Lemon juice
30g Lime juice
400g Fresh apple juice
2g Salt
40g Fresh root ginger juice
10g Olive oil

Apple and soy purée
250g Bramley apples, peeled and diced
12g Sugar any particular type?
3 tbsp Soy sauce

Scallops
10 King scallops
Salt
20g Enoki mushrooms
1 Apple, cut into long sticks 1cm thick
1 stick Salsify, thinly sliced into 12cm long ribbons, then cooked in salted water
Maldon salt
Coriander cress, as required
Few drops Sunflower oil
1 Lemon

To serve
1 leaf Spring cabbage, thinly sliced and deep fried

METHOD

Lime and ginger infusion
In a pan dissolve the sugar into the lemon and lime juices. Remove from the heat, add the apple juice, salt, ginger juice and olive oil, and whisk in well. Pass through a fine sieve and place into the fridge to cool.

Apple and soy purée
Place the apples and sugar into a pan, covering with a lid or clingfilm. Cook on a medium heat for 8-10 minutes until the apples have broken down. Remove from the pan and place into a liquidiser, add the soy sauce and blitz to a smooth purée. Pass through a fine sieve. Leave to cool. Once cooled check the seasoning and put into a squeezy bottle.

Scallops
Roll 6 of the scallops in clingfilm into a cylinder, then place into the freezer to semi freeze (this is to ensure perfect slices of scallop of the same size). Once the scallops are semi frozen slice on a slicing machine ½ cm thick – you need 5 slices per portion. Place the sliced scallops onto a small flat tray, covering all the surface area. Season with salt then spoon over 100ml of the lime and ginger infusion. Leave to marinate in a warm area for 4 minutes.

In a small bowl mix together the mushrooms, apple and salsify with a small amount of dressing, and season with salt.

Place the sliced scallops overlapping each other in the bottom of the serving bowls. Carefully place on top the salsify/apple mixture, and season with Maldon salt. Spoon over one tablespoon of lime infusion. Finish with the coriander cress.

Heat a medium non-stick pan and add a small amount of oil. Lightly season the four remaining scallops. Place the scallops into the pan, press lightly and cook for 1-2 minutes until golden on one side, then turn them over and cook for a further minute. Add a squeeze of lemon juice. Immediately remove the scallop from the pan onto a piece of absorbent paper and season with Maldon salt.

TO SERVE

On a flat rectangular plate place the glass bowl of marinated scallops to the left-hand side. Put four dots of apple and soy purée across the plate, moving diagonally away from the bowl. Place a scallop onto the first dot of the purée. Finish with a small amount of the crispy cabbage on top.

TRIO OF LISSARA DUCK
Serves 3

Lissara ducks are from Ireland from a company called Crossgar just outside Belfast – visit www.crossgar.ie for more information. I am very keen to use them as they are such a fantastic product.

INGREDIENTS

Duck confit and rillette
4 x 255g Duck legs
75g Sea salt
1kg Duck fat
Milled pepper
25g Flat leaf parsley, chopped
Honey, for drizzling

Parsnip purée
250g Parsnips, diced
2 Golden delicious apples, peeled, core removed and diced
Milk (enough to cover the parsnips and apples)

Girolles
200ml Rice wine vinegar
30g Brown sugar
25g Pink peppercorns, crushed
1 Cinnamon stick
2 whole Cloves
Salt & pepper
300g Girolles, cleaned

Duck breast
2 Duck breasts
Salt & pepper
25g unsalted Butter
Olive oil

To serve
200g Spinach, cooked and buttered
100ml Red wine jus
50g Coriander cress

METHOD

Duck confit and rillette
Preheat the oven to 180°C.

For the duck confit and rillette, dust the legs with the sea salt, place on a tray, cover and leave for 8 to 10 hours or overnight, in a cool place.

Wash the salt off the duck legs with cold water. Dry the meat.

Melt the duck fat in a heavy-bottomed pan and then submerge the duck legs in the fat. Cover with a lid, place over a medium heat and cook for about 1½ to 2 hours or until the meat is tender – the temperature may need to be adjusted to a gentle simmer as you do not want the fat to boil.

When the duck legs are cooked allow them to cool in the fat until they can be removed from it and picked up by hand. Pass the fat through a fine sieve and retain, but discard the contents of the sieve. Retain the leg whole but remove the thigh, discard the skin and any bones, keep the drumstick whole and set to one side. Then shred the meat from the thigh into a bowl, pour some of the fat over and mix in well. Season with salt and pepper to taste, and add the parsley. Place this shredded duck mix (rillette) into either a metal tray lined with clingfilm or if using oblong moulds (approximately 4 x 7.5cm) spoon in about 1 tablespoon of the rillette mix, press flat and allow to set in the fridge.

When required remove from the fridge and bring up to room temperature, slice as necessary then place on the serving plate.

Place the duck leg in a pan and season with milled pepper. Drizzle a little honey over and place into the oven to glaze, then remove and place on top of the rillette.

Parsnip purée
Place the parsnips and apples in a saucepan and cover with milk, bring to the boil over a medium heat and allow to cook until tender. Then drain, retaining the liquid. Place the cooked parsnips and apples into a blender and slowly add the liquid back in to form a purée. Set to one side.

Girolles
Place the vinegar in a saucepan then gently warm. Add the sugar, peppercorns, cinnamon and cloves, and allow to infuse for 2 to 3 minutes. Season, add the mushrooms and place back on the heat for 1 minute. Remove and keep warm.

Duck breast
Take a non-stick pan and heat it up over a medium heat. When it's hot add the breast skin-side down and season with salt and pepper. Allow to colour for 3 to 4 minutes. When a nice even golden brown colour is achieved turn over and add the butter and a little olive oil. Cook for 4 to 5 minutes or until the medium-rare stage is reached, then remove from the heat and continue to spoon over the cooking juices. Allow to rest.

TO SERVE

Slice the duck breast and serve with
the whole leg and the buttered
spinach next to the rillette. Drizzle
with the jus, arrange some pickled
girolles around and garnish with the
coriander cress.

Mutton with Beer, Shallots and Herbs
Serves 10

INGREDIENTS

Mutton
2kg Mutton shoulder
White chicken stock, as required
Brown chicken stock, as required
Olive oil, as required

Caramelised shallot purée
10 Shallots, chopped
50g Olive oil
50g Butter
100ml Dark chicken stock
Salt, to taste

Braised shallots
500g Shallots
50g Butter
50g Maple syrup
50g Demerara sugar
Salt, to taste

Green onion powder
50g Chives
50g Leek tops
50g Fresh onion tops
250g Sunflower oil
1 pinch salt
Maltodextrin

Jus noisette with capers
300ml Brown chicken stock
150ml Browned butter
Lemon juice, to taste
1 tbsp Green elderberry capers
1 tsp Shallots, finely chopped

METHOD

Mutton
Cut the shoulder into 500g pieces, brown on all sides and place into a pressure cooker. Add enough of each stock to cover the meat. Place on the heat and when up to full pressure cook for 45 minutes. Strain the liquid from the pan and reduce by two-thirds, pick the meat and gently break down. Add the reduced stock and season to taste. Roll the meat into cylinders in cling film and leave in the fridge until cold. Remove the clingfilm, slice and sear in some hot olive oil then finish in the oven for 6 minutes at 180°C just before serving.

Caramelised shallot purée
Sweat the shallots in the oil and butter. When the moisture has evaporated, lower the heat and gently caramelise for 1¾ -2 hours. Deglaze the pan with stock and blend to a smooth purée. Push through a mesh if necessary and season with salt.

Braised shallots
Cover the shallots with the other ingredients in an ovenproof dish, seal first with wet baking paper, then foil and bake at 160°C for 1 hour or till the liquid has caramelised.

Green onion powder
Blitz the chives, leek and onion tops together for 5 minutes, then strain and leave overnight. Mix the oil and salt with the maltodextrin until a powdered texture is achieved then combine with the chive mix.

Jus noisette with capers
Heat the stock and butter in a pot and bring almost to the boil. Add the rest of the ingredients and stir.

TO SERVE

Pour the jus over the mutton and serve with the purée, braised shallots and green onion powder.

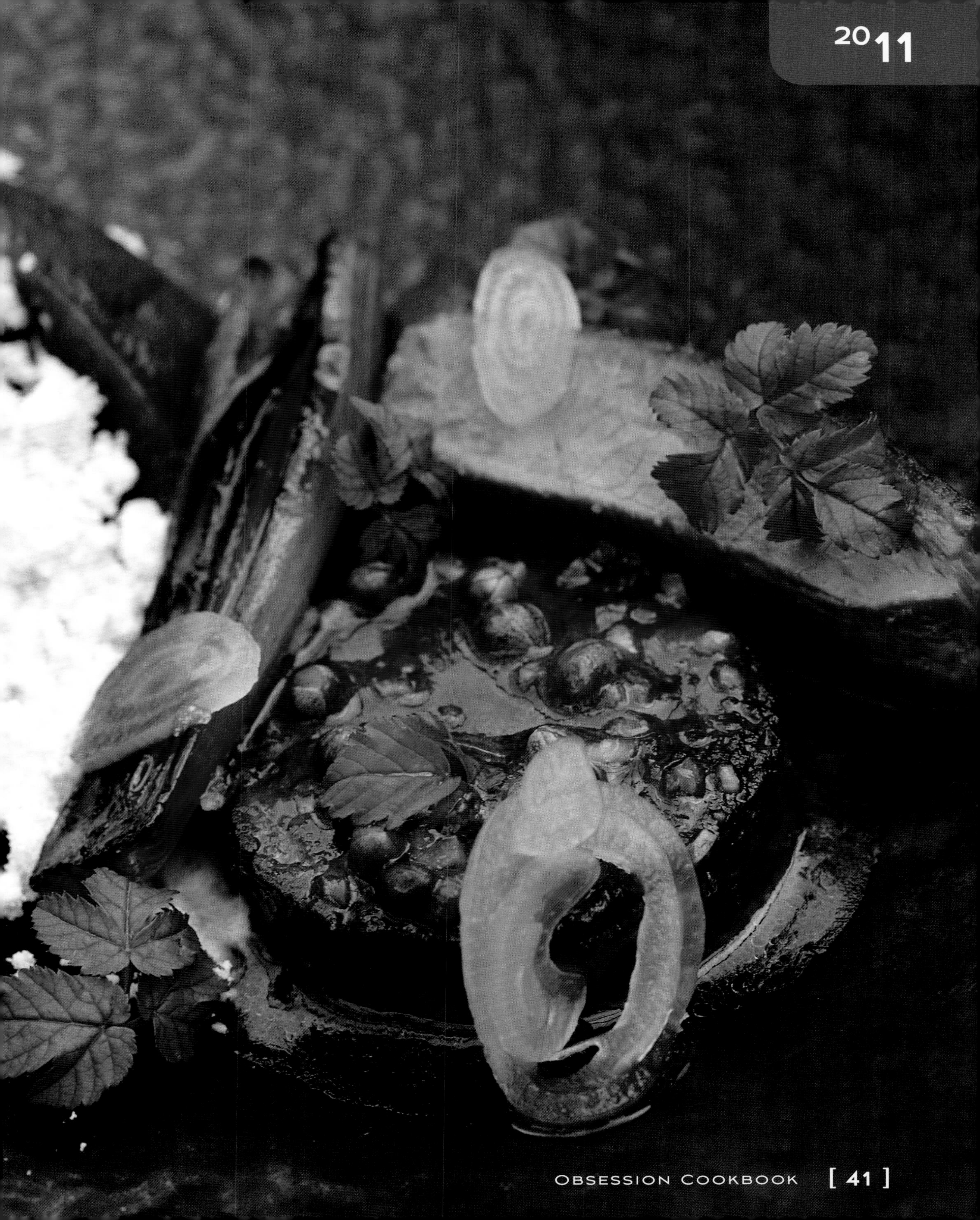

TANDOORI BREAST OF SQUAB PIGEON, SMOKED PAPRIKA RAITA

Serves 4 as a starter and 2 as a main

Although pigeons are eaten throughout the sub-continent, you rarely see them on restaurant menus. I simply love the taste and texture of good quality pigeon, which is unusual and lot more interesting than the regular chicken you find on all menus!

This recipe uses most of the flesh on the squab but requires a friendly butcher to take the pain out of the preparation. The breast of the pigeon gets the tandoor treatment and the rest is minced into a stunning kebab. This is a user-friendly way of eating such a small bird that many are put off by because of dealing with the bones.

This version may be served with a little salad as an accomplished starter or with small quantities of black lentils and pilau rice as a stunning main course.

INGREDIENTS

Pigeon breasts
2 Pigeons, breasts de-boned but with the skin and the leg meat, liver and heart minced (for the kebabs)
5g Ginger paste
5g Garlic paste
5g Chilli powder
3g Salt
15ml Lemon juice
30g Crisp fried onions, blended into a paste
15g Yoghurt
3g Garam masala
15ml Oil

Kebabs
15ml Oil
2g Royal cumin seeds
50g Onions, finely chopped
30g Beetroot boiled, peeled and cut into ½ cm dice
2g Red chilli powder
2g Cumin seeds, roasted and ground
10g Ginger, finely chopped
5g Green chillies, finely chopped
5g Fresh mint, chopped
3g Salt
2g Garam masala
1 Egg, beaten
100g Golden breadcrumbs
Oil for frying

Smoked paprika raita
100g Cucumber, deseeded and cut into ½ cm dice
50g Red onion, finely chopped
500g Greek style yoghurt, drained overnight in muslin
5g Fresh mint, chopped
2g Sugar
5g Salt
3g Smoked paprika powder

METHOD

Pigeon breasts
Pat dry the breasts and marinate with the ginger paste, garlic paste, chilli powder, salt and lemon juice and leave aside for 20 minutes. Then add the rest of the ingredients and set aside for another 10 minutes.

Kebabs
Heat the oil in a pan, add the cumin seeds and when they splutter, add the onions and sauté till golden brown. Add the minced pigeon and beetroot and sauté for about 3 minutes. Now add the chilli powder and cumin powder and cook further till the mixture is almost dry. Add the ginger, green chillies, mint and salt. Remove from heat and allow the mixture to cool.

Smoked paprika raita
Combine all the ingredients in a mixing bowl and refrigerate until ready to use.

TO SERVE

Cook the pigeon breasts in a hot tandoor for 2-3 minutes or in an oven preheated to 200°C for 5 minutes. Allow to rest for a couple of minutes.

To finish the kebabs shape the cooked pigeon mince into four cakes. Dip each in the egg, then roll in the breadcrumbs and deep fry till golden brown. Serve the pigeon breast along with the fried kebabs and smoked paprika raita.

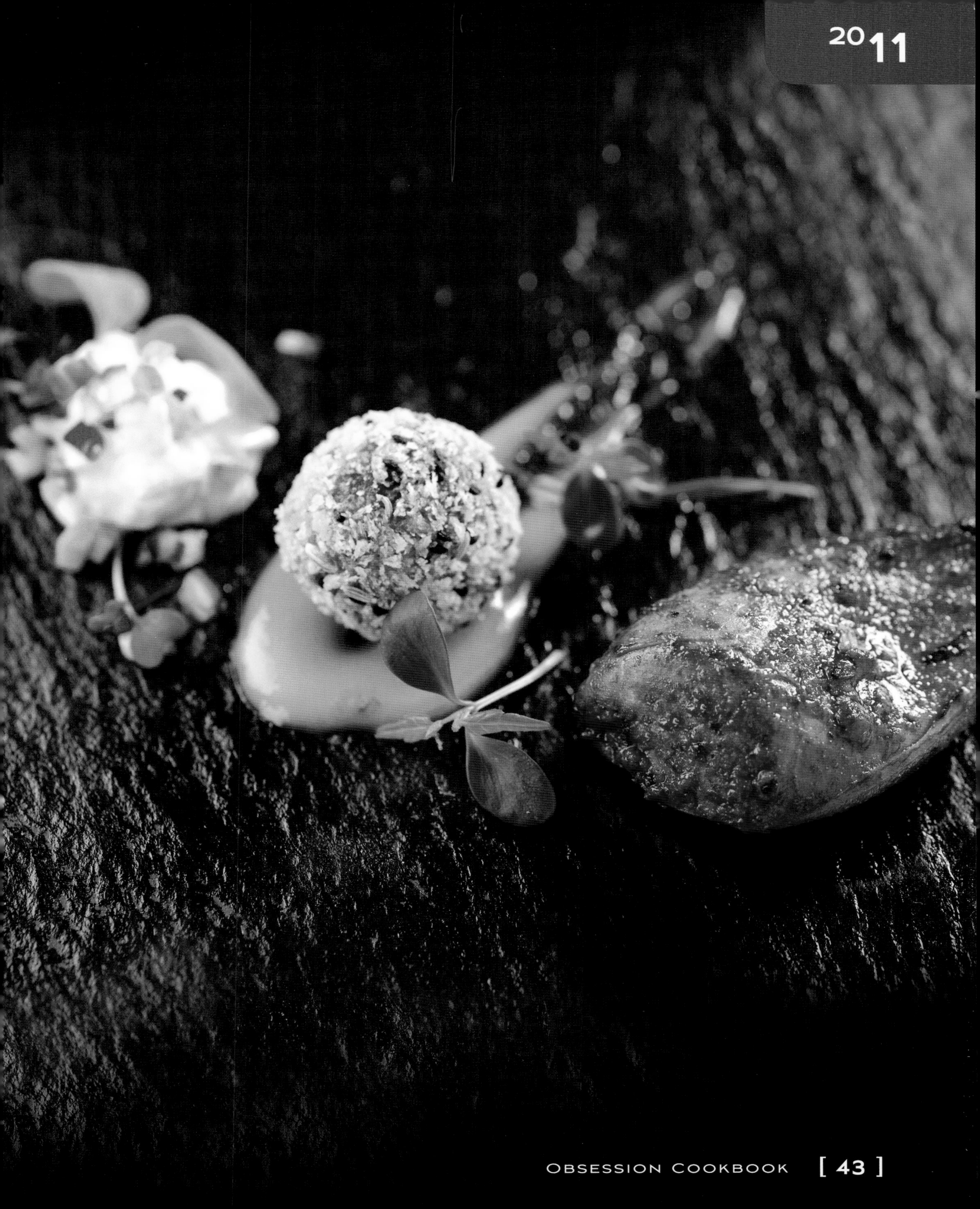

FREE-RANGE CHICKEN 'INDIAN GAME', BLACK PEAS, BACON, MEDJOOL DATES, GAME CHIPS

Serves 2

FREE-RANGE CHICKEN 'INDIAN GAME', BLACK PEAS, BACON, MEDJOOL DATES, GAME CHIPS

Serves 2

INGREDIENTS

Chicken
1 Free-range 'Indian Game' Chicken
Salt
1 Sprig of rosemary, picked and chopped
20g Medjool dates, stones removed and cut in half
300ml Olive oil
Butter

Black peas
10g Bacon
40g Mirepoix (assorted) vegetables (celery, carrot, leek and onion)
200g Black peas, soaked
1 Bay leaf
2 Parsley stalks
800ml Chicken stock

Chicken and parsley broth
500g Ground Goosnargh chicken mince
250g Finely chopped vegetables (onion, carrot, celery and leek)
2 Parsley stalks/chervil
1 Sprig of thyme
1 Bay leaf
6 Black peppercorns, crushed
80g Egg whites
5g Chicken bouillon
2g Salt
1 litre Black pea stock
1 litre Good white chicken stock
30g Parsley, picked
20g Spinach, picked and washed
5g Chervil, picked

Black pea purée
250g Black peas, soaked overnight and steamed for 1 hour until soft
1g Dried chillies, crushed
1 Clove garlic, roasted
1 tsp Salt
50ml Olive oil
150ml Tomato juice
100ml Sunflower oil
100ml Vegetable bouillon

Black pea, Medjool dates and bacon broth
30g Bacon, diced ½ cm x ½ cm
60g Black peas, cooked – see above
16 Button onions, roasted and peeled
?g Medjool dates any preparation required?
?ml Chicken and parsley broth - see above
Salt
2 tsp Parsley, finely chopped

Game chips
1 large Maris Piper chipping potato, peeled
Salt

METHOD

Chicken
Remove the wishbone, then the breast and legs, from the chicken. Roll the breast in clingfilm tight to a cylinder, put in a vac bag and seal tight. Cook at 68°C for 30 minutes.

Leave the leg and thigh attached together and remove the bone as a whole, keeping the skin on. Once the bone is removed check for any excess sinew and remove, place the legs between a piece of parchment paper and bat flat with a meat hammer; repeat this on the other leg. Lightly season each leg with salt, flesh side up. On one of the legs sprinkle the rosemary. Cover with an even layer of dates. Place the other leg on top to make a sandwich, then put into a vac bag with olive oil and seal tight. Place into a water bath at 70°C for 14 hours. Once cooked remove the legs from the bag, cover in clingfilm and press flat – this is to set the legs together. Once they are set cut into 3cm thick and 5cm long pieces.

Black peas
In a large pan, lightly sweat the bacon and mirepoix of vegetables for 2-3 minutes, no colour. Add the black peas, bay leaf, parsley stalks and chicken stock and bring to the boil. Cover and reduce to a simmer, then cook for 20-30 minutes until the peas

are just cooked. Once the peas are cooked remove from the pan, strain the remaining stock and reserve for the broth.

Chicken and parsley broth

Combine the mince, chopped vegetables, herbs (not the 5g chervil), egg whites, bouillon and seasoning in a mixing bowl. Mix well. Put the black pea and chicken stocks into a large heavy-bottomed pan. Carefully mix in the mince mixture. Mix well and check the seasoning. Place the pan onto the stove and bring to a simmer over a medium heat, stirring the contents of the pan frequently until the 'pad' starts to set on the surface of the stock. Once the pad has risen give it a final stir and then allow the pad to set, make a small opening to the side and allow the broth to boil. Gently simmer for 1½ hours. Once the broth is done remove from the heat and carefully strain through a tammy cloth, being careful not to disturb the pad too much. Place the broth, parsley, spinach and 5g chervil into a Thermomix or food processor and blitz until the herbs have all been incorporated – this should make a lovely green colour. Pass the broth back through the tammy cloth and check the seasoning.

Black pea purée

Place all the ingredients into a Pacojet beaker and freeze to –20°C. Once frozen Paco 3 times, remove from the beaker and reheat to serve. Use a food processor if you do not have a Pacojet.

Black pea, Medjool dates and bacon broth

Put the diced bacon into a pan and just cover with cold water. Bring to the boil and cook for 1-2 minutes, until the bacon fat is cooked. Remove from the pan and refresh in cold water (this is to prevent the final broth from having any fat). In a pan add the black peas, bacon, onions, dates and broth, and a little salt to taste. Heat until hot but do not boil. Check the seasoning and add the parsley.

Game chips

Thinly slice the potato on a mandoline to about 1mm thick. Put the slices of potato between two flat metal plates and place into a fryer at 180°C for 1-2 minutes until golden. Remove from the fryer onto absorbent paper and season with salt. Serve two chips per person

TO SERVE

Preheat the oven to 180°C .

Put the pieces of the chicken leg into a pan with a knob of butter, heat gently then place in the oven for 5 minutes until crispy. Season the cooked chicken breast and place into a hot pan skin-side down with a little oil and cook for 2-3 minutes until golden. Turn the breast over and add two knobs of butter and baste for a further 2-3 minutes, then remove from the pan. Slice the chicken breast into six pieces.

In a stone bowl place the chicken leg pieces just off centre. Put two spoons of black pea and Medjool date broth just coming off the leg, then put one spoon of purée next to the broth. Place three slices of the chicken breast on top of the leg and garnish with the game chips and an extra spoon of broth.

2010

2010

The arrival of the 2010 festival after ten years was potentially daunting with our decision to run for ten nights to celebrate our tenth anniversary.

Tom Kitchin, ably assisted by his team Dominic, Sebastian and David, arrived on Sunday night with his wife and business partner Michaela. It was great to see Tom and the team who enjoyed dining in the Northcote restaurant on the Sunday evening.

The following day Tom was up early, and on top form, he needed to be as there were record numbers for a first night – 98. I had talked to Tom briefly before about the adventurous nature of his menu with octopus, pig's head and razor clams, but he was confident that all would be well and he was right: the customers loved it. He also served his famous Great British Menu dish of beef wellington – a truly great dish that was just pipped to the post by that equally famous hot pot in the final. To finish he did chocolate and sea buckthorn – what a great ingredient – it's a berry that grows on the coast with a sort of earthy passion fruit flavour, harvested by Tom's personal forager – the must-have accessory of today's leading chefs.

Matthew Fort arrived the night before and in his own inimitable style he entertained the Northcote guest table on Tom Kitchin's night with his gastronomic stories. Tom Parker Bowles arrived at 4.30pm the following afternoon. Matthew was a little perturbed at the lateness of Tom's arrival as he had been toiling all afternoon preparing for their menu, but Tom hit the kitchen at full throttle. He swung on to his ceviche of bream and Morecambe Bay shrimps which proved to be a winner. Next up was John Dory with zabaglione, which I have to say would have got an eight or more on the Great British Menu. Duck on barley, then Eccles cake ice cream rounded off the evening in a fittingly Lancashire style. It goes without saying that the bar was full until the early hours and legend has it that Tom nearly missed his train the next morning. A great night was had by all.

Theo Randall travelled up from London on Tuesday and arrived with his assistant, Sanjeewa Thommadura. Theo, a connoisseur of Italian cuisine, dined at Matthew and Tom's evening and thoroughly enjoyed it, in fact, he was incredibly complimentary. Simplicity with confidence was the start of Theo's menu, chicory shoots with red wine vinegar dressing, anchovies and capers. The scallops and veal pasta were outstanding but wonderfully rustic. To finish was the fantastic and memorable Amalfi lemon tart – a perfect conclusion especially with the Moscato d'Asti wine.

Ken Hom flew in from Rio with no jet lag, he was full-on from the start. Intense, articulate and, above all, very passionate about his food. Ken is a very naturally talented man who truly understands his food culture.

Ken was assisted by Lee Williams who had prepared the way for his arrival. Crispy Vietnamese spring rolls, wrapped in soft herbs and lettuce leaves. Hot and sour soup came next, then steamed turbot which, with a touch of Hom magic, was transformed into a bubbling, spicy Chinese dish. Roast belly pork (which we dried for 24 hours with electric fans) was sublime and to finish was warm mango, basil and vanilla ice cream – a refreshing end to a stunning night.

Angela Hartnett and our very own Lisa Allen made for the biggest night of the festival: 'girl power'. When Angela is at Northcote it's always a time for laughter with serious cooking. Angela arrived late the night before, just catching the main course of Ken's evening. She and Lisa joined forces in the bar after service with several drinks and decided to have an early trip to Bury Market, perhaps, in hindsight, not the best plan. Angela, who was assisted on the night by ex-head chef Neil Borthwick, started her menu with scallops, Pata Negra and butternut squash, followed by one of her famous risottos, this time with black truffles and artichoke, with roasted local lamb, all brilliantly executed and cooked to perfection.

Home-grown Lisa Allen wowed us all with her duck consommé and crispy duck skins, then sent us into heaven with two desserts, a lime and pineapple cream and then a brilliant chocolate cylinder with a very silky sheep's milk ice cream.

Nathan Outlaw had just finished filming the Great British Menu and had travelled up from London on the late train, just arriving in time to have drinks with Angela and Lisa. He might be an 'Outlaw', but he is a true gentle giant and certainly a chef to watch. His night was packed to the rafters and a very fishy night was in store. Nathan kicked off with a beautiful crab salad, followed by lemon sole on potato dumplings – a dish that was incredibly well received. Next was his signature dish wreck fish with mussels – a blend of the Cornish and Normandy shores. Venison was the main course with chicory, then to finish the night, a cosy rhubarb sponge with ginger ice cream. Wow – what a great night. Those Cornish chaps can drink – we limped to bed at 4.30am!

For the first time in ten years Phil Howard sent up assistant James Salkald who started his mise en place allowing Phil to arrive by train the next day. Having worked with Phil over the past ten years, you notice the true style of the man: confident, comfortable and really accomplished. He kicked off the night with beetroot and goat's cheese, to be followed by a sublime combination of Dover sole, oysters and smoked eel. Ravioli of calves' tail with chanterelles was real comfort food. Venison Wellington was a classic dish, followed by a beautiful taste of Roquefort, pear and port, and then a perfect ending of a memorable and warming rhubarb tart. Somehow life at the festival will never be the same – thank you, Phil.

Jacob Jan Boerma and I quickly became friends after cooking at the Vila Joya Food Festival together in 2009. Jacob's food was really outstanding and I was so pleased when he accepted my invite to cook at the 2010 festival. Jacob was accompanied by his partner, Kim, and Ewout, Marco and Arturo. We were not to be disappointed. Jacob is a chef that can really hit the high notes, with a delicacy of touch. We started with an amazing oyster Tokyo-style, unbelievably tasty, moved on to North Sea Crab and warm Dublin Bay prawns, followed by slow-cooked lobster – a real star of a dish, with great textures and flavours. Grilled turbot with pumpkin, scallops and black truffles came next, followed by French pigeon and than an Obsession of desserts. A real surprise as Jacob hadn't really explained what this Obsession of desserts

entailed, but we were soon to find out. Three desserts, one after the other, were the climax to the evening. The first was a small selection of chocolate desserts – followed by red fruits and sorbet, then basil mousse with tropical fruits and basil oil. What an end to a truly hectic, frantic and all-absorbing evening.

It took me an awfully long time to get Andrew Fairlie down to the festival – nearly six years – but it was well worth the wait. He was assisted by Ian Scarramuzza, one of the chef de parties from Fairlies. Andrew launched the night with a stunning smoked eel and foie gras terrine, beetroot and apple. He had the balance of the terrine just perfect – what a brilliant start. Baked king scallops were followed by a beautifully delicate cep tart with roasted sweetbreads and ceps, which Andrew tells me had been picked with his own fair hands. His assiette of pork consisted of confit of belly pork, a small croquette of brawn, pork filled with some smoky cabbage and apples, along with a beautiful bacon from Alsace. These were really great combinations and very well received by an adoring public. Andrew wrapped the night up with a carpaccio of pineapple and coconut parfait: a refreshing end to another great night. The bar afterwards was extremely full and Andrew and I relaxed and enjoyed a few beers, a great atmosphere and a brilliant night.

And so finally, the last night was here – after nine fantastic evenings, it was up to us to go out on a high, which was no mean feat after such a gastronomic journey. We started with the venison carpaccio, pickled damsons and hazelnuts, followed by goose consommé with faggots which Craig matched memorably with his infamous Madeira. My main course was Lakeland veal with trotters and sweetbreads which, although daring, was very well received. Finally, the menu was completed with a rhubarb and marshmallow dessert.

There was a special atmosphere on this final night, and the realisation of what had been achieved and how brilliantly the staff had pulled together in supporting our guest chefs through this marathon of ten days was incredible. To top things off, along the way we had managed to raise money for charity and I'd like to take this opportunity to thank you all for your support in raising over £10,000 for Hospitality Action.

NIGEL HAWORTH

"To be obsessed by something you love is wonderful, some people work just for money."

OBSESSION FESTIVAL

2010

PHIL HOWARD

"My life has seen many interesting moments, but none more significant and random than the all-consuming Obsession with food and its production while I was at university. Furthermore, many interests, some fanatical, have come and gone but my interest and love of food is as intense now as it ever was. For me it is all an internal and intuitive thing – there is simply no desire to innovate or impress – my fulfilment has always been derived from the simple pleasure of cooking delicious food and the satisfaction that it has the capacity to give to its consumers.

Well, here it is, the 10th year. It is testament to Nigel's status in the industry, to the fact that he has managed to keep a full house of impressive chefs for a decade. It is easy to pull it off for a year or two but 10 is another story.

I have had many, many fantastic times cooking at Northcote and have to confess to having my professional life enriched by the relentless displays of welcoming northern hospitality and the variety of cooking going on in that kitchen. Nigel and Craig have become great mates and people for whom I have the utmost respect."

ANGELA HARTNETT AND LISA ALLEN

"I'm passionate about food because you get the chance to express your character, ability and flair in a plate of food. For me cooking is very emotional — there are so many emotions you go through: frustration, joy, passion and love, and that all comes through in cooking. You have to be obsessed to be a chef."

Lisa Allen

"I'm obsessed with food because I like to eat — simple as that. I was fortunate as a kid to grow up in a household that cared a lot about what we ate, and when you have that as a child it spoils you and becomes a part of what you want to do. I love my job, and I love cooking, end of story."

Angela Hartnett

ANDREW FAIRLIE

"I was very fortunate at a young age to find something that I had a natural talent for and that's continued to grow — the more I discovered, travelled and the harder I worked, the more passionate I became about it. At this level it's become a lifestyle. If you're a chef restaurateur you're in a fortunate position to be enjoying it 25 to 30 years later. If the food is right then everything else falls into place. The noise and the buzz got me into the job in the first place — now it's double the pleasure."

THEO RANDALL

"I'm obsessed with food and cooking because when I was very little my family instilled in me a love of food. It's always been a part of me and it's the tasting I love — remembering a flavour or smell. I knew it's something I really liked so I started working in kitchens and I cooked at home a lot, and used to help my mother bake and cook. We used to grow lots of produce in the garden and it was very common for me to go out into the garden and pick fresh vegetables to cook. Then I really got into it and loved the idea of being a chef, because it's not regular hours and there's this amazing pressure and the fulfilment at the end of the day when you make people happy — then start over the next day. It's the simplicity of food I love."

JACOB JAN BOERMA

"Food is a human interest and to cook serves man's survival. Professional cooking came in my life by chance. From the beginning the work in the kitchen obsessed me. I loved the richness of smells, tastes, textures and colours of the ingredients and the dishes that came from them. I perceived my capacity to make things with my own hands and to be original and imaginative. Cooking proved to be a way of pleasing others and get appreciation, eating together is a social activity. Every year my ambition is to be better than the year before; you may call it an Obsession, for me it is a lifetime vocation."

OBSESSION
FESTIVAL

"I am often asked what is it that motivates me to cook and without hesitation I always say it's an Obsession which is defined as a strong and barely controllable emotion. This strong feeling is hard to quantify but it has guided me throughout my life and career whether it be cooking, learning, writing or broadcasting.

Without a doubt, there have been many trying times when I questioned my Obsession with food and cooking and was unsure if I should continue to follow it. Even my mother had her doubts. She kept asking me for years when I was going to give up my passion for cooking and get a normal job. Finally, after 23 years, I got the chance to cook for the Chinese president at No 10 on his first ever state visit to this country which resulted in global headlines that reached even Chinese newspapers. My mother called and said perhaps I should keep my day job. That is when Obsession pays off!"

KEN HOM

MATTHEW FORT AND TOM PARKER BOWLES

"To adapt an observation of the great Liverpool manager, Bill Shankly, 'food isn't a matter of life and death. It's more important than that'."

Matthew Fort

"Greed is the root of all my passion for food, and the endless quest for great food, be it in the Michelin-starred glory of Northcote, or the most humble of Laotian noodle stores. I want good ingredients, cooked with love and skill."

Tom Parker Bowles

TOM KITCHIN

NATHAN OUTLAW

"Food and cooking have always been an Obsession for me, since I was a small boy. Watching my dad prepare and cook in his kitchen always got me excited and from his point of view I probably got in his way! The most exciting thing about cooking is the eating and I definitely have an Obsession for that – as you will have noticed if you have met me. There aren't many people in this world who can say they are obsessed with their work, but I am one of those lucky people who can say they are. Being obsessed with something cannot be taught, it comes from within. A hunger to learn more and get better and better produce from my area is what drives my passion to cook every day. The day that passion isn't there is the day I hang up my whites."

"I am completely obsessed with seasonality in my cooking. It is all about working with nature and understanding where produce comes from. My passion in cooking is all about appreciating and understanding beautiful fresh seasonal ingredients and creating new exciting taste sensations.

As a chef, it doesn't matter what level you're cooking at, if your heart doesn't start beating when you get the first asparagus of spring or the first woodcock in autumn, then you're not doing it for the right reasons."

RAZOR CLAMS
Serves 4

INGREDIENTS
1 Carrot
1 Courgette
100ml Vegetable oil
1 Lemon
8 Razor clams
2 Shallots, peeled and finely chopped
100ml White wine
100ml Whipping cream
50g Chopped chives or parsley
Knob of unsalted butter
Salt & pepper

Garnish
Bunch of chives, chopped
3 Sprigs of dill, chopped
Bunch of fresh amaranth leaves
2 Sprigs of chervil, chopped

METHOD

Vegetables
Peel the carrot and cut into 5mm dice. Cut the green skin off the courgette and dice into 5mm pieces – you don't need the white part for this recipe. Gently sauté the diced carrot and courgette in 1 teaspoon of vegetable oil for 3-4 minutes and set them aside.

Zest the lemon and squeeze the juice. Set aside for later.

Razor clams
Wash the razor clams well in cold running water, making sure you rinse away any sand and grit. Take a pan large enough to hold all the razor clams and place it over a high heat. Add the clams, shallots and white wine and immediately cover the pan with a tight fitting lid so the clams steam. The razor clams should be cooked in 1 minute – don't be tempted to cook them any longer or they will become rubbery. Discard any clams that don't open.

Remove the clams from their shells – keep the shells for serving. Slice the razor clam meat thinly at an angle around the brown intestine. Set aside.

Reduce the white wine cooking liquor by half. Then add the cream and diced vegetables and chopped chives or parsley while the liquid is simmering, stirring constantly. Once the cream thickens slightly, add the sliced razor clams, lemon juice and zest, and finish with a knob of butter. Season to taste.

TO SERVE

Place some shells on each plate and pile in the razor clams, vegetables and creamy juices. Garnish with fresh herbs for decoration and added flavour.

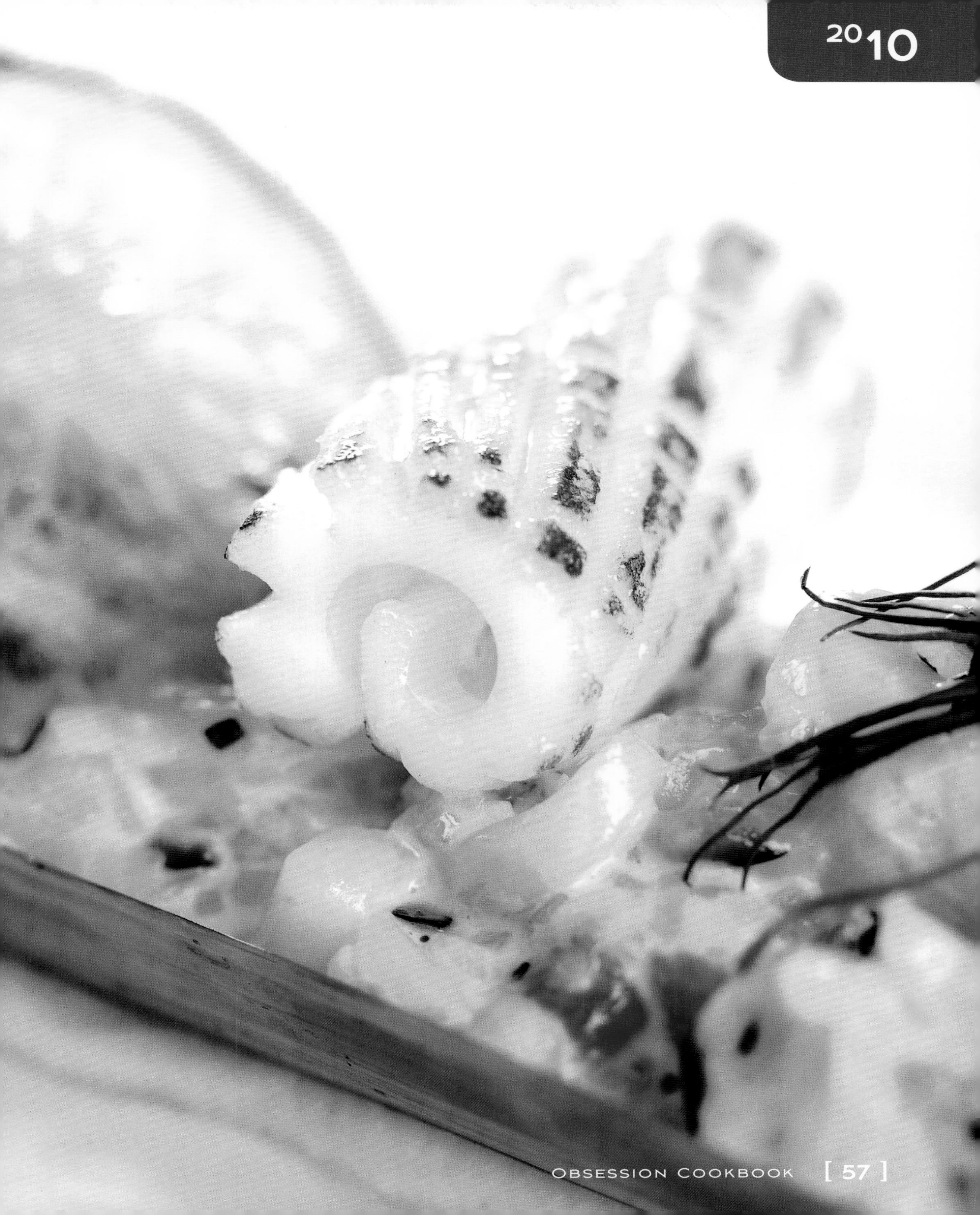

PETTO D'ANATRA CON ORZOTTO E ZUCCA (DUCK BREAST WITH BARLEY RISOTTO AND PUMPKIN)

Serves 4

INGREDIENTS

1 Reg Johnson supreme duck
Fat (preferably duck fat)
Oil
1 Carrot
1 Onion
1 Leek
1 Celery stick
1 Bay leaf
1 Bottle full bodied red wine
1 tsp Black peppercorns
1 tsp Juniper berries
100g Red onion marmalade
Handful deep-fried salsify

Barley risotto and pumpkin

140g Barley (35g per person)
2 ltr Stock (vegetable if you're a vegetarian; chicken, quail or game if you're not)
600g Pumpkin or butternut squash flesh
30g Butter
Handful of kale
Salt & pepper
30g Grated parmesan

METHOD

Preheat the oven to 230°C/450°F/gas mark 8. Brown the duck crown in hot fat by slipping it into the oven skin side down for 15-18 minutes. Remove from the oven and allow to cool.

Cut the legs off the duck. Cut the undercarriage of the duck away, leaving the crown. Chop up the undercarriage and brown in hot oil. Add the vegetables. Turn in the hot fat for a few minutes. Pour over the red wine and bring to the boil. Skim off the disagreeable foam. Turn down to a gentle simmer. Add the spices and bay leaf and the duck legs. Simmer for 1½ hours. The duck legs may possibly fall apart before this, in which case take them out, take off the skin and shred the flesh. Strain the duck stock into a clean pan and reduce to the desired intensity.

Barley risotto and pumpkin

Put the barley and stock in a saucepan. Bring to the boil. Simmer gently until the barley is cooked – about 40 minutes. Peel, de-seed and chop up the pumpkin flesh into chunks. Put inside a roasting bag or bowl and microwave for 8 minutes at full power until soft (or cook in a saucepan with a little water and the butter, remembering to boil off the water; or roast until soft). Liquidise in a food processor along with the butter. Season to taste. Stir the liquidised pumpkin into the barley. Blanch the kale until well cooked and cut up finely. Stir into the orzotto con zucca (pumpkin risotto) along with the shredded duck's legs. Season again. Beat in the parmesan.

TO SERVE

Remove the duck breast from the crown and keep warm. Place the orzotto con zucca in the centre of a plate. Slice the duck breasts and place on top, dividing them equally between the plates. Place the duck liver at the side, garnish with the onion marmalade and deep-fried salsify. Sauce around.

PAN FRIED SCALLOPS WITH CHILLI, SAGE, CAPERS AND ANCHOVIES

Serves 4

INGREDIENTS

250g Cima di rapa or purple sprouting broccoli, tough stems removed
600ml Water
Salt & pepper
1 Garlic clove, sliced finely
Olive oil
12 Cleaned large scallops
1 Red chilli – sliced and seeds removed
1 tsp Capers
8 Sage leaves
4 Anchovy fillets, salted in oil
250g White polenta flour
½ tsp Red wine vinegar

METHOD

Blanch the cima di rapa in salted boiling water. Remove when tender and cool down in a colander.

Fry the garlic in a saucepan and add the cima di rapa and cook for 3 minutes. Season and put to one side.

In a deep saucepan boil the water and add a pinch of salt then whisk the polenta into the boiling water and cook for 30 minutes. Season and add 2 tablespoons of olive oil.

Heat a frying pan until it smokes. Toss the scallops with salt and pepper and a little olive oil. Place in a hot pan carefully and colour on one side. Turn over, add the chilli, capers, sage and anchovy and a dash of olive oil then take off the heat and add half a teaspoon of red wine vinegar.

TO SERVE

Plate up by putting the polenta in the middle of the plate. Place the cima di rapa on top followed by the scallops, sage, anchovy and capers.

SPICY HOT AND SOUR SOUP
Serves 4

INGREDIENTS

1.2 ltr Homemade chicken stock
2 tsp Salt
125g Lean boneless pork,
finely shredded
1 tsp Light soy sauce
1 tsp Shaoxing rice wine or dry sherry
½ tsp Sesame oil
½ tsp Cornflour
Pinch of salt
Pinch of sugar
2 Eggs, beaten with a pinch of salt
2 tsp Sesame oil
25g Dried Chinese mushrooms,
soaked, stems removed and finely
shredded
15g Dried 'tree ear' mushrooms,
soaked, stems removed and
finely shredded
250g Fresh firm beancurd, drained
and shredded
1½ tbsp Light soy sauce
1 tbsp Dark soy sauce
1 tsp Freshly ground white pepper
6 tbsp Chinese white rice vinegar or
cider vinegar
2 tsp Sesame oil
2 tsp Chilli oil
2 tbsp Fresh coriander, finely chopped

METHOD

Bring the stock to a simmer in a large
pot and add the salt.

Combine the pork with the
soy sauce, rice wine, sesame oil,
cornflour, salt and sugar. Mix well and
set aside.

In a small bowl, combine the eggs
with the sesame oil and set aside.

Stir the pork into the stock
mixture and simmer for 1 minute.
Then add the two types of
mushrooms with the beancurd and
continue to simmer for 2 minutes.
Add the egg mixture in a very slow,
thin and steady stream. Using a
chopstick or fork, pull the egg slowly
into strands. Remove the soup from
the heat, and stir in the soy sauces,
pepper and vinegar. Give the soup a
good stir, then finally add the sesame
oil, chilli oil, fresh coriander and stir.

TO SERVE

Ladle into individual bowls or in a
large soup tureen and serve at once.

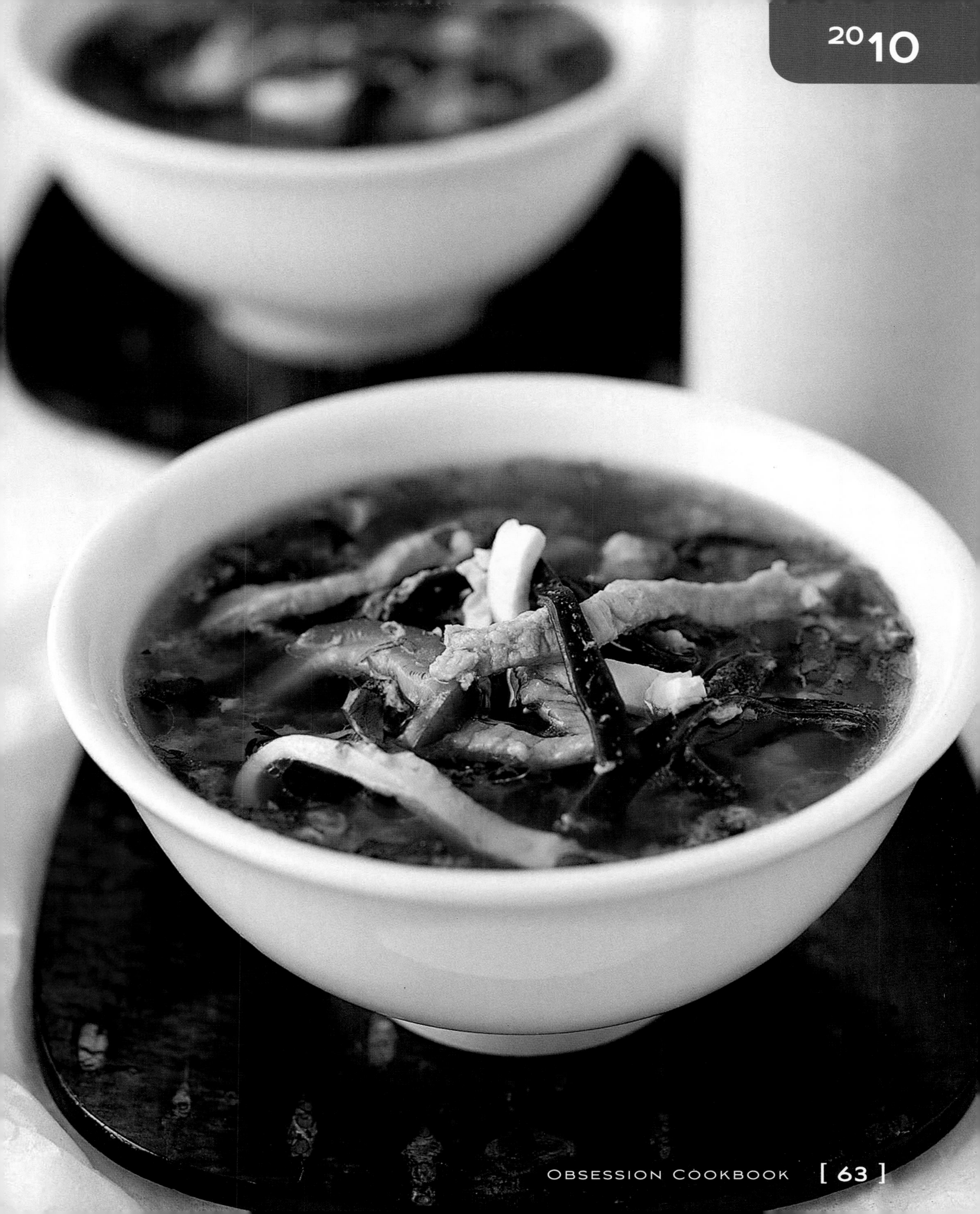

SEARED WEST COAST SCALLOPS, PATA NEGRA AND BUTTERNUT SQUASH

Serves 4

INGREDIENTS

Apple vinaigrette
(makes more than enough for 4)
1 ltr Apple juice
500ml Olive oil
70ml Cider vinegar
Salt

Butternut squash purée
(makes more than enough for 4)
1kg Ripe pumpkin diced
50g Butter

Candied walnuts
100g Shelled walnuts
200g Sugar
Butter

Shallot chutney
3 Shallots
100ml Chardonnay vinegar
Salt
Thyme
Bay leaf

Scallops
8 Large scallops
Olive oil
Curry seasoning
(1:1 mild curry powder to salt)
1 Granny Smith apple
½ Cucumber, peeled
Chopped chervil
Pata negra ham sliced
Mixed cresses

METHOD

Apple vinaigrette
Bring the apple juice to the boil and reduce to 100ml.

Mix the olive oil, cider vinegar and salt together with the reduced apple juice.

Butternut squash purée
Sweat the butternut squash dice in butter and season with salt.

Cover with a lid and let it steam for 15 minutes, or until the butternut squash has released its juices.

Take the lid off and cook on a medium heat until the butternut squash has gone soft and the liquid has evaporated.

Blend in a Vitamix (liquidiser) adding some of the diced cold butter.

Season and pass through a chinoise (conical sieve).

Candied walnuts
Toast the walnuts in the oven at 180°C/ 350°F/gas mark 4 for 2 minutes so that the walnuts are hot.

Heat the sugar to make a caramel.

When golden, add the walnuts, a pinch of salt and enough butter to cover the walnuts.

Mix for a few seconds and then pour onto parchment paper.

Leave to cool then roughly chop.

Shallot chutney
Dice the shallots into 2cm cubes.

Cover with the vinegar, add the aromats, season and cook at a very low heat, until the liquid has evaporated and the shallots are cooked.

Scallops
Cut the scallops in half, sprinkle with curry seasoning and pan fry in a hot pan with the olive oil.

Dice the apple and cucumber into equal cubes (roughly 0.5cm³).

Mix the diced apple and cucumber with a spoonful of shallot chutney, walnut crunch, chopped chervil and the apple vinaigrette.

Arrange the purée on the plate, scallops on top, spoon the apple garnish on and around.

Finish with a slice of pata negra on top and then the cresses.

Valrhona Chocolate Cylinder, Smoked Nuts, Salted Organic Sheep's Milk Ice cream
Serves 4

Valrhona Chocolate Cylinder, Smoked Nuts, Salted Organic Sheep's Milk Ice cream
Serves 4

INGREDIENTS

4 Chocolate cylinders (see below)
Chocolate mousse (see below)
Condensed milk caramel (see below)
Salted sheep's milk ice cream
(see below)
Sugar pull (see below)
Vanilla soaked sultanas (see below)
Smoked nuts (see below)
Chocolate paint (see below)

Chocolate cylinders
600g Valrhona 55% Equatorial
Chocolate Pistols

Chocolate mousse
140g Valrhona chocolate
30g Butter
60g Egg yolks
15g Caster sugar
50ml Cream
100g Egg whites
60g Icing sugar

Salted sheep's milk ice cream
½ ltr Sheep's milk
¼ ltr Cows' milk
75g Glucose
75g Milk powder
2.5g Stabiliser – stab 2000
75g Sugar
5g Maldon sea salt

Condensed milk caramel
400g Carnation condensed milk or
a can of ready caramelised
condensed milk

Sugar pull
200g Fondant sugar
40g Glucose syrup
10g Smoked nut dust

Vanilla soaked sultanas
100g Water
50g Sugar
½ Vanilla pod
5g Minus 8 vinegar
60g Yellow sultanas

Smoked nuts
30g Roasted pecan nuts
30g Roasted hazelnuts
30g Roasted walnuts

Chocolate paint
62g Sugar
62g Water
20g Cocoa powder
62g Double cream

To serve
1 Cylinder
1 Sugar pull
Smoked nut dust
Melted chocolate
Salted sheep's milk ice cream
Condensed milk caramel
Chocolate paint

METHOD

Chocolate cylinders

Melt 200g of the chocolate to 55°C. Stir in the remaining 400g of pistols, work briskly to melt the beans but be careful not to incorporate any air. The chocolate should end up at around 33°C. Leave the chocolate in a cool dry place to cool to 28°C. The chocolate will begin to set around the outside. Gently heat the chocolate back up to 31°C, stirring in the solidified chocolate as you go. IF YOU EXCEED 32°C THE PROCESS WILL HAVE TO BE REPEATED.

To make the cylinder, cut pieces of acetate to 18x15cm and attach parcel tape to one of the longer sides. Spread the chocolate across half of the acetate away from the tape and roll, securing with the tape at the other side. If necessary, drizzle a little more chocolate down the tube to seal the edge of the cylinder. Allow to set in a cool dry place, preferably for 24 hours. To assemble the cylinder pipe a little condensed milk caramel into the tube, try to get some running the full length. Pipe chocolate mousse into the tube. Follow by adding some of the nuts and sultanas. Repeat the process until the tube is filled. Cap each end with condensed caramel and refrigerate.

Chocolate mousse

Melt the chocolate and butter, mix until fully incorporated. Whisk egg yolk and sugar until light and double in size. Boil the cream and pour over the chocolate and butter. Fold the yolk mixture into the chocolate. Whisk egg whites until soft peaks, slowly adding icing sugar. Fold into the above. Lastly, refrigerate until cold and ready to use.

Salted sheep's milk ice cream

Bring both milks to the boil. Add the glucose, milk powder, stabiliser and sugar and simmer for a further 2 minutes then blitz with a hand blender, pass through a fine sieve and mix in the Maldon sea salt. When cool, place into the Pacojet and freeze to –20°C. Once frozen, paco once then paco again before serving. An ice cream maker could be used for this.

Condensed milk caramel

Place an unopened tin of condensed milk in a pan of boiling water and simmer for 4 hours.

Check the pan occasionally to ensure it doesn't boil dry. When cooked, leave the tin to cool completely before opening. Open the tin, empty the contents into a bowl and stir to ensure an even colour. Put into a piping bag ready for use.

Sugar pull

Bring both sugar and glucose syrup to the boil and cook to 121°C. Stop the cooking by dipping the base of the pan into cold water, add the nut dust, pour out onto a silpat mat. When cooled a little, pull thin sheets of sugar and form over a rolling pin or other cylindrical object. Dip your thumb into one end of the sugar pull to provide space to place the ice cream.

Vanilla soaked sultanas

In a small pan bring to the boil the water, sugar and vanilla pod and boil for 3-4 minutes.

Remove from the heat, add the minus 8 vinegar and the yellow sultanas. Leave to cool and marinate for at least 1 day.

Smoked nuts

Place the nuts onto a tray and into a smoker with hickory smoking tablets for 45 minutes.

Once smoked cut the nuts into bite-size pieces. Reserve for the cylinder and the small nuts for the nut dust.

Chocolate paint

Bring the sugar and water to the boil. Add the cocoa and whisk in well, pour into a small bowl and place on ice water. Once cool, whisk in the double cream, pour into a squeezy bottle and refrigerate.

TO SERVE

Brush the plate with the chocolate paint. Pipe a little condensed milk caramel to secure the cylinder. Unwrap the cylinder, be careful not to mark or get fingerprints on the surface of the chocolate. Dip the ends in the smoked nut dust, secure on the plate with the condensed milk caramel. Place the sugar pull over the cylinder. Finally position a quenelle of ice cream in the end of the sugar pull and serve.

WRECKFISH, MUSSELS AND SAFFRON WITH RED PEPPER AND BLACK OLIVES
Serves 4

INGREDIENTS

Mussels
500g Live mussels
Water to cook

Saffron sauce
750ml Fish stock
250ml Shellfish stock
2 Chopped ripe tomatoes
1 Sprig tarragon
Pinch of saffron
50ml Unsalted butter

Shellfish stock
1 Onion, chopped
2 Carrots, peeled and chopped
4 Ripe tomatoes, chopped
6 Garlic cloves, halved
1kg Frozen shell-on prawns
1 Orange, zest and juice
Few knobs unsalted butter

Potatoes
16 Medium Roseval (salad) potatoes
100ml Olive oil
Pinch of salt

Red pepper
1 Large red pepper

Wreckfish
4 x 200g Fillet portions of wreckfish
Oil for cooking
Salt for seasoning

Garnish
600g Washed baby spinach
40g Pitted black olives, roughly chopped
Extra virgin olive oil

METHOD

Mussels
Heat a pan with a tight fitting lid until it is very hot. Add the mussels and carefully add the water. Place the lid on and steam open the mussels for 2 minutes. Drain the mussels, reserving the juices. Pick the mussel meat out of the shells and wash off the sand and grit, if any. Chill down the mussels and place in the fridge.

Saffron sauce
Place all the ingredients into a pan and reduce to a sauce. Pass through a sieve and keep warm.

Shellfish stock
Place the prawns onto a tray and roast for 45 minutes. Sweat off the vegetables and orange zest in a pan until coloured and add the prawns. Cover with water and juice and simmer for 1 hour. Pass the stock through a sieve and reduce by half in a fresh pan. Chill and refrigerate.

Potatoes
Peel the potatoes and place them in a vacuum pack bag with the oil and salt. Seal the bag and place it into a water bath at 95°C. They will take 30-40 minutes to cook. To serve add a little of the oil to a pan, add the potatoes and colour them all over. Season and serve.

Red pepper
Place a wire rack or trellis over a naked flame. Place the pepper over the flame and blacken all over. Transfer the pepper to a tub and cover with cling film. Leave for 20 minutes then peel the black skin away and de-seed the pepper. Cut the pepper into 1cm squares. Reserve.

Wreckfish
Preheat the oven to 180°C/350°F/ gas mark 4. Heat a non-stick pan on the stove and add some oil. Place the fish skin side down into the pan and season with salt. Cook the fish on the skin until it starts to turn golden, then place it in the oven and cook for 4-5 minutes. Remove from the oven and flip the fish over on to the flesh side and remove from the heat. This should be cooked at the very last moment and served immediately.

TO SERVE

Bring the shellfish stock to the boil and whisk in the unsalted butter. Warm 4 bowls. Place the potatoes in the centre of the plates. Add a little shellfish stock. Mix together the spinach, olives and red pepper and wilt in a pan, add the mussels and warm through. Season and plate up around the potato. Warm the sauce and spoon over the garnish and finish with the extra virgin olive oil. Finally, top with the fish.

TERRINE OF DOVER SOLE WITH SMOKED EEL AND OYSTERS
Makes one terrine (12-14 portions)

INGREDIENTS

3 Large Dover soles (1.2kg skin removed both sides)
Salt & pepper
Juice of a lemon
150ml Crème fraîche
3 Leaves of gelatine

Garnish (for 8)
20 Large rock oysters, carefully shucked, juice retained
2 Egg yolks
200ml Grapeseed oil
Juice of ½ lemon
75g Sugar
1 tbsp Lemon olive oil
½ bunch of chives, finally chopped
¼ tsp Sosa Gelespressa or xanthan gum
1 x 330ml Bottle of beer
12g Fresh yeast
1 tsp Sugar
280g Flour
1 Smoked eel, skinned
1 Cucumber, peeled and cut into 3x5cm lengths
100ml White wine vinegar
24 Sprigs of chervil, to garnish

METHOD

Season the Dover soles, vacuum pack them individually and cook for 15 minutes at 65°C in a water bath. Remove from the bath and leave to rest for 10 minutes. Remove the soles from the bags, reserving the juices, and carefully lift the fillets from the bone. Lay them all out on a tray and lightly season with salt and pepper and give them a squeeze of lemon juice. Measure out 150ml of the sole juices, add the crème fraîche and warm, whisking to combine.

Soften the gelatine in cold water and dissolve in the crème fraîche mix to make a jelly. Set aside and keep warm.

Line a standard terrine mould with cling film. Place two sole fillets in the base, trimming as required, and spoon over ½ tablespoon of crème fraîche jelly. Continue filling the terrine with sole fillets making sure you add a small quantity of crème fraîche mix between each layer. Once all the fillets are in, wrap the terrine in cling film and chill overnight.

Place 4 oysters and the egg yolks in a blender and blend until smooth. Add 50ml oyster juice and re-blend. Now gradually add the grapeseed oil. This will give a creamy oyster mayonnaise. Check and adjust the seasoning with salt, pepper and lemon juice. Set aside in the fridge.

Make the beer batter by gradually whisking the beer into the yeast, sugar and flour. Whisk until homogeneous and leave to prove in a warm place.

Cut the eel in 3, blast chill until firm and, with the use of a slicer, slice wafer thin slices of eel from each side of the central spine. You will need 16 slices. Lay on parchment paper and set aside in the fridge.

Cut a total of 16 thin slices off the cucumber blocks. Dissolve the sugar in the vinegar, add the cucumber and leave for 1 hour.

Chop 8 of the oysters into quarters. Thicken the remaining oyster juice (about 100ml) by blending with the Sosa Gelespressa. Add the chopped oysters, the lemon olive oil and chives and stir gently to combine. Dip the remaining 8 oysters in the beer batter and deep fry at 180°C until crisp and pale golden. Drain on absorbent paper.

TO SERVE

Remove the terrine carefully from the moulds and, using a sharp carving knife, take 8x1cm slices from the terrine. Place one on each of 8 plates and drape over 2 slices of cucumber. Place small dots of oyster mayonnaise onto the plates and spoon some of the oyster vinaigrette over the terrine. Garnish with a deep fried oyster and sprigs of chervil.

LIGHTLY GRILLED TURBOT WITH BUTTERNUT SQUASH, TWO PREPARATIONS OF SCALLOPS, WINTER TRUFFLE, PURSLANE AND JUS OF TRUFFLE AND OLIVE OIL

Serves 4

INGREDIENTS

1 White onion
6 Pieces of lemongrass, chopped
1 Piece ginger
Olive oil
Salt & pepper
2 Laurel leaves
2 Pieces of lemon peel
1 tsp Curry powder
Small amount of curry paste
150ml White wine
400ml Chicken fond (bouillon made from chicken meat and carcasses)
8 Scotch scallops
Mayonnaise
1 Winter truffle, chopped
1 Piece of parsley
500g Butternut squash, half diced and half sliced
4 x 100g Pieces of turbot
Japanese vinegar
Natural fish sauce, to serve
Truffle vinegar, to serve
Purslane or lettuce leaves, to serve

METHOD

Cook the onion with chopped lemongrass and the ginger in olive oil with some pepper and salt, then add the laurel leaves, lemon peel, curry powder, curry paste and white wine and wait until it is reduced. Put in the chicken fond and cook until boiled. Remove the ginger and the laurel leaves. Blend the juice in a thermo blender.

Make a scallop tartare sauce by taking 4 scallops and mixing them with some mayonnaise, chopped truffle and parsley.

Boil the butternut squash squares and slices in salted water until almost well done and then marinate them in Japanese vinegar and olive oil.

Put some salt, pepper and olive oil on the turbot, grill them then put into the oven to steam at 120°C/250°F/gas mark ½ for between 2½ and 4 minutes.

Cut the other 4 scallops in half, season and sauté on one side.

TO SERVE

Place 2 sautéed scallops on a plate, sautéed side up, then put some scallop tartare on top followed by a slice of marinated butternut squash. Put some stripes of butternut squash purée around the plate with some squares of butternut squash. Place the turbot in the middle, then put some natural fish sauce on top of it. Dot truffle vinegar around and garnish with purslane or salad leaves.

Cep Tart, Roasted Calf's Sweetbread

Serves 1

INGREDIENTS

2 Sheets of filo pastry
50g Melted butter
1 Sprig of thyme
70g Grated parmesan
250g Firm ceps
150g White button mushrooms
150g Butter
Salt
2 tbsp Lemon juice
2 Shallots, finely chopped
1 Small garlic clove, crushed
75ml Chicken stock
1 tbsp Double cream
Vegetable oil
1 Large nugget of soaked and trimmed calf's sweetbread
1 tsp Chopped tarragon
Flat parsley
2 tbsp Madeira sauce

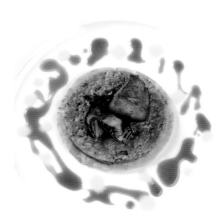

METHOD

Preheat the oven to 180°C/350°F/gas mark 4.

Brush one sheet of filo pastry with melted butter, remove the thyme leaves from the sprig and sprinkle over the filo with 20g of the grated parmesan. Place the other sheet of filo on top and run your hand over the top to dispel any air that may be trapped. Brush this top sheet with the remaining butter. Cut out a large round using a pastry cutter or cut round a saucer. Place the round in between two silpat mats (silicon paper can be used) and bake for exactly 8 minutes. Remove the crispy rounds and place on a wire rack to cool.

Pick out one perfectly shaped cep for roasting and presentation. Cut the remaining ceps into 3mm dice, keeping all the trimmings to one side.

Finely slice the button mushrooms.

Melt 50g of the butter in a small saucepan, add the cep trimmings and the button mushrooms, season with a little salt and the lemon juice, cover with a lid. Cook gently over a medium heat until the mushrooms are completely soft. Blend to make a very smooth purée. Keep until needed.

Melt another 50g of butter in a saucepan, add the chopped shallots and crushed garlic, sprinkle with a little salt and cook gently for 4 minutes. Add the diced ceps, turn the heat up a little and cook until the ceps just begin to take colour. Add the stock and cream and boil until almost evaporated. Remove from the heat until needed.

Heat a small frying pan with a little vegetable oil. Season the sweetbread and fry over a medium heat until golden brown, add the whole cep and continue to cook until both are nicely caramelised. Add the remaining butter and baste continuously until both the sweetbread and cep are cooked. Remove from the pan and drain on a cloth.

TO SERVE

Put the filo disc into the oven to reheat.

Heat the diced cep mixture; when hot fold in the mushroom purée and the grated parmesan. Check the seasoning and add the chopped tarragon.

Place the warmed disc onto a tray, place a cutter slightly smaller than the disc onto the disc and press the mushroom mixture into the cutter and smooth with the back of a spoon.

Place this mushroom tart onto the centre of a warmed plate, place the caramelised cep and sweetbread on top and garnish with a piece of flat parsley.

Drizzle a little Madeira sauce around and serve immediately.

VENISON CARPACCIO, MUSHROOM PÂTÉ, PICKLED DAMSONS, HAZELNUTS

Serves 4

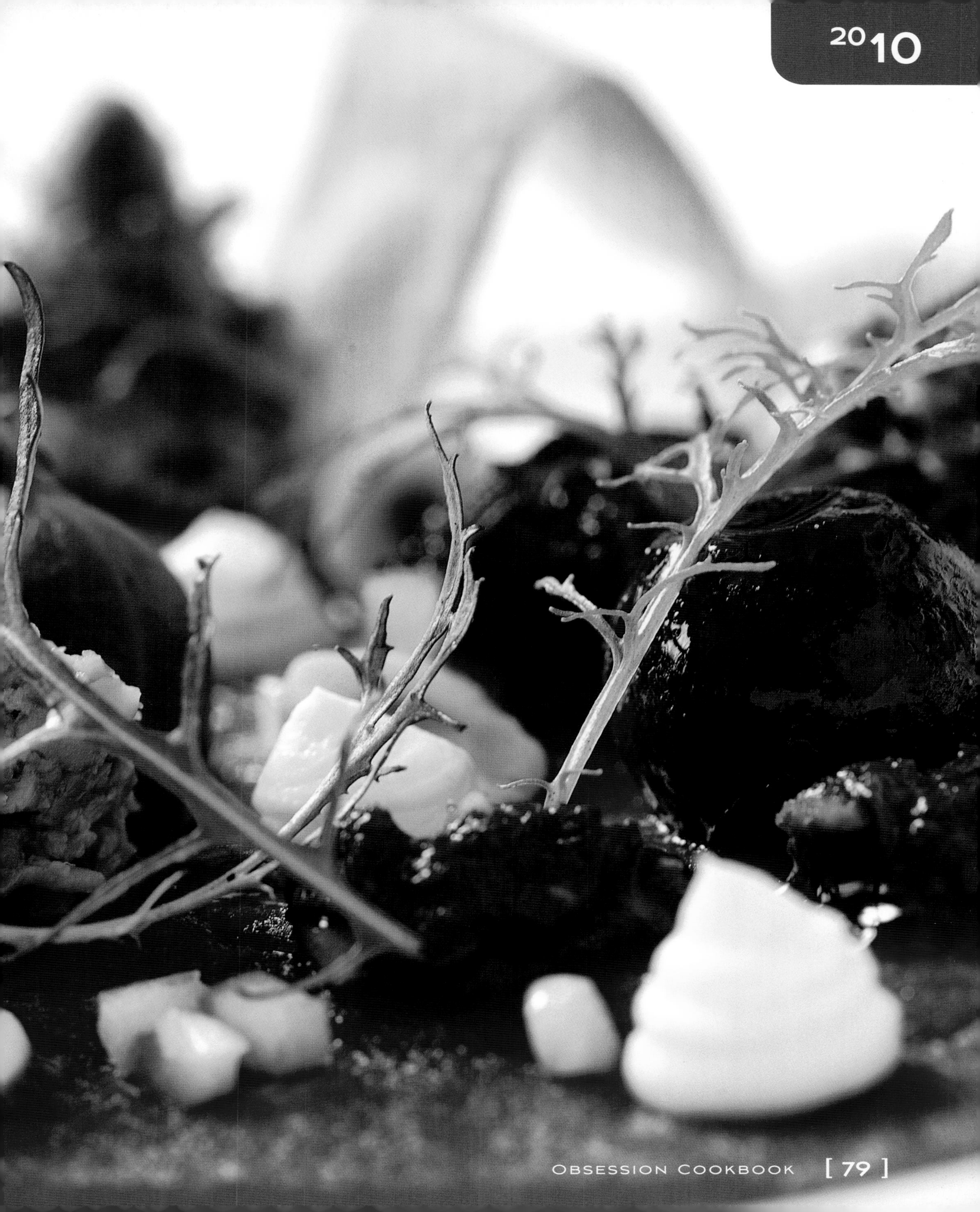

VENISON CARPACCIO, MUSHROOM PÂTÉ, PICKLED DAMSONS, HAZELNUTS

Serves 4

INGREDIENTS

1 x 300g Piece of venison cushion
(silverskin removed and trimmed)
Tarragon pesto (see below)
8 Pickled damsons, deseeded and cut
in half (see below)
Mushroom pâté (see below)
Crème fraîche and horseradish cream
(see below)
4 Bread wafers (see below)
Few drops lemon olive oil
Maldon salt
20g Red onions, finely diced
8 Whole smoked hazelnuts, roasted
and halved
4 Caper berries
Salad leaves

Mushroom pâté

100g Sliced white button mushrooms
25g Shallots, finely sliced
1 tbsp Olive oil
½ Garlic clove, crushed
Salt & pepper

Pickled damsons

225g Damsons
110g Sugar
1 Cinnamon stick
3 Cloves
10g Fresh root ginger, peeled
and sliced
150ml White wine vinegar

Tarragon pesto

50g Tarragon (picked and cut
with scissors)
10g Roast pine nuts
1 Garlic clove, finely chopped
150ml Olive oil
60g Parmesan
Pinch of salt

Crème fraîche and
horseradish cream

50g Crème fraîche
20g Horseradish sauce
25g Whipping cream, semi-whipped
Salt
Pinch of cayenne pepper

Bread wafers

100g White bread dough
Salt & black pepper

METHOD

Roll the venison cushion tight in
cling film, place in a blast chiller to
semi freeze. Remove from the chiller
and cut ½cm off each end to form a
rectangle 11cm long and 6cm wide.
Slice at number 1 (approx 1cm thick)
on the meat slicer, then place directly
on to the plate, overlapping slightly,
three slices per plate.

Mushroom pâté

Sweat the mushrooms and shallots
in the olive oil in a pan for 2-3
minutes until soft, add the garlic
and season with salt and pepper.
Cook for a further 8-10 minutes until
all the liquid has evaporated. Place
into a food processor and blitz to a
rustic pâté, check the seasoning and
remove from the food processor.

Pickled damsons

Preheat the oven to 140°C/275°F/
gas mark 1.
    Prick the damson skins with a
needle to prevent them splitting,
then put into an earthenware dish
and sprinkle with sugar. Scatter the
cinnamon, cloves and ginger over
the fruit and cover with the vinegar.
Put the dish at the bottom of a warm
oven and leave to cook very slowly for
about 20 minutes. Remove when the
damsons begin to feel soft and the
juice is running and set aside to cool.
When cold, strain the juice, boil it for
5 minutes and pour over the damsons.
Put them into a jar. They are best kept
for two weeks before use.

Tarragon pesto

Place all the ingredients into a
liquidiser, blend well to make the
pesto. Remove from the liquidiser
and check the seasoning. Reserve.

Crème fraîche and
horseradish cream

Mix together the crème fraîche
and horseradish sauce. Pass the
mix through a fine sieve. Place into
a bowl, fold in the semi-whipped
cream, season with salt and cayenne
pepper. Put into a piping bag ready
for use.

Bread wafers

Roll the dough through a pasta
machine, working down the numbers
to number one. Dust the dough
lightly with flour to prevent it from
sticking. Once the dough is thin (you
should be able to see your hand
through it) lay it flat on to a dusted
tabletop. Cut into long rectangles
16cm long by 2½cm wide. Season
with salt and black pepper. Place
the cut bread dough on to a metal
wavy rack, bake in the oven at
190°C/375°F/gas mark 4 for 8-10
minutes until golden. Remove from
the oven, leave to cool then remove
from the wavy rack.

TO SERVE

Lightly brush the venison with the
lemon olive oil and season with
Maldon salt.
    Take the bread wafers and put
on two small spoons of mushroom
pâté and a little horseradish cream,
reserve.
    Put 2 small teaspoons of
mushroom pâté on to the venison,
pipe 6 tiny cones of horseradish
cream and sprinkle around the diced
onion. Also place on the plate some
hazelnuts, a caper berry and pickled
damsons. Add a bread wafer and
finish with the tarragon pesto and
salad leaves.

20O9

aniel opened the 2009 Festival. I had met Daniel Clifford at Midsummer House while visiting St John's College, Cambridge where I was doing a talk on provenance. His first dish was cep, pumpkin and parmesan with fantastic flavours. This dish was followed by scallops and bay leaves, venison was the main course with a stunning chestnut ravioli and to finish a top dessert of roasted pineapple on a coconut and lime gateau.

Shaun Rankin was our next guest, probably a chef whose food we have eaten more of than many with our trips to Jersey. Shaun cooked his signature dish of a lightly poached royal bay oysters with sevruga caviar and they went down a treat. Jersey has some incredible seafood. Shaun's main course was a combination of raw and cooked beef with woodland mushrooms and winter truffles which took a few people by surprise but the result was a winner.

Where was Glynn Purnell? Glynn was due to arrive the night before, rooms were booked, Hot Pot prepared, staff on stand by, but there was no sign of Glynn. Alas, we went to bed at 2am, thinking that it could be a worrying day, but he arrived the next day with a full brigade, having closed his restaurant and it was an absolute joy. Of course he cooked a version of his fish curry that won the Great British Menu in 2008. Glynn's flavours really shone through, everyone loved it, a really star dish. His famous egg dish with blackberries and crystallised tarragon was a beauty of a dessert.

It was great to have Phil Howard and Brett Graham – Brett opened the night with the warm game canapés and pigeon tea that was garnished with smouldering bay leaves which wafted throughout the room in an ecclesiastical way. He followed with Pyrenean lamb and truffled potato which was a delight. Phil reworked kedgree and I had to remind him it was a dinner, not a breakfast; joking aside it was a fabulous interpretation. Foie gras is always a feature and it made its way back on the menu to great acclaim; salted

caramel nougatine was a modern twist on a great dessert.

Atul Kochhar arrived with his wife and children and his two trusted assistants from Benares. Atul cooked a fantastic carpaccio of venison with subtle spicing and great flavour. The Goan spiced lobster was an incredible dish with fresh flavours and soft spices. Then he finished with an interesting interpretation of a classic bread and butter pudding, introducing the flavours of fennel and ginger.

Jason and his team delivered his formidable repertoire in a precise and focused way. Tongue in cheek, a classic Atherton dish, was particularly well-received. Sweetcorn panna cotta followed, with salted caramel and popcorn sherbet – an unusual dish that was brilliantly delivered with real theatre. Jason finished with bitter chocolate and hazelnut parfait with a milk mousse, a wonderful way to close a great menu.

To wrap it up in 2009, I cooked with my old friend Paul Heathcote. I had always wanted Paul to take part in the festival but had never managed to squeeze in the invitation in-between his many skiing holidays. This year we were in luck and finally we were cooking together. Preparation done and all in place we joined a fellow chef and great friend, Michael Golowitz, who was staying at Northcote, for a few minutes relaxing and watching football before service. Paul cooked braised turbot and scallops with leeks and wild mushrooms, a classic Heathcote dish from his former two Michelin star repertoire. He closed with Heathcote's bread and butter pudding, one of Paul's signature dishes and renowed for its depth of flavour and lightness. I cooked a beef tea then Herdwick mutton and smoked mash potato. Finally, tiny melting Valrhona chocolate desserts which were inspired by Lisa Allen. A final night at the bar saw us sipping a stunning red Vinha Pan from Luis Pato in front of the fire.

obsession
northcote
FESTIVAL OF FOOD & WINE, TWO THOUSAND & NINE

DANIEL CLIFFORD

"When I fall in love with something I give it 100 per cent. Food has always been my first love and it was the first thing that I found in life that I truly enjoyed. Every day I am learning. It's not a job, it's a lifestyle."

OBSESSION
FESTIVAL

ATUL KOCHHAR

"I was fortunate to be born in a family where food and family were the most important things. My dad was a connoisseur in his own right and his values got instilled in me and my siblings right from childhood. Since I've become a professional, I have always worked my food around agriculture and natural cycles. Food is a passion for me and its natural character motivates me to cook with the seasons. I dream of the seasons in terms of their produce and the end products I would create next time. I think of good food markets in terms of fashion show ramps; I imagine food flavours as if they were new perfumes for the season. So if people think I am obsessed, then so be it."

JASON ATHERTON

"I became obsessed with food from an early age of about 16, so I was lucky I knew I wanted to become a chef and was dedicated to my craft. I came from a modest background and cooking gave me a foot in the door into a world like no other. The smells, the tastes, the most amazing ingredients. I couldn't stop eating, sleeping, breathing my new love which to this very day is still embedded in my soul. I can't walk past a bistro, shop or farm for that matter without getting lost in the romance of our beautiful world which is cooking."

SHAUN RANKIN

"My Obsession is really with ingredients because it all starts with them. Ingredients define what I do. I call Jersey my nine-mile kitchen garden and for me it's all about sourcing local produce and ingredients. I started cooking because I loved the whole thing - I used to love cooking with my mum and that took me into catering, but from the age of 16 it's a job and you're cutting your teeth, I think a deeper understanding of ingredients doesn't come until a later age. My passion is growing more and more and I source better produce the older I get - it's a life work."

GLYNN PURNELL

"I got into cooking when I was about 10 and the Obsession started when I went to the market with mum. It was wild: food had faces and from then I was obsessed with the way food changes when it's cooked - like when you fry an egg and how cheese goes stringy when it's hot. Then it really kicked in when I walked into my first kitchen at 14 and I realised it's not a job; it's a way of life. First I thought, why are all these people shouting? But it was instant - the hair on the back of my neck was standing up and it was a total buzz. You can't describe the feeling, but I knew that's what I'd do for the rest of my life and that Obsession has never been dampened - if anything it's grown. Even when I'm away from the restaurant I think about food. It's food, food, food! You can't be any more intimate with someone (other than sex) than when you're cooking for them."

PHIL HOWARD AND BRETT GRAHAM

OBSESSION
FESTIVAL
2009

"In 2008 I told Nigel and Craig I would retire from The
Festival after 10 years and give way for a more youthful
star to shine! I genuinely thought this was the 10th year,
so I brought Brett Graham with me to pass the baton to.
We shared the dinner and our food dovetails perfectly but
it was swiftly explained to me that this was only the 9th
year. One more to go then. Quite how local legend Paul
Heathcote managed to slip through the net for 9 years,
I do not know!"

Phil Howard

"I'm obsessed with the seasonality of the food I cook. I
take a very seasonal approach and enjoy sourcing, shooting
and preparing some fantastic wild British ingredients."

Brett Graham

Nigel Haworth

Paul Heathcote

"Finding the best piece of meat or fish over and over again is not easy, it is like trying to replicate the right company; ambience; mood – it is a difficult marriage. But when it happens it is magical, and we always want to better this – it is what drives us: for great chefs it is an obsessive pursuit."

Paul Heathcote

"To be obsessed with food is to be obsessed with the fruit of life."

Nigel Haworth

AMUSE BOUCHE CEP, PUMPKIN AND MUSHROOM

Serves 8

INGREDIENTS

Mushroom purée
1kg Mushrooms, roughly chopped
Oil or clarified butter
2 Shallots, sliced
2 Garlic cloves
Thyme and bay leaves
170ml Vegetable stock
50ml Madeira
Salt & pepper
1 tbsp Whipping cream per serving
1 tsp White truffle oil per serving

Cep jelly
300ml Cep essence, seasoned
(see below)
15g Vegi Jell (Sosa)

Cep essence
1 Onion
½ Shallot
1 Garlic clove
1 Stick of celery
600g Button mushrooms
50g Dried ceps
150ml Madeira
500g Fresh chicken stock

Gnocchi
140g Potatoes
Salt
55g Pasta flour
5g Cep powder
Salt & pepper
½ Egg
Olive oil
Butter

Pumpkin soup
2 Onions, chopped
4 Garlic cloves
140g Pumpkin, chopped
190g White chicken stock
Small pinch of saffron
100ml Double cream
50g Beurre noisette
Sherry vinegar
50g Pumpkin seeds

METHOD

Mushroom purée
Sauté the mushrooms in very hot oil, so they colour quickly. Continue cooking until they start to render their juices. Strain off the liquid, but reserve it. Add the shallots and garlic to the pan and cook with the mushrooms. Add the stock, thyme and bay leaves and simmer until well reduced. Flavour the mushrooms with Madeira. Season.

Add back the reserved juice. Remove the bay leaves and liquidise the mushrooms, add the whipping cream and truffle oil, and pass through a tammy cloth.

Cep jelly
Whisk the cep essence and vegi jell/Sosa together. Boil, pass through a sieve and onto a small shallow tray and allow to set. Dice.

Cep essence
Sweat the onion, shallot, garlic and celery until soft, add the mushrooms and ceps and sweat again. Add the Madeira and reduce by half. Add chicken stock and boil.

Simmer for 2 hours then pass through muslin.

Gnocchi
Bake the potatoes on salt. Once cooked pass through a drum sieve. Add the flour and cep powder and season. Bind with the half egg. Pipe into shapes of ½ cm diameter. Blanch in salted boiling water until the gnocchi float. Lightly coat in olive oil and pan fry in foaming butter.

Pumpkin soup
Sweat the onions with the garlic. Add the pumpkin and cook for a couple of minutes. Add the white chicken stock and boil for 7 minutes with the saffron, then add the cream and cook for a further 2 minutes. Add the beurre noisette and blend, pass twice through a sieve.

Boil the sherry vinegar and add to taste. Pour 500g into a foam machine, gas with one cartridge, shake and keep at 57°C until needed.

TO SERVE

Take a glass and add pumpkin seeds, diced jelly, gnocchi then the soup. Put foam on the soup and serve.

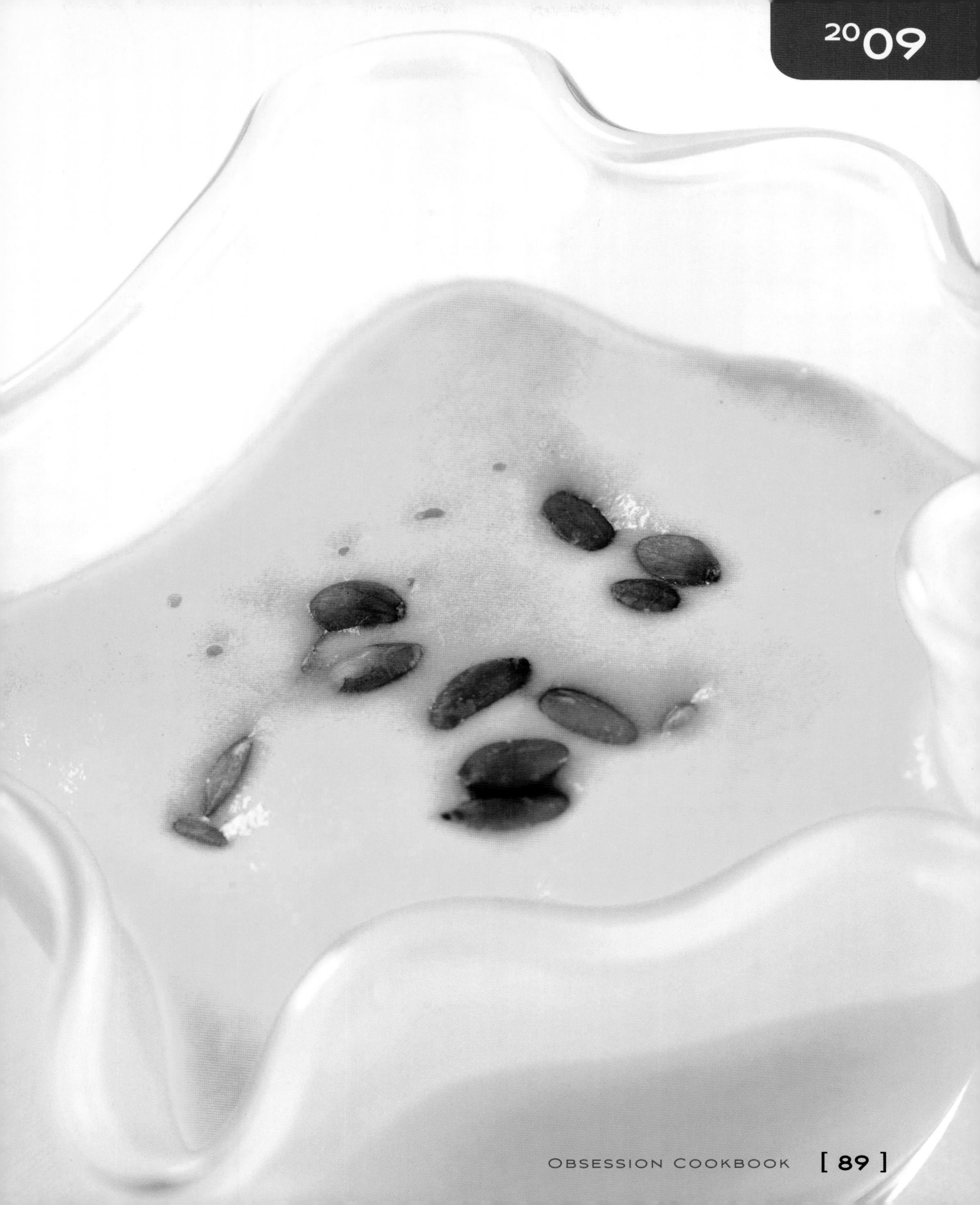

LIGHTLY POACHED ROYAL BAY OYSTERS WITH SEVRUGA CAVIAR, SAFFRON NOODLES AND LEMON BUTTER SAUCE

Serves 4

INGREDIENTS

Oysters and caviar
12 Fresh oysters
1 Cucumber
Sevruga caviar
Chives
Micro celery

Butter sauce
300ml White wine
6 Black peppercorns
1 Sprig of thyme
1 Bay leaf
1 Shallot, finely chopped
2 tbsp Double cream
250g Diced unsalted butter
Lemon juice

Pasta
600g Pasta flour
Pinch of salt
3 Eggs
6 Egg yolks
3 tbsp Saffron reduction
1tsp Olive oil

METHOD

Pasta
Sieve the flour and salt together and place in a food processor along with the eggs, egg yolks, saffron reduction and olive oil.

Process until the mixture comes together. Stop the machine, tip the ingredients onto a board and knead well until you have a firm smooth ball of dough.

Wrap in cling film and leave to rest for a minimum of 30 minutes.

On a lightly floured surface divide the dough into 4 equal pieces.

Take one part of the dough and roll out with a rolling pin to a rectangle approximately 5mm thick.

Feed the dough through the pasta machine several times on the thickest setting, adjusting the setting by one notch each time.

Finish with the thinnest setting, then using the linguine attachment run the dough through the machine.

Let the linguine hang over a wooden pole to dry before cooking in boiling salted water.

Drain and refresh in iced water then drain and toss with a little olive oil and set aside until needed.

Butter sauce
Take a small sauce pan, add the white wine, peppercorns, thyme, bay leaf and chopped shallot.

Bring to the boil and reduce the liquid by half its volume.

Pass through a fine sieve into a clean saucepan.

Add the cream, bring back to the boil then pull the pan to the edge of the stove.

Keeping warm, slowly add the diced butter a little at a time making sure the sauce does not boil.

Add the lemon juice, season with pepper and keep warm until needed.

Oysters
Carefully open and cut out the oysters, place in a bowl with their juices. Peel and cut the cucumber into small batons for the top of the oyster.

TO SERVE

When ready, reheat the noodles in boiling salted water.

Drain and, with a carving fork, make three little bobbins for each plate.

Warm the oyster juice in a saucepan and drop the oysters in for approximately 8 seconds.

Spoon them out onto a clean cloth and drain well. Place on top of each pasta bobbin.

Top with the cucumber batons and caviar.

Chop the chives and place in the warm lemon butter sauce.

Spoon over the oysters and noodles, garnish with the micro celery and caviar, and serve straight away.

Poached Egg Yolk, Smoked Haddock milk Foam, Cornflakes, Curry Oil

Serves 4

INGREDIENTS

Curry oil
300ml Sunflower oil
2 tbsp Medium curry powder

Haddock
400ml Whole milk
250g Undyed smoked haddock, skin on
½ tbsp Xanthan gum (available from health food shops and online)
4 Free-range egg yolks
20 Cornflakes

METHOD

Curry oil
Place the oil and curry powder into a small pan over a very low heat and heat gently for one hour. Allow to cool, then strain.

Haddock
Place the milk into a wide deep pan over a low heat and bring to a gentle simmer. Add the smoked haddock and poach until the fish begins to flake and the milk has taken on the flavour of the fish.

Strain the haddock through a fine sieve into a bowl, squeezing as much moisture from the haddock as possible. Transfer the milk to a clean pan over a low heat. Discard the haddock (or use in other dishes, such as kedgeree).

Add the xanthan gum to the milk and whisk to dissolve and thicken it. Pour into a siphon, then place the siphon into a jug or bowl of hot water to keep the milk mixture warm.

Poach the egg yolks in gently simmering water for 1-2 minutes, then remove with a slotted spoon.

TO SERVE

Pipe out the thickened milk from the siphon into each serving bowl into a round shape. Place an egg yolk into the centre of the milk (so the milk and yolk resemble a fried egg).

Place or sprinkle the cornflakes over the milk, then drizzle the curry oil over the egg in a zig-zag pattern.

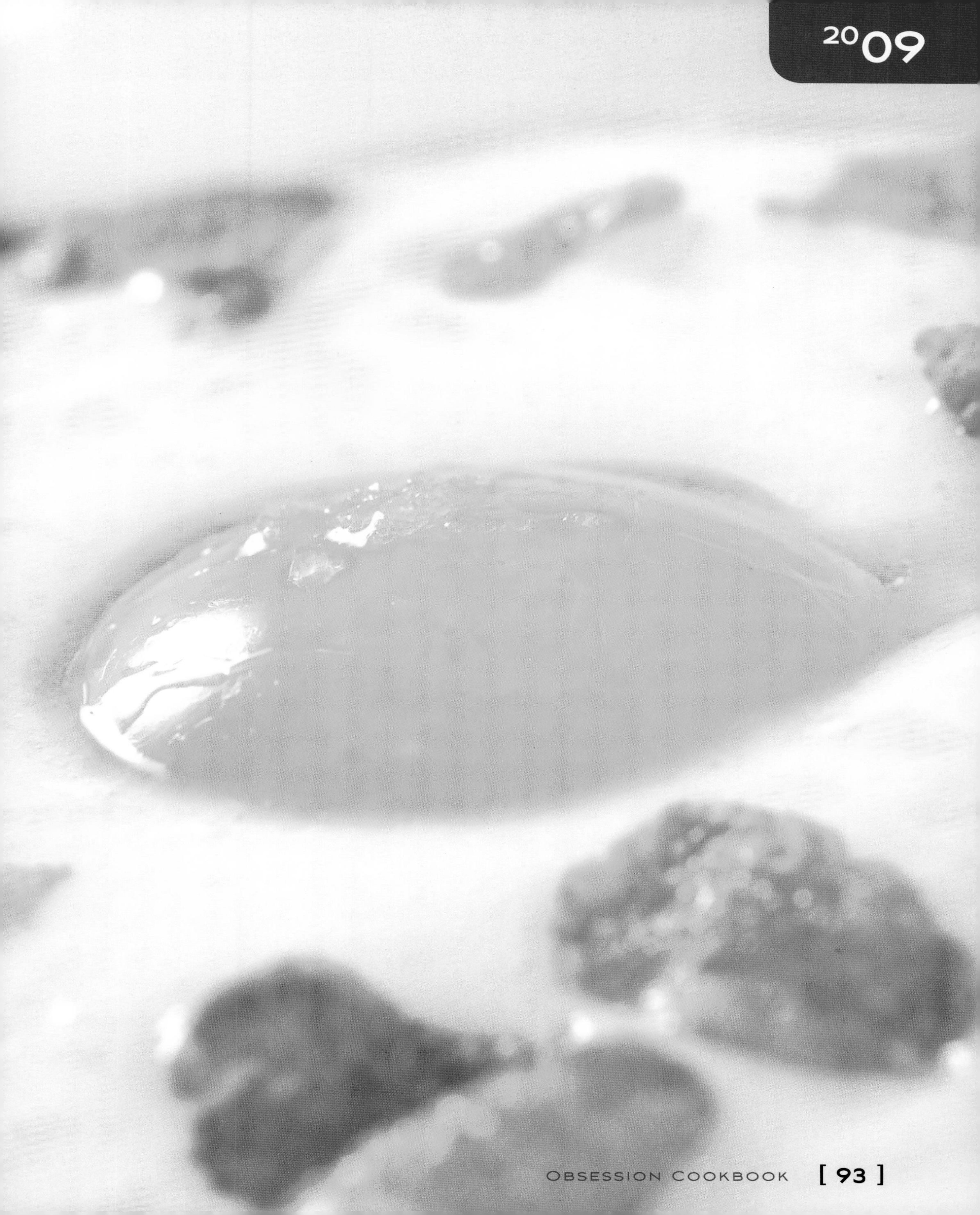

PIGEON TEA WITH WARM GAME CANAPÉS

Serves 4 - 6

INGREDIENTS

Consommé
10 Wood pigeon carcasses with legs attached (ask your butcher to chop them and save them in the freezer for you)
Vegetable oil
2 ltrs Chicken stock
1 Brown onion, sliced
6 Button mushrooms, sliced
200ml Madeira
100ml Oloroso sherry
3 Slices dried ceps

To clarify the consommé
2 Wood pigeon breasts
1 Chicken breast
4 Egg whites
Pinch of salt

CANAPÉS
Pheasant and quince beignet
1 Pheasant breast with skin sealed in a hot pan, cut into 24 pieces
Quince paste cut into 12 small squares
100g Plain flour
100g Cornflour
Sparkling water
Salt
1 ice cube
1 bunch of bay leaves

Wild boar rillette on toast
200g Confit of boar
1 tsp Tarragon mustard
25g Fresh duck fat
Chopped parsley
Freshly ground pepper
6 Fingers of Poilâne bread, toasted
Freshly grated parmesan

Partridge sausage roll
1 White onion
50g Butter
Salt & pepper
1 Sprig of sage
1 tbsp Breadcrumbs
2 Rashers of smoked bacon
200g Diced fatty pork belly (no skin)
2 Partridges – meat only (no skin, sinew or bones)
3 Rolls puff pastry cut into 10cm squares
Eggwash

To serve
Herbs (rosemary, thyme, bayleaf, juniper)
Cilass tea pot with fine mesh
Tea cup
Wooden board
Quince paste

METHOD

Consommé
For the consommé, roast off the chopped carcasses in some vegetable oil until golden brown. Remove from the pan. Add the chicken stock, onions and mushrooms and cook until lightly coloured. Deglaze with the Maderia and Oloroso, add the dried ceps and cook for 2 hours, strain through a fine sieve and cool.

To clarify the consommé
Blend the wood pigeon breast, chicken, egg whites and salt in a food processor to make a paste. Whisk this mix into the consommé, place in a heavy bottomed pan and bring up to a light simmer. Pass through a fine cloth and chill.

CANAPÉS

Pheasant and quince beignet
Mix the plain flour, cornflour, sparkling water, salt and ice cube together to make a batter one hour before serving.

Cut the bay leaves into skewer size with a leaf on top and a sharp base. Skewer one piece of pheasant breast, then a quince paste square, then follow with another piece of pheasant. Season lightly, dust in flour, then dip in the batter and deep fry until golden. Drain well. Light the top of the bay leaf, then blow it out so it smokes.

Wild boar rillette on toast

Mix the mustard, duck fat, parsley and pepper together with the confit of boar. Roll this mix between two pieces of greaseproof paper and set in a fridge. Cut to appropriate sizes, place on the toast and warm briefly in the oven. Sprinkle with freshly grated parmesan.

Partridge sausage roll

Sweat the finely diced white onion in the butter with a pinch of salt. When soft add the sage and cool. Add the breadcrumbs and a grind of pepper. Dice all the meat and put through a mincer. Add the meat to the breadcrumbs, mix well. Test for seasoning. Pipe some mix near to one end of each puff pastry square. Fold over the top and crimp with a fork. Eggwash the top lightly and place in an oven for about 12-14 minutes until crisp.

TO SERVE

Bring the consommé up to the boil and pour it into a herb-filled pot. At the table, pour into the guests' cups and serve on a wooden board with a selection of the canapés and some quince paste.

KEDGEREE
Serves 8

KEDGEREE
Serves 8

This is a modern take on a well known classic. There are many opinions about what constitutes a proper 'kedgeree' and in my opinion the four ingredients which must be present are smoked haddock, rice, eggs and curry. The rest is open to debate. In this version the eggs and the haddock play the star roles and I have added mussels because their affinity with curry is phenomenal. It is not possible to make small quantities of the creams and rice balls, but these items will just have to be enjoyed elsewhere!

INGREDIENTS

8 Quails' eggs
8 Small hens' eggs
1 Long leek
1 Stick celery
24 Mussels, cleaned
2 Granny Smith apples
16 Celery leaves
1 ltr Milk
2 Finnan smoked haddock fillets, skinned, trimmed and cut into 110g pieces – reserve the skin and trim for the stock (see below)
150g Curry cream (see below)
150g Mussel cream (see below)
50g Raisin purée (see below)
24 Smoked haddock rice balls (see below)

Smoked haddock rice balls
450ml Smoked haddock stock (simply made by covering the smoked haddock skin and trim with water and adding some onion, leek and celery)
3 Shallots, finely chopped
50g Butter
Salt
10g Raz el hanout curry powder
150g Risotto rice
25g Parmesan
Whisked egg
Flour
Breadcrumbs

Curry cream
125g Finely chopped onions
1 Garlic clove, crushed
10g Raz el hanout curry powder
250ml Grapeseed oil
Salt & pepper
200ml Apple juice
3 Egg yolks
Squeeze lemon juice

Mussel cream
100ml Mussel juice (from cooking of mussels)
Lemon juice
½ tsp Dijon mustard
3 Egg yolks
Salt & pepper
200ml Grapeseed oil

Golden raisin purée
50g Sugar
250g Golden raisins
150ml Apple juice

Mussel beignets
1 x 330ml Bottle of beer
300g Plain flour
50g Yeast
Pinch of salt and sugar
24 Cooked mussels
Bunch of celery leaves, to garnish

METHOD

The rice balls and creams can be made the day before.

Cook the quails' eggs in boiling water for 2 minutes and 20 seconds and refresh in cold water. Peel and reserve. Similarly cook the hens' eggs for 9 minutes, peel and reserve. Cut the leek into ½cm rounds, peel the celery and cut into 3mm crescents. Blanch both, separately, in boiling salted water until just tender. Thoroughly drain and chill on a flat tray or plate in a fridge. Do not refresh in iced water – this will leach out flavour.

Briefly cook the mussels by placing in a preheated covered pan with a splash of water, allowing them to steam open. Pick the mussels from the shells and reserve in the fridge along with the juice.

Smoked haddock rice balls

Heat up the smoked haddock stock. Sweat the shallots in a heavy based pan with some butter, a pinch of salt and the curry powder. After 3 or 4 minutes add the rice and cook for a further 2-3 minutes to seal the rice. Now, gradually add the hot smoked haddock stock over a period of about 10 minutes until the rice has just a bit of a bite left. Never swamp the rice with stock – add it gradually as the rice absorbs the previous addition. Finish off the risotto by adding the remaining butter and parmesan. The end result should be a rich, mellow, creamy smoked haddock risotto where the rice is fully, but not over, cooked. Pour this risotto into a shallow dish and chill. Roll into 24 little balls 2.5cm in diameter. Coat them in flour, then egg and finally in the breadcrumbs.

Curry cream

Sweat the onions, the garlic and the curry powder in a splash of the oil with a generous pinch of salt. Once softened and translucent add the apple juice and simmer for 2-3 minutes. Allow to cool, place in a blender, add the egg yolks and blend to a smooth purée. Gradually add oil with the blender running on maximum and you will end up with a smooth curry cream. Check the seasoning and adjust with salt, pepper and lemon juice if necessary. This should be the consistency of a thick pouring cream.

Mussel cream

Place the mussel juice, a squeeze of lemon juice, the mustard and the egg yolks in a blender and blend. Season with salt and pepper. With the blender on maximum add the grapeseed oil until a thick cream is achieved. Check the seasoning and adjust if necessary. This should be the consistency of a thick pouring cream.

Golden raisin purée

Cover the raisins in apple juice and soak overnight. Take the sugar to a caramel in a heavy based pan over a flame. Drain the raisins and add them to the caramel. Stir until the caramel has dissolved, add the drained apple juice and bring to the boil. Place in a blender and purée until smooth.

Place the curry and mussel creams and this purée into plastic 'squeezy' bottles.

Beer batter for mussel beignets

Make a simple batter with the beer, the flour, the yeast, sugar and the salt by whisking all the ingredients together. Set aside in a warm place.

TO SERVE

Bring a pan of vegetable oil to 180°C.

Cut the apple into matchstick-size batons.

Dip the mussels in the beer batter, coating them lightly, and deep fry until golden.

Deep fry the rice balls until golden and deep fry the celery leaves until they are crisp. Reserve and keep warm.

Bring the milk to simmering point in a shallow pan. Remove from the heat and drop in the pieces of smoked haddock. Drain the smoked haddock after 4 minutes, at which point it should break into beautiful translucent flakes. Using an old fashioned egg slicer ideally, slice the hens' eggs into thin slices. Place these onto the plates – do not use the slices with no yolk. Place the flaked haddock on top. Dress this with both the curry and mussel creams and garnish with the leeks and celery. Finish with 'dots' of raisin purée, the mussel beignets, rice balls, celery leaves and julienne of apple and finish each plate with a quail's egg cut in half and seasoned with salt.

GOAN SPICED LOBSTER WITH COCONUT SAUCE AND YOGHURT RICE
Serves 4

INGREDIENTS

4 x 700-800g Lobster
Salt
Water

Goan spice paste
100g Fresh coconut, grated
3 Dried red chillis
3 tsp Coriander seeds
1 tsp Black pepper
4-6 Cloves
1 tsp Cumin seed

Sauce
Oil
2 Large onions
1 Green chilli
1 tsp Ginger and garlic paste
½ tsp Turmeric powder
1 tsp Coriander powder
¼ tsp Red chilli powder
Water
2 Tomatoes, chopped
40g Tamarind paste
200ml Coconut milk
2sp Finely chopped coriander leaves

Tomato rice
Oil
½ tsp Mustard seeds
10 Curry leaves
1 tsp Garlic clove, chopped
½ tsp Ginger, chopped
¼ tsp Green chilli, seeds removed and chopped
1 Onion, chopped
½ tsp Turmeric powder
1 tsp Coriander powder

1 tsp Red chilli powder
10ml Lemon juice or water, to dilute
100g Tomatoes, chopped
2 tsp Tomato paste
200g Basmati rice (cooked)
Butter
1 tbsp Coriander, chopped
¼ tsp Black pepper

Tail meat and claw
Oil
50g Butter

Asparagus
12 Asparagus spears
Water
Micro cress, to garnish

METHOD

Lobster
Boil water in a large pan with salt. Add the lobster for 4-5 minutes and simmer. Remove from the pan and immerse in cold water with ice for 30 minutes. Drain the water then split the tail using scissors. Remove the tail meat and pat dry. Wash the tail in running water and dry it using a cloth. Crack the claws and remove the meat. Break the knuckles, remove the meat and set aside. Add most of the spice paste (below) to the tail and claw meat and pack in bags, sealed to make them air tight. Reserve for 30 minutes.

Goan spice paste
Lightly toast the grated coconut, dried red chillis, coriander seeds, black pepper, cloves and cumin seeds in the pan until lightly coloured, remove from the pan and leave to cool. Put the mixture in a food processor with a little water and blend to a smooth paste.

Sauce
Heat the oil in a large pan, add the onions and green chilli and sauté until brown. Stir in the ginger and garlic paste, turmeric powder, coriander powder, red chilli powder, add water and sauté for a few minutes. Add the chopped tomatoes and cook gently. Add any remaining spice paste and cook for 4-5 minutes. Add the tamarind paste and simmer for 3-4 minutes then pour in the coconut milk and simmer for another 10 minutes. Sprinkle in the chopped coriander and remove from the heat.

Tomato rice
Heat the oil in a pan, add the mustard seeds, curry leaves, garlic, ginger, green chilli and stir over a medium heat until the mustard and curry leaves begin to pop. Then add the onion and stir fry until translucent, add the turmeric powder, coriander powder, red chilli powder, lemon juice or water and stir until the moisture

evaporates. Add the chopped tomatoes and tomato paste, stirring with a spatula until nicely cooked. Add the cooked rice, a little bit of butter, all of the chopped lobster meat, coriander and mix well. Adjust the seasoning. Remove the pan from the heat and fill the lobster tail with the rice.

Tail and claw meat

Heat the oil in a non-stick pan. Cook the lobster meat from both the tail and claws. Cook until soft and tender, constantly basting with butter. Remove and serve.

Asparagus

Peel the asparagus heads and retain the tips up to 3cm. Blanch in boiling salted water and when crisp, remove and refresh in iced water. Strain and reserve.

TO SERVE

Arrange the different elements of the dish on a round plate. Use some micro cress to garnish.

Sweetcorn Vanilla Panna Cotta
Serves 10

INGREDIENTS

400g Sweetcorn purée
700g Cream
120g Sugar
5g Salt
4 Vanilla pods
4 Gelatine leaves

Clear caramel jelly
4 Gelatine leaves
400g Sugar
870g Water

Popcorn granite
70g Butter
50g Popcorn
750ml Milk
20g Sugar
2g Salt
Vanilla powder, to serve
Caramel popcorn, to serve

METHOD

Put the purée, cream, sugar, salt and vanilla into a pan and bring to the boil. Soak the gelatine in ice water. Whisk the gelatine into the mix, pass through a sieve and chill over ice until the vanilla seeds are suspended in the mix and then set in the glasses. When the panna cottas are set put a thin layer of caramel jelly on the top.

Clear caramel jelly
Soak the gelatine in ice water. Make a caramel in a pan by gently melting the sugar and add the water. Measure out 1 litre of this liquid, add the softened gelatine and pass through a sieve.

Popcorn granite
Melt the butter in a large pan and add the popcorn. Cook for 10 minutes on a medium heat, stirring occasionally. Add the milk, sugar and salt. Bring the mix back up to the boil and simmer for 10 minutes. Remove from the heat and cover for 10 minutes. Pass the mix through a sieve, refrigerate until the butter sets on the surface, pass again through a sieve then freeze in a large tray.

TO SERVE

Put the granita on top of the panna cotta. Sprinkle with the vanilla powder and serve with caramel popcorn.

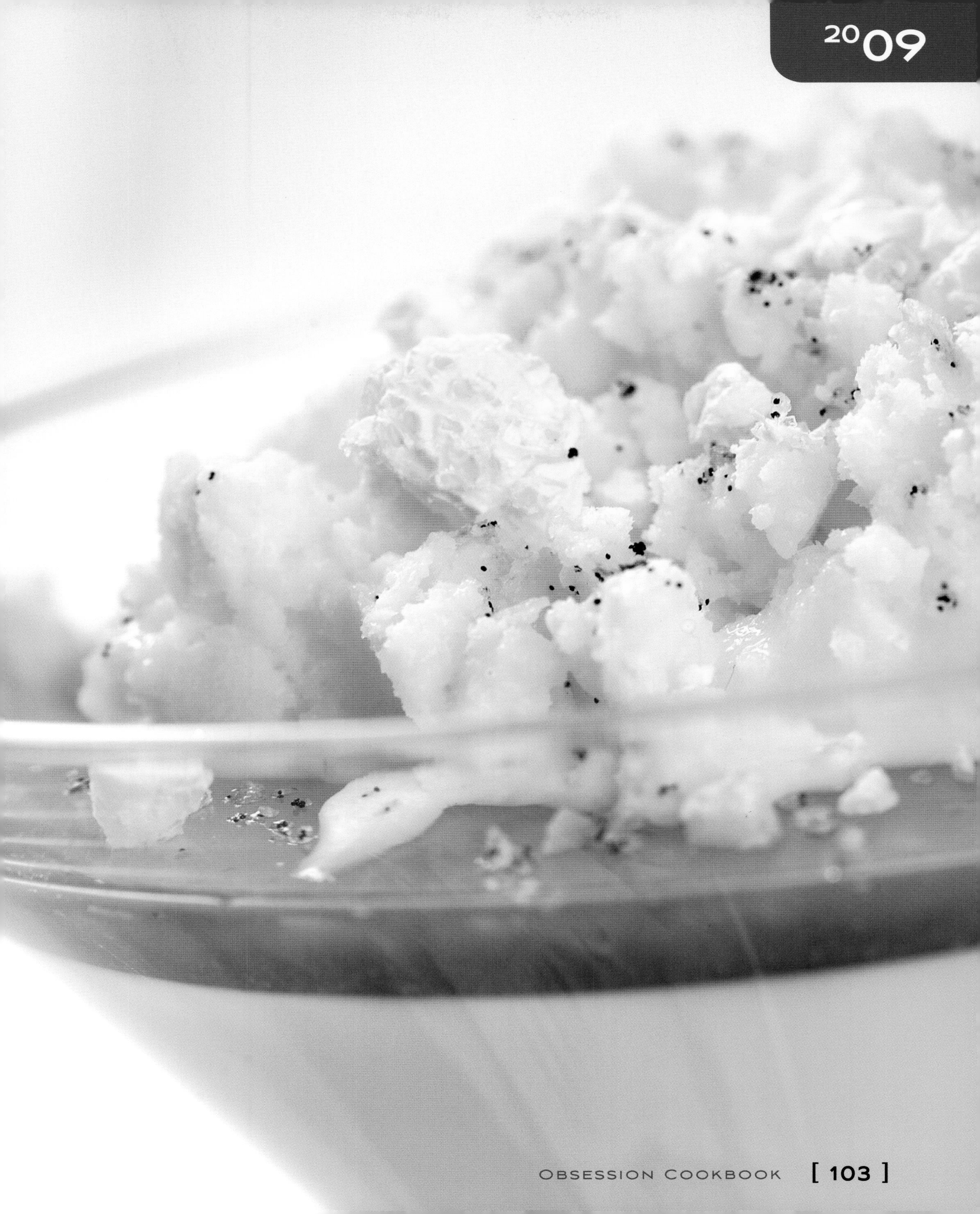

HEATHCOTE'S BREAD AND BUTTER PUDDING, APRICOT COMPOTE, CLOTTED CREAM

Serves 4

INGREDIENTS

75g Butter
5 Thin slices of white bread
100g Sultanas
220ml Cream
220ml Milk
50g Sugar
1 Vanilla pod split and seeds removed
3 Eggs
25g Icing sugar
50g Apricot jam
Clotted cream
8 Dried apricots

METHOD

Butter the bread and remove the crusts. Place one layer of bread in the base of a dish and cover with a layer of sultanas. Place the rest of the bread on top of the sultanas.

Bring the cream, milk, sugar and vanilla to the boil in a pan, place the eggs in a bowl and whisk the hot liquid into them. Pour over the bread and place the dish in a bain-marie, put in a moderate oven for about half an hour until cooked.

Dust with icing sugar and glaze under a grill until golden. Brush with jam.

TO SERVE

Serve with clotted cream and a compote of dried apricots.

Tiny Melting Valrhona Chocolate Desserts

Serves 10

TINY MELTING VALRHONA CHOCOLATE DESSERTS
Serves 10

INGREDIENTS

Liquid chocolate
60g Valrhona 70% chocolate, chopped
40g 33% milk chocolate, chopped
175g Double cream
75g Milk
25g Honey
Seeds of ½ vanilla pod
Pinch of salt

Chocolate spray
250g Valrhona 70% chocolate, chopped
25g Cocoa butter

Chocolate custard
100g Full fat milk
190g Double cream
1 Vanilla pod
10g Caster sugar
60g Egg yolks
12g Caster sugar
25g Valrhona 55% chocolate (Equatorial Noire)
20g Demerara sugar
20g Crackling candy

Pulled sugar
10g Sugar
200g Water
30g Glucose
½ tsp Lemon juice

Cherry sorbet
200g Fresh cherry juice
200g Cherry purée – Boiron
100g Stock syrup
12g Sour cherry purée
20g Lemon juice

Cherry jelly
150g Cherry juice
50g Cherry purée – Boiron
5g Sour cherry purée – MSK
6g Lemon juice
30g Stock syrup
2g Agar agar

Chocolate paint
62g Sugar
62g Water
20g Cocoa powder
62g Double cream

Kirsch foam
4g Gelatine leaves (2½ bronze leaves)
150g Whole milk
40g UHT 55% whipping cream
30g Caster sugar
15g Kirsch

Dipped cherries
10 Cherries with stalks
100ml Valrhona chocolate 55%

Chocolate swirl
25g Tempered chocolate

METHOD

Liquid chocolate
Makes 12 portions. Melt the chocolate in a medium heatproof bowl over warm water (or in a microwave). In a pan bring to the boil the cream, milk, honey, vanilla pod seeds and salt. Remove from the heat and pour over the chocolate – leave to stand for 1 minute then

blend with a hand blender until fully incorporated. Skim off the foam from the top of the chocolate then strain through a fine chinoise (conical sieve).

Spray a tray approximately 22x13cm and 2cm deep with a non-stick cooking spray to hold a sheet of silicon paper in place – make sure the edges of the silicon paper come up the side of the tray by at least 2cm.

Pour the liquid chocolate into the tray, then place in a blast chiller and freeze until solid. Remove the chocolate from the tray and cut into 4x4cm squares. Then place the chocolate squares carefully on to a tray lined with parchment paper, return to the freezer and reserve.

Chocolate spray

Makes 20 portions. Carefully melt the chocolate and cocoa butter together. Once melted, put into a chocolate sprayer (paint spray gun). Remove the liquid chocolate squares (silicon sheet) from the freezer and place on a silpat then spray with the chocolate taking care to coat evenly. Return the squares to the freezer to set for approximately 10 minutes then turn the squares over and spray the other side, keep the liquid chocolate squares in the freezer until required. N.B. When spraying the chocolate you must protect the area in which you are spraying. One way to protect it is to break up a large cardboard box and remove one side and spray into the v-shaped box.

Chocolate custard

Makes 10 portions. Bring to the boil the milk, cream and 10g sugar. Whisk together the egg yolks and 12g sugar until light and fluffy (to make a sabayon). Once the milk and cream has come to the boil add the chocolate and melt carefully. Then pour the mix onto the egg yolks and sugar, gently whisk until all the mix

has been incorporated. Place the mix onto an ice bath and cool.

Line the bottom of 10 stainless steel custard moulds with cling film and put onto a flat tray with acetate on the bottom. Once the mix is cool, fill the mould three-quarters of the way up. Put into a convection oven for 28 minutes at 94°C; when ready remove and allow to cool and refrigerate. To make the caramel top, sprinkle on the sugar and caramelise with a blow torch then, while still warm, sprinkle on the crackling candy and reserve.

Pulled sugar

Boil all the ingredients together to make a golden 'caramel' at 170-175°C then pour onto silicon paper and leave to set. To use, warm in the oven until the sugar is pliable, then pull the sugar as required.

Cherry sorbet

Will make approximately 20 large teaspoons of sorbet. Mix all the ingredients together cold. Pass through a muslin cloth or a fine sieve. Churn in an ice cream machine, remove and reserve until required.

Cherry jelly

Makes 20 jellies. Place all the ingredients, except the agar agar, into a pan, bring to the boil and once boiling whisk in the agar agar and re-boil. Pass through a fine sieve. Pour the mix into a deep tray with acetate on the bottom. Put in the fridge to set. Remove the jelly, carefully cut into 2.5cm squares and reserve.

Chocolate paint

Makes 25 portions. Bring the sugar and water to the boil. Add the cocoa and whisk in well, pour into a small bowl and place on ice water. Once cool, whisk in the double cream, pour into a squeezy bottle and refrigerate.

Kirsch foam

Makes 20 portions. Soak the gelatine leaves in cold water. Bring the milk, cream and sugar to the boil. Dissolve in the gelatine off the heat. Pass through a fine chinoise (conical sieve) and add the kirsch. When cool, load into a kisag gun and load with two cartridges. Keep in the fridge.

Dipped cherries

Simply dip the cherries in the chocolate and then place them on silicon paper to set.

Chocolate swirl

Spread a thin layer of tempered chocolate over a sheet of acetate 21x6cm. Leave for 2-3 minutes until the chocolate is nearly set (still needs to be flexible). Cut into half-width strips (without cutting through the acetate). Take the acetate and roll in opposite directions to form a curl. Place the chocolate covered acetate into a ring to hold the shape, leave until set. Once the swirls are set remove from the ring and carefully peel away the acetate.

TO SERVE

Take an oblong plate and pipe a small round of chocolate paint at the top of the plate and then pull with the nozzle to create a swirl. Put the liquid chocolate square in the middle of the plate and the jelly below. With a blow torch warm the exterior of the stainless steel custard moulds then place onto the plate above the liquid chocolate and remove the mould. Place the pulled sugar on top of the custard. Place the chocolate-dipped cherry to the right of the jelly. Spoon the sorbet onto the liquid chocolate, spoon over the kirsch foam and place the chocolate swirl on top. Serve immediately.

20O8

This was the year when I possibly realised we had created something special; to manage to attract the iconic chef Pierre Koffmann out of retirement for one special evening was truly a remarkable achievement.

Anthony Flinn kicked off on the Monday with his influences of El Bulli where he had spent more time than any other British chef. The first dish of risotto of white onion parmesan air espresso was Antony's signature dish. Other dishes included cured squab, foie gras macaroon, chocolate soy dressing, carton of milk ten different techniques, a truly fascinating dish which had the customers excited, perplexed and intrigued all at the same time. He finished the night with pumpkin cheesecake, a memorable finish to a fascinating start to the festival. The following week we competed against each other in the Great British Menu billed as the War of the Roses.

Next up was Mark Edwards. Mark hails from Wigan and oversees the kitchens for Nobu restaurants worldwide, an incredible job. Mark cooked an array of Japanese food which included two sashimi dishes which went down fantastically well even though many of our diners had never eaten sashimi or sushi, but they tried it for the first time and loved it. He also served the world renowned blackened cod which is actually sable fish. Wagyu beef was as expected outstanding and he finished on a Suntory Whisky cappuccino, which rounded off the night a real treat.

Pierre's main course on the night was the classic hare royale. Pierre was struggling to get hares in London, so he contacted me to see if we could get the hares. We did and actually ended up with hares from all over the north of England, so many that we were using hare royale for weeks to come. Pierre closed his menu with his famous pistachio soufflé, which is so well known throughout the culinary world, it's a masterpiece. Assisting Pierre came two members of his old brigade at La Tante Claire, his old head chef Eric Chavot and one of my first brigade members Tim Payne, who went on to become Marco Pierre White's right-hand man and of Hell's Kitchen fame.

Angela arrived via Liverpool Lime Street station as I arrived in Preston Station. She had been talking on the phone at Euston and got on the wrong train. I was on the phone saying to her "whereabouts are you, I can't see you?" and she was saying "I'm on the platform!" – I realised she was on the wrong platform at the wrong station. A few hours later we finally got Angela to Northcote. Angela wowed us with white truffle risotto and everyone wanted an extra bowl so Angela toured the restaurant serving the extra helpings as required. Angela was a little disappointed with the frugal amount of white truffles available as I had mis-calculated the cost. To follow was braised halibut with oxtail ravioli, we finished with lemon panna cotta and Grappa granite, a truly memorable night.

Phil arrived for the first time in his Maserati; the old Aston had finally been retired along with its accumulated points. Phil cooked with rock oysters, foie gras and used British White Beef which he absolutely loved; it may not conform but it certainly performs. The night was wrapped up with Bakewell tart and rhubarb ice cream, a simple finish to another brilliant Howard night.

Shane Osborn from Pied à Terre and his family came next and had a fantastic time. Shane prepared an unbelievable scallop ceviche especially for a man who has an intolerance to fish. His pumpkin soup was superb and his herb-crusted venison saddle a real treat. To finish bitter sweet chocolate tart with a stout ice cream was a great dish with a humorous Antipodean twist.

I finished off the year with my first use of goat at the festival; the Boer goat from Sharon and Chris Peacock in Cockerham are superb and the consommé was well received. I finished the evening with Lancashire curd tart which turned out to be not one of Oliver Peyton's favourites on the Great British Menu that year.

MARK EDWARDS

"The greatest satisfaction one gets from cooking is other people's enjoyment."

OBSESSION FESTIVAL
2008

ANGELA HARTNETT

"I'm obsessed with food because I like to eat — simple as that. I was fortunate as a kid to grow up in a household that cared a lot about what we ate, and when you have that as a child it spoils you and becomes a part of what you want to do. I love my job, and I love cooking, end of story."

PIERRE KOFFMANN

"Since early in my childhood I was surrounded by good food and great ingredients — I simply want to carry on the tradition."

SHANE OSBORN

"There are so many reasons for my Obsession. I've loved my job since I was 15 and being an Australian working in the UK, the seasonality is fantastic. Every season offers exciting ingredients – from game to chervil; that's what keeps me inspired and engaged, and the changing of the seasons gets me excited. Being immersed in food, meeting producers and finding out where it comes from is a part of that. I'm very lucky to have a talented and enthusiastic young team with a thirst for knowledge who keep me on my toes so I have to keep pushing the food and not resting on my laurels. It's always moving forward."

ANTHONY FLINN

"I'm obsessed by food because there is no boundary to it, you can do exactly what you want. There are rules to the science of food, but who says you can't put certain things together? It's the playful experimenting that I enjoy."

PHIL HOWARD

"Over the years of visiting Northcote and Lancashire in general, I have come to appreciate how much they love their food. I always try to propose a menu that not only showcases what we do at The Square but includes dishes that will have a natural affinity with what local folk will want to eat. The field mushroom veloute is a classic example of this. The great old master Pierre Koffman was "in the house" this year – always a pleasure to see him delivering his well honed classics!"

NIGEL HAWORTH

"To be obsessed by the seasons is to capture the moment."

Risotto of White Onion, Parmesan Air, Espresso

Serves 4

INGREDIENTS

Risotto base
50g Chopped onion
300g Risotto rice
1 ltr Vegetable stock

Onion purée
2 Onions
100g Cream
Salt
Oil

Parmesan air
500g Water
500g Grated parmesan
Pinch of lecithin

Other ingredients
Chives
Espresso coffee

METHOD

Risotto base
Sweat the onions in a little oil without colour. Add the rice and cook for 1 minute to toast the rice a little. Add the stock a little at a time until three-quarters cooked. You may use all the stock or only half; it all depends on the temperature and speed in which you cook it. Once three-quarters cooked pour on to a tray and cool.

Onion purée
Peel and slice the onions. Place in a pan with a little oil and salt. The salt will start to extract the moisture and sweat them down quicker. Keep cooking them until they are golden brown and fully caramelised. Then add the cream. Blitz to a smooth paste. Store in the fridge.

Parmesan air
Bring the water to the boil and add the parmesan. Simmer for 30 minutes. Strain off the liquid and discard the mass that is left. Chill in the fridge until the fat and liquid separate, then remove the fat from the top. Add the lecithin to the liquid and blitz with a stick blender. Slowly move the blender around to create foam.

TO SERVE

Place the rice in a pan with the purée and some more of the vegetable stock. Mix all together and continue to cook the rice leaving a slight crunch to it. Fold through the chives and season. Sprinkle a little coffee at the bottom of the bowl. Pour the risotto over the coffee and aerate the parmesan foam with the stick blender. Spoon just the froth over the rice and sprinkle with a little more coffee. Serve immediately.

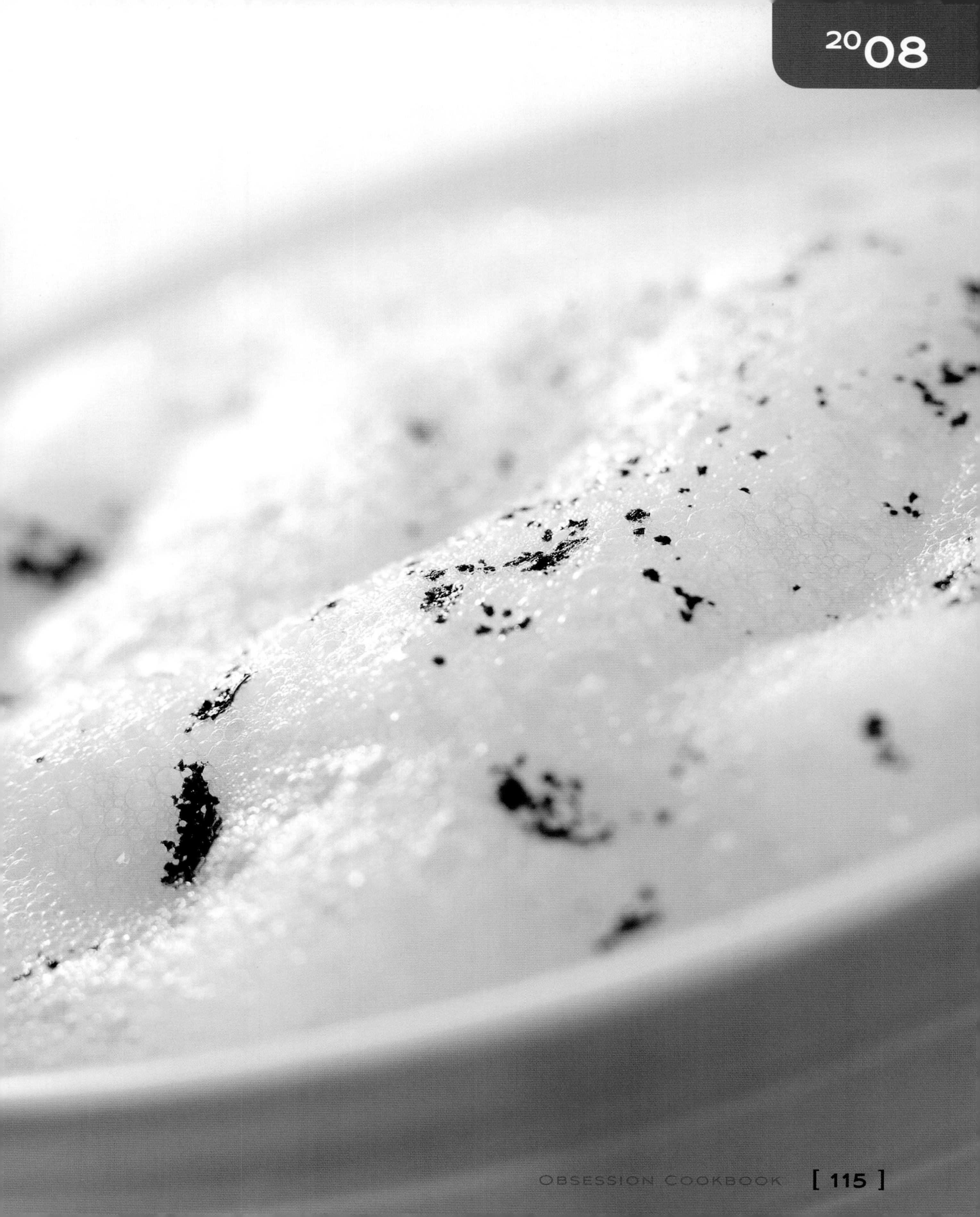

Black Cod with Sweet Miso
Serves 1

The Black Cod (sable fish) with Miso has become one of the most famous dishes at all the Nobu restaurants around the world. Some of our customers like to squeeze some fresh lemon over the top to balance the sweetness out but this is down to your own personal taste.

INGREDIENTS

Den Miso
100ml Sake
100ml Mirin
150g Caster sugar
300g White Miso paste
200g Sable fish fillet with the skin intact
Sliced lemon, to serve
Galangal stem

METHOD

Bring the Sake and Mirin to the boil in a thick bottomed, non-reactive saucepan for 2-3 minutes to allow the alcohol to evaporate. Add the sugar and allow to dissolve, slowly mixing in the Miso paste a little at a time using a wooden spoon. Continue to cook on a medium heat stirring constantly so as not to let the mixture burn in the pan for a further 10-5 minutes. Strain the mixture through a sieve to remove any lumps, allow to cool and then refrigerate.

Marinating and cooking
Place the sable fish in a non reactive container and pour over a little of the Den Miso and marinate for 1-2 days in the refrigerator. Preheat the oven to 200°C/400 °F/gas mark 6 and place the fish on to a non-stick baking sheet and cook in the oven for 10-12 minutes until cooked through and golden on the outside.

You can cook the sable fish under a grill or Salamander with the same results but care must be taken that it does not burn before it is cooked through to the centre.

TO SERVE

Place on to a serving dish and dress the plate with a little extra Den Miso and serve with some sliced lemon and galangal stem.

PISTACHIO SOUFFLÉ
Serves 4

INGREDIENTS

500ml Milk
½ Vanilla pod
120g Egg yolks
100g Caster sugar
50g Plain flour
40g Pistachio paste
25g Butter, softened
25g Dark chocolate, grated
4 Egg whites
1 tbsp Caster sugar
Icing sugar, to serve

METHOD

Boil together the milk and vanilla pod. Simultaneously whisk together the egg yolks and caster sugar, whisk until the mixture slightly thickens and turns light in colour.

Sieve the flour and add into the mixture, whisk until smooth. Add half of the milk to the base, whisk until there are no lumps. Sieve through a fine strainer, remove the vanilla pod and return the mixture back to the pan and add the remaining milk. Using a whisk, stir the mixture. When it comes to the boil, bring the temperature down to a simmer. Continue to stir and cook out for 8-10 minutes and mix in the pistachio paste.

Pour the pastry cream onto a shallow tray, wrap with cling film and cool rapidly.

Generously butter 4 individual soufflé dishes. Put the grated chocolate inside and rotate the moulds so that the chocolate completely covers the inside, sticking to the softened butter.

Beat the egg whites until firm, add the tablespoon of caster sugar and whisk until stiff. Add a small quantity of the whites to the pistachio mix to soften it, then fold in the rest of the egg whites and pour into the soufflé dishes.

Bake in a hot oven 240°C/475°F/ gas mark 9 for 15 minutes or until well risen.

TO SERVE

Dust the top with icing sugar and serve with ice cream of your choice.

Glazed Halibut with Oxtail Ravioli

Serves 4

Glazed Halibut with Oxtail Ravioli
Serves 4

INGREDIENTS

Pasta dough
600g Pasta flour '00'
Salt
5-6 Large Italian eggs
Extra virgin olive oil

Braised oxtail
1 Carrot
1 Onion
1 Stick celery
1 Stick leek
½ Head garlic
Thyme
Bay leaf
Peppercorns
2 bottles Red wine
1 bottle Port
1 Oxtail, chopped
½ ltr Veal stock
½ ltr Chicken stock
Parsley, chopped
2 Shallots, chopped

Parsnip purée
1kg Parsnip (peeled and chopped)
1 ltr Milk
Thyme
Bay leaf
50ml Double cream
Butter

Halibut
4 120-130g piece halibut
Olive oil
Butter
Chopped chervil
Fish stock
1 Bunch baby spinach
8 Baby leeks

METHOD

Pasta dough

Mix the flour with a pinch of salt in the Robot Coupe (food processor).

Mix the eggs with a squirt of olive oil and start adding into the Robot Coupe slowly.

When the crumble starts to climb the walls and does not collapse any more, the dough should be ready to knead.

Turn the dough onto a work surface and start kneading.

Knead for 10 minutes or until it is smooth. Cover with cling film and let it rest in the fridge for at least 1 hour.

Braised oxtail

Dice the vegetables (all except the shallots) into a bowl, add the oxtail together with the aromats (herbs), port and wine, and leave to marinate overnight.

Once marinated, drain off the liquid and separate the oxtail from the vegetables.

In a hot pan, colour off the oxtail on all sides and set aside.

In the same pan, colour off the vegetables and add the oxtail back in.

Deglaze with all the alcohol from the marinade and reduce until sticky and glazed.

Add the stocks and simmer for approximately 2 hours or until the meat is coming off the bone.

Leave to cool then pour into a colander over a bowl.

Discard the vegetables and let the oxtail slightly reduce in temperature.

Pick the meat off the bone and shred it down and pass the juices through a chinoise (conical sieve). Divide into 2, keep half as it is to be used later as a sauce. Reduce the remaining half down until sticky and add to the meat. Add the chopped parsley. Cook down the chopped shallots in olive oil and butter until golden brown and almost sweet, then season and also add to the meat.

Let the farce cool down until it is possible to shape into balls, and leave to set in the fridge.

Roll out the dough and make into ravioli with the oxtail as a filling.

Parsnip purée

Bring the milk together with all the ingredients to the boil and simmer for 30 minutes or until the parsnip is soft.

Pass through a chinoise (conical sieve), keeping the milk and the parsnip.

Place the parsnip in Vitamix and blend, adding the milk as needed so as to get a smooth purée.

Season, add a few cubes of butter and pass mixture through a chinoise (conical sieve). Add a touch of cream if it isn't runny enough.

TO SERVE

Season the fish, and colour in olive oil on both sides. Once coloured, with presentation side up, add a spoonful of butter, chopped chervil and a ladle of fish stock.

Cover and finish cooking in boiling salted water.

Cook the baby leeks until a knife can go through the centre then shock in ice water. Once cold trim so that they all have the same shape.

Warm the baby leeks in foaming butter.

Warm the parsnip purée.

Boil the ravioli.

Cook the spinach in butter, season and drain on kitchen paper.

Finish with the oxtail cooking juices as a sauce.

Field Mushroom Velouté, English Breakfast Garnish

Serves 4

INGREDIENTS

100g Butter
1 White onion, finely sliced
Salt & pepper
6 Large field mushrooms, finely sliced
500ml Chicken stock
100ml Double cream
1 Bay leaf
Garnish
2 Cumberland sausages
1 tbsp Grapeseed oil
4 Small eggs
4 Lambs' kidneys, quartered

METHOD

Place a large, heavy based pan over a medium heat, melt 50g of the butter and add the onion with a generous pinch of salt. Cook until the onions are soft and translucent. Turn the heat up, add the mushrooms and cook, stirring frequently for 5 minutes, or until all the moisture has evaporated.

Add the chicken stock, cream and bay leaf, bring to the boil and cook at a bare simmer for 15 minutes. Remove from the heat, lift out the bay leaf and blend to a smooth, homogeneous soup. Adjust the seasoning, chill over ice and set aside in the fridge.

Garnish
Colour the sausages in half a tablespoon of grapeseed oil and finish in an oven at 160°C/325°F/gas mark 3 for 15 minutes. Remove from the oven, take the sausages out of the pan and keep warm.

Place the same pan over a gentle heat, add 50g of butter and crack the four small eggs into it and gently cook. Remove from the pan, season the eggs and cut the yolk out with a pastry cutter, slightly larger than the yolk itself. Set aside in a warm place, covered. Finally, sauté the lambs' kidneys in a hot pan with the remaining grapeseed oil. Season with salt and pepper.

TO SERVE

Into each of 4 prepared soup bowls, place an egg yolk, two slices of sausage and some kidney. Heat up the soup to near boiling point and serve it in a jug on the side.

VENISON WITH CELERIAC AND CHANTERELLES
Serves 4

INGREDIENTS

1 tbsp Butter
½ Celeriac, peeled and diced
Salt & pepper
4 x 120g Boneless venison loin portions
50g Pasteurised egg white
8 tbsp Green herb crumb (see below)
1 tbsp Olive oil
100g Butter
150g Chanterelles
200g Shallot stock

Green herb crumb
2 Sprigs of thyme
2 Sprigs of rosemary
1 Garlic clove
300g Japanese breadcrumbs (Panko)
2 Bunches of flat leaf parsley

Shallot stock
2 Large shallots, peeled
30g Butter
2 Garlic cloves
1 tsp Fresh thyme, chopped
Salt
500ml White chicken stock
8 Pomme soufflés, to serve

METHOD

Heat a frying pan and add the butter, when golden brown add the celeriac and a pinch of salt. Sauté over a medium heat until the celeriac is golden brown and soft. Drain the butter and add water to cover the celeriac. Bring to a simmer and cook for 5 minutes. Pour into a blender and purée until smooth. Adjust seasoning.

Heat the oven to 140°C/275°F/gas mark 1.

Season the venison well with salt and pepper. Roll through the egg white then through the green crumb.

Warm a non-stick frying pan and add the oil. Place the venison in the pan and gently fry the meat on all sides for 30 seconds.

Place in the oven and turn after every 30 seconds. The meat should take between 6-8 minutes for medium rare. Allow to rest for 5 minutes in a warm place.

For the mushrooms heat a frying pan over a high heat and add 30g of butter. When golden brown add the mushrooms and sauté until all the water has evaporated. Add the shallot stock and reduce by two-thirds. Add the remaining butter and stir in well. Adjust seasoning and keep warm.

Green herb crumb
Pick the leaves off the thyme and rosemary and place in the Robot Coupe (food processor) with the garlic and breadcrumbs. Blend for 3 minutes.

Pick the leaves off the parsley then add slowly to the breadcrumbs while the machine is on.

Blend until the crumbs are bright green. Pass over a fine sieve.

For the shallot stock
Chop the shallots finely. Melt the butter in a small pan. Then add the garlic, thyme and shallots and a sprinkle of salt. Sweat without colour until soft. Add the stock and simmer for 20 minutes.

TO SERVE

Swipe a spoonful of celeriac purée on a plate. Cut the venison in half. Spoon the chanterelles over the meat and top with the pomme soufflés.

LOCAL GAME BAKED IN BUTTER PUFF PASTRY, CELERIAC PURÉE

Serves 4

INGREDIENTS

Game roll

160g/9 slices (1mm thick) Sliced rindless streaky bacon (must be 28cm long, slice while frozen)
2 x 100g Pheasant breasts (skinless)
2 x 100g Wild duck breasts (skinless)
4 x 50g Partridge breasts (skinless)
10g Salt
400g Chicken mousse (see below)
500g Puff pastry
Egg wash

Celeriac purée

20g Butter
200g Celeriac, diced
100ml Milk
100ml Cream
Salt to taste

Madeira sauce

50g Shallots
100g Mushrooms, sliced
35g Unsalted butter
200ml Strong Madeira
400ml Brown chicken stock
Salt & pepper, to taste

Chicken mousse

200g Chicken breasts, diced
250ml Cream
1 Egg white
4g Salt
10g Chives, chopped
5g Chervil, finely chopped

METHOD

Game roll

Place a sheet of cling film flat onto the table, line it with streaky bacon to form a square 25x25cm.

Check the game breasts for lead shot then season lightly with salt.

Place the pheasant breasts exactly in the middle of the bacon, overlap slightly, spread a layer of chicken mousse 1cm thick on top of the pheasant breasts.

Place the wild duck breast on top of the chicken mousse then spread another even layer of the chicken mousse on top of the duck breasts.

Place the partridge breast on top of the chicken mousse, fold the bacon over to wrap completely around the game.

Wrap the cling film around the game roll and refrigerate. Remove the cling film before using.

To complete the game roll, roll out the puff pastry on a clean surface to a 3mm thick 25x25cm square. Place onto a flat tray lined with parchment paper and put in the blast chiller for 20 minutes (this is to ensure a perfect shape for the pastry).

Once chilled place back onto a clean surface and allow to semi defrost, then cut the pastry with a lattice cutter width ways. Carefully open the lattice, then fold the pastry over and around the game roll. Place onto the tray lined with parchment

paper and put into the fridge and chill for 20 minutes.

Once chilled again completely egg wash the pastry and put into the oven at 200°C/400°F/gas mark 6 for 14 minutes. Remove from the oven, place on a wire rack and rest for 5-8 minutes. It is now ready to serve.

Celeriac purée
In a heavy bottom pan, melt the butter then add the diced celeriac. Sweat for 2-3 minutes then cover with cling film, cook for a further 10-15 minutes without colouring and until the celeriac is tender. Remove the cling film, add the milk and cream, season with salt and bring to the boil. Remove from the pan, place into a Thermomix and blitz until smooth, pass through a fine sieve, check seasoning and reserve.

Madeira sauce
In a heavy bottom pan, sweat off the shallots and mushrooms in 25g of butter for 2-3 minutes. Add the Madeira and reduce by two-thirds, once reduced add the chicken stock and reduce by half. Pass through a fine sieve, add the remaining 10g knob of butter and whisk well, check seasoning.

Chicken mousse
Place the diced chicken, 100ml of cream, egg white and salt into a Pacojet beaker and freeze to -20°C. Once frozen Pacojet three times (a food processor can be used). Place into a metal bowl over ice and beat in the remaining 150ml of cream until smooth and shiny. Mix in the chives and chervil, check the seasoning and reserve.

TO SERVE

Put a medium sweep of celeriac purée on the plate, add the hot butter puff pastry wrapped game, finish with the lightly foamed Madeira sauce.

20O7

Andrew Pern arrived with his brigade from Yorkshire with the biggest bottle of Rhubarb Schnapps I have ever seen in my life; needless to say, most of it was drunk on the night, and many of the chefs were a little the worse for wear. Andrew cooked his signature dish of black pudding and foie gras that later became the title of his award-winning book. His main course was a selection of Yorkshire beef with Hambleton ale and root vegetables and he finished with a magnificent plate of various desserts using Yorkshire rhubarb – rhubarb and custard, my favourite.

Raymond Blanc had already sent an advanced posse led by his development chef, Adam, and a team of three; all was well. The great man himself arrived late afternoon checking everyone from top to bottom in his flamboyant and exacting style; the team had done a great job and approval was given. There was a moment of anxiety when he asked to taste the wines alongside the food. Raymond questioned some choices but, after Craig had advised him that he had chosen alongside his then sommelier Xavier, he was reassured. It turned out to be another amazing Blanc night with classics from the Le Manoir stable. The turbot with cucumber and seaweed was sensational and the squab pigeon classically brilliant, one of my favourite ingredients.

Michel Roux Jr arrived and Craig organised flowers, hair and spa for his wife Giselle. Michel was happy and is a true gent, which reminds me of the time Craig, Paul Heathcote and I came back from a trip to France, penniless, and Michel rescued us, feeding us and putting us up over night at Le Gavroche. Michel cooked along classical lines, making the legendary lobster cassoulet with pigs' trotters – a combination perhaps you wouldn't normally put together but ate incredibly well. He did a lovely veal and morel dish, and finished with the most perfect chocolate tart with pears and lashings of cream.

Paul Cunningham was introduced to me through Sat Bains, two great characters who typify the phrase that genius is close to insanity – their energy and humour is always endless. Paul has been in Copenhagen for a number of years and has established a fantastic reputation at The Paul in Tivoli Gardens. He cooked some extraordinary food – the rabbit dish will live with me forever, probably one of the most surprising combinations that was truly outstanding, in terms of favour and balance the star of the show. What a character, what a night! Paul took loads of photos and brought a ridiculously expensive Danish wine that no one drank or liked, and that is still in this cellar today.

Michael Caines cooked solid food from the Gidleigh Park repertoire, a classic ballontine of foie gras with Madeira jelly – perfection – and the slow poached sea bass with Thai purée and lemongrass foam was exquisite and the fillet of beef and smoked belly pork was to die for. We drank rum and coke into the early hours by the roaring fire in the bar, reminiscing about time spent at Robuchon, Ramsay and the like, a fascinating night.

Phil cooked on Saturday night in his own formidable style. He broke all records that night with 108. Phil kicked off with a warm game jelly with chanterelles, bacon foam and frazzles which was a fantastic start to the night followed by pan roast foie gras – perfection with the raisin pain d'epice one of our ultimate favourite ingredients. Finishing off with a pave of bitter chocolate and roast madadamias. A rich evening, not for the faint hearted.

Life was difficult following Phil that particular festival. All the extra staff had gone and the place was crammed with 105 on a Sunday night. But hey, that's life. I cooked game for the first time at the festival and the partridge went down incredibly well.

Obsession 07
FOOD
of the Gods
FESTIVAL OF FOOD & WINE 22ND - 28TH JANUARY 2007

RAYMOND BLANC

"My earliest learning in the kitchen was as chef's apprentice to Maman Blanc. I worked as a minion, with the tasks of peeling and preparing vegetables, plucking chickens and so on, all ready to give to my mother for her to perform the simple creative act of cooking. These were truly my formative years with food, because I am totally self-taught and have never worked under a chef in my life. I learned the seasons of the garden and the nobility of produce; I connected with the woods and fields, which were full of delightful wild produce, and partook in the feast of cooking and sharing around the table. This training formed the basis of the simple food philosophy which permeates Le Manoir aux Quat' Saisons: seasonality; simplicity; fresh produce; cooking and giving. As children we would mostly eat only seasonal food which came either from our garden or from the farms around us. Everything we grew was organic – although the word didn't exist back then. This is why food is my Obsession."

OBSESSION FESTIVAL

PAUL CUNNINGHAM

"I wouldn't really say that I am obsessed. It's more of a passion, and not only for food. For me food, and in particular cooking, is more of an artistic expression — an extension of my creative self. The only wish that I have for my children, apart from obvious good health and happiness, is that their chosen professions are creative and that they are able to use their hearts as well as their heads. I photograph as much as I cook nowadays. My photography enables me to keep a more permanent record of my emotions. Our problem as creative chefs is the fact that our art is displayed, destroyed and digested within minutes — seconds even. Not really a problem — as long as we move our guests with what we do. As long as they understand and appreciate the reference point and where we're coming from.

I am driven, inspired by everything I am in contact with. Every day at the restaurant I cook within a glass pavilion, within a private garden. Wooden floors, white walls and glass ceilings surround my chefs and I — we are constantly inspired by the change of light, temperature and the weather. Using each other as catalysts for inspiration is also a most important factor. We are all moved and inspired in very different ways. We work as a team, but are very much inspired as individuals — for me it is most important to pick up on this.

I love what I do; I love to create ... if love is an Obsession then, yes, I am obsessed."

MICHEL ROUX JR

"Food is my life. There isn't a moment in the day or night that it isn't on my mind. Cooking or eating gives me equal amounts of pleasure; I suppose you could call it an Obsession, though I prefer to call it my life."

MICHAEL CAINES

"My love for food came from being within a large family and enjoying meals around the table. My time was spent helping my mother cook for these occasions using the crops that father lovingly tended from our garden. So the love came from here and the Obsession grew from my desire to cook to the best of my ability, using the best ingredients. By the nature of the trade that we are in, food becomes an Obsession and a quest for excellence in all you do. I'm lucky to have found my Obsession in food for others to enjoy!"

OBSESSION
FESTIVAL

"To be obsessed by perfection and its demands is unrelenting and never ending."

NIGEL HAWORTH

PHIL HOWARD

"One of the great benefits of participating in an event such as Northcote Food Festival is the fact that you get to see what is happening outside your own world. It is so easy to be too introspective in this industry. For me, Paul Cunningham's menu was one of the greatest displays of cooking I have witnessed at Northcote over the years. A larger than life Lancashire lad cooking world class food."

"I've always been obsessed with food from an early age. I was born and brought up on a farm in the Esk Valley and many of my childhood memories are the tastes and smells from the farm. I can instantly recall the waft of bacon frying; the aroma of roasting beef; the gamey scent of partridge in the oven; the smell of warm straw as I gathered eggs and the tang of blackberries plucked — purple-fingered — from the hedgerows. The North Yorkshire moors was, and still is, an idyllic place to live and learn about nature's larder — be it seafood from the north sea or lamb, beef and pork reared by people with pride in their produce. This in turn makes my Obsession a very nice reality."

ANDREW PERN

GRILLED BLACK PUDDING WITH PAN-FRIED FOIE GRAS, SALAD OF PICKERING WATERCRESS, APPLE AND VANILLA CHUTNEY, SCRUMPY REDUCTION

Serves 1

INGREDIENTS

10g Washed and trimmed watercress
Salt & pepper
A dash of vinaigrette
Apple and vanilla chutney
(see below)
Sprigs of thyme for garnish
Scrumpy reduction – made with apple juice and a splash of cider vinegar.
2 Slices black pudding
Knob of butter
1 Slice caramelised apple
1 Decent slice of duck or goose foie gras

Apple and Vanilla Chutney
1k Granny Smith apples with skin, ½ - 1cm diced
3 Medium shallots, finely diced
200ml Cider vinegar (or white wine, if you wish)
1 Fresh vanilla pod – split and de-seeded
400g Caster sugar
Pinch of salt

METHOD

Place five small piles of apple chutney at intervals around the plate; garnish each pile with a sprig of thyme. In the centre of the plate dress a few seasoned leaves with vinaigrette to form a little 'salad'. Drizzle the reduction around the side of the plate.

Lightly brush the slices of black pudding with melted butter and grill for 3 to 4 minutes. While this is cooking heat a frying pan and pan-fry the foie gras for 1½ minutes each side.

When cooked, stack alternatively: black pudding, foie gras, black pudding. Top with the slice of caramelised apple. Serve immediately. Drizzle the scrumpy reduction.

Apple and Vanilla Chutney
Place everything into an ample-sized thick-bottomed pan and reduce down until thickened and starting to caramelise. Cool down and tub up ready for using. Keep in a cool place.

BRAISED FILLET OF TURBOT, OYSTER; CUCUMBER AND WASABI JUS

Serves 4

It has been a classic dish at Le Manoir for many years. But as with all Le Manoir dishes it is about details which are not always easy to duplicate in your own home. I have 40 chefs in my kitchen. Maybe the best way to enjoy it is at Le Manoir.

INGREDIENTS

Fish

50g Shallots, peeled and sliced
20g Butter, unsalted
120g Button mushrooms, washed and sliced
100ml Dry white wine eg. Chardonnay
4 150g each turbot, filleted and portioned, brushed with melted butter, lemon, salt & pepper. Can be prepared a few hours in advance and refrigerated
2g Sea salt
0.5g Pepper, freshly ground white
80ml Water

Vegetable garnish and oysters

20g Butter, unsalted
30ml Water
200g Spinach, washed
85g Cucumber ribbons
60g Samphire grass
Salt
120g Native Colchester oysters, size 2, opened and kept in their juices in a small saucepan

To finish the sauce

200ml Strained cooking liquor, see above
60g Cucumber skin
12g Wasabi paste
1g Lecithin, soya based (optional)
40g Butter
1g Lemon juice

METHOD

Sauce and fish

Preheat the oven to 190°C/375°F/Gas mark 5.

In a sauté pan on a medium heat, sweat the shallots in the butter for 2 minutes.

Add the sliced mushrooms and sweat for a further minute. Add the wine and water and bring to the boil.

Place the fillets of fish on the mushrooms and cover with a lid.

Cook in the preheated oven for approximately 5 minutes. Remove from the oven, spoon out the fish on to a large buttered serving dish and keep warm. Strain the juices into a large jug blender, pressing on the shallots and mushrooms to extract as much juice as possible. Reserve.

Finishing the sauce

In a large jug blender, blitz together the hot cooking juices, cucumber skin, wasabi paste, lecithin, butter and lemon juice. Strain and reserve.

Cooking the vegetable garnish and heating the oysters

Divide the butter and water into two saucepans. Place the spinach in one and cucumber and samphire in the other. Add a tiny pinch of salt to the spinach. Cover with a lid. On a high heat bring the pans of vegetables to a quick boil. The spinach will take 1 minute, the cucumber and samphire 30 seconds. Just barely warm the oysters in their own juices. Place the turbot back in the oven for 1 minute. Bring your sauce to the boil.

TO SERVE

Place the spinach in the middle of each plate, with the cucumber and samphire spread around. Top with the fish and oyster, spooning the sauce over and around.

BITTER CHOCOLATE AND PEAR TART, WHITE CHOCOLATE ICE CREAM

Serves 8-10 cold and on the day it is made, otherwise the pastry will go soft.

INGREDIENTS

300g Caster sugar
2 Cinnamon sticks
400ml Water
4 Williams pears, peeled, cored and halved

Sweet pastry
120g Butter, softened
250g Plain flour
60g Caster sugar
1 Egg yolk
½ tbsp Double cream

Chocolate filling
120ml Double cream
60g Butter, cut into small pieces
250g Extra-bitter dark chocolate, chopped

White chocolate ice cream
½ ltr Milk
6 Egg yolks
50g Caster sugar
350g White chocolate, broken into pieces

METHOD

Put the sugar and cinnamon in a pan with the water and bring to the boil. Add the peeled, cored and halved pears. Cover and simmer for 10 minutes or until the pears are tender. Leave to cool in the syrup.

Sweet pastry
Mix the soft butter, flour and sugar together using your fingertips. Gradually add the yolk and cream until the pastry comes together. Do not overwork. Wrap in cling film and refrigerate for at least a couple of hours.

Preheat the oven to 180°C/350°F/ gas mark 4. Butter a fluted tart tin, 22cm in diameter. Roll out the pastry on a lightly floured surface and line the tin. Cut the edges flush with the sides and prick the base with a fork. Line with greaseproof paper and dry beans, then bake for 15 minutes. Remove the paper and beans and put back in the oven until golden and fully cooked, about another 10 minutes. Leave to cool in the tin.

Chocolate filling
Bring the cream to the boil. Add the chopped butter and chocolate and whisk well until completely melted Pour the chocolate filling into the tart.

Drain the pears on a tea towel until completely dry. Slice them across, fan out and place on the tart, keeping their shape. Refrigerate for 45 minutes before taking out of the tin and serving.

White chocolate ice cream
Boil the milk. Meanwhile whisk the yolks and sugar together until pale, add to the boiling milk and cook as an 'Anglaise' then pour onto the chocolate, mix well and pass through a sieve. Churn in an ice cream machine or freeze overnight.

TO SERVE

Serve each slice with the ice cream.

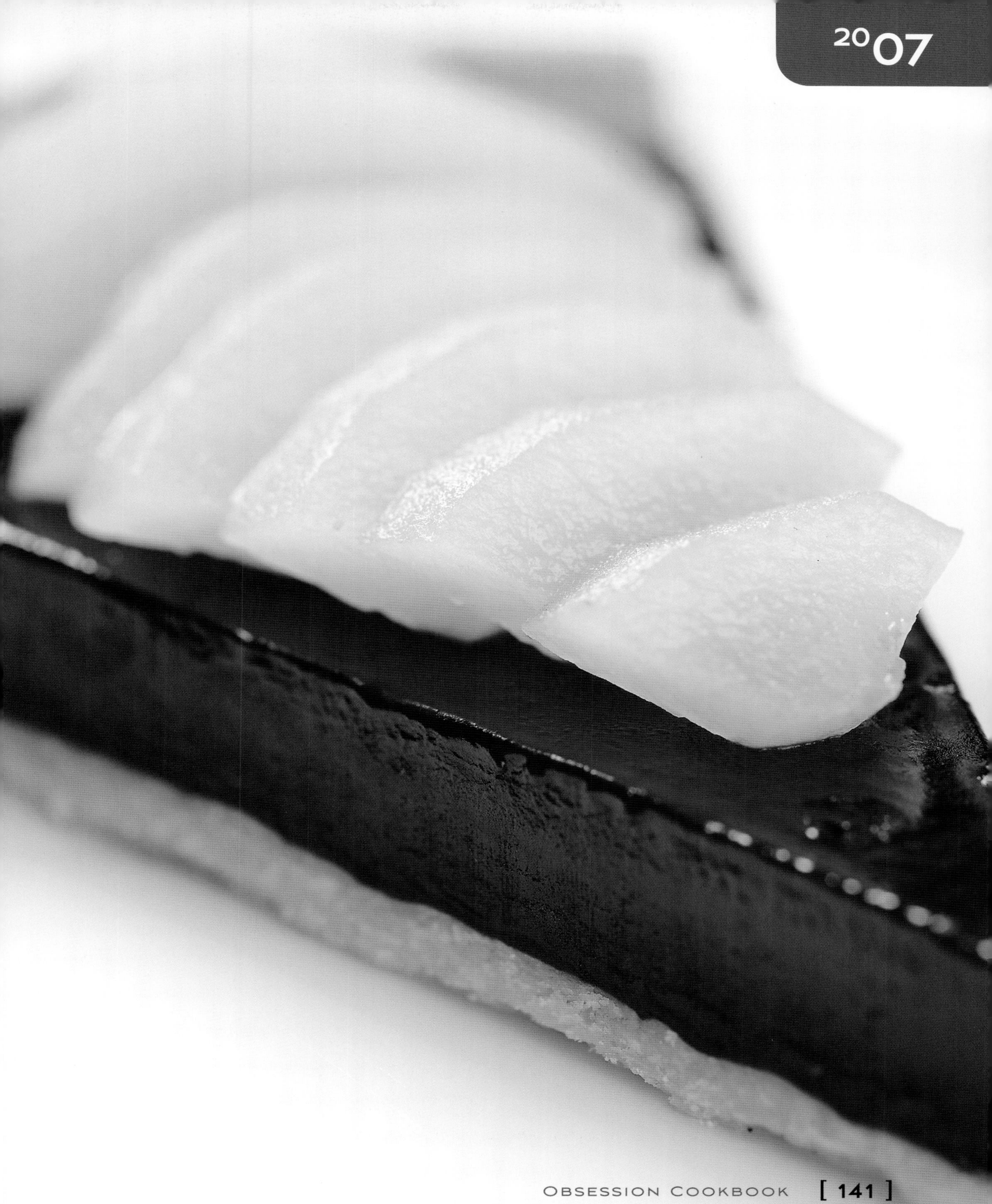

LOCAL RABBIT GRILLED WITH LANGOUSTINES FROM LÆSØ

Serves 4

INGREDIENTS

4 Gigantic fresh langoustines from the Danish island of Læsø
2 Saddles of medium-sized local rabbit
1 tsp Roasted, crushed fennel seed
Poul's Læsø sea salt

Chutney
4 Green tomatoes, diced
2 Green apples, diced
2 Gotland shallots, finely diced
100g Sugar
100ml Lilleø apple vinegar
1 tsp Roasted, crushed fennel seed plus more to serve

Aioli
4 New potatoes
1 Fennel
Water
Olive oil
100ml Olive oil mayonnaise
2 Garlic cloves
Lemon juice
1 tbsp Pastis
Garlic salt from Læsø

Salad
1 Bunch fennel
1 Bunch wild rocket leaf from Gotland
Rapeseed oil from Bornholm
1 Lemon

METHOD

Chutney
Boil the tomatoes, apples and shallots together with the sugar, vinegar and the fennel seed for about 10 minutes until thick and well reduced.

Aioli
Braise the potatoes with the fennel in a touch of water and olive oil. Blend together with the mayonnaise until smooth. Finish with a little lemon juice, pastis and fresh garlics salt from Læsø.

TO SERVE

Dress the rabbit and the langoustines with the crushed fennel seed and sea salt. Grill rare over hot coals.

Dress the finished dish with the salad ingredients and a little roasted fennel seed to enhance the aromas.

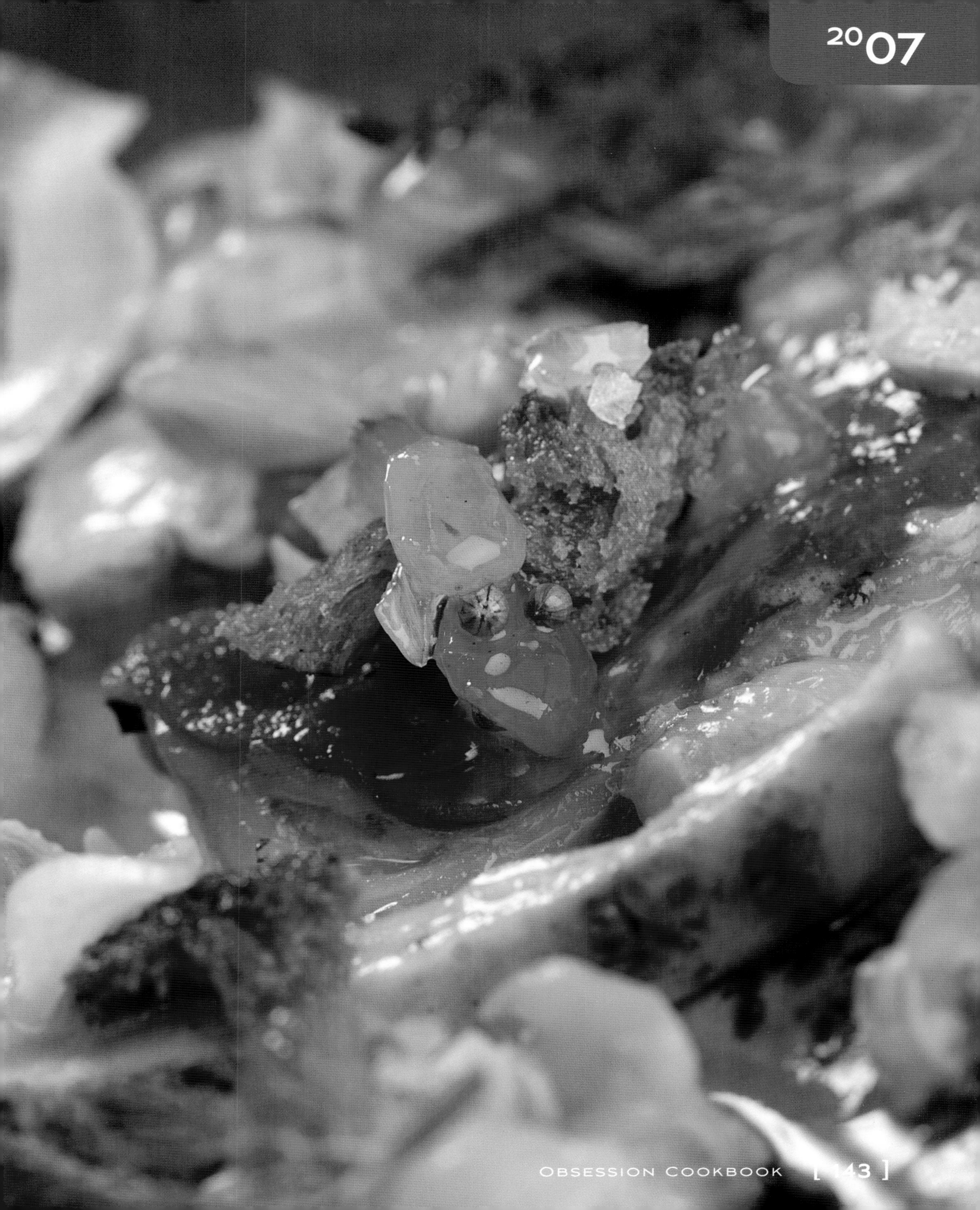

PAN FRIED SCALLOPS WITH CELERIAC PURÉE AND TRUFFLE VINAIGRETTE

Serves 4

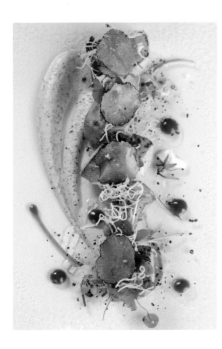

INGREDIENTS

12 Scallops
Olive oil
Mixed salad
Chopped chives

Celeriac purée

15g Onions, chopped
15g Celery, chopped
Salt and pepper
25g Unsalted butter
150ml Milk
150ml Chicken stock
150ml Water
200g Celeriac, chopped
25g Unsalted butter
Pinch of salt & pepper to season

Soy & truffle vinaigrette

25g Shallots sliced
130ml Olive oil
Salt & pepper
50g Button mushrooms
2 sprigs of fresh thyme
10ml Soy sauce
20ml Truffle juice
25g Veal glace
5ml Truffle oil

French vinaigrette

300ml Vegetable oil
100ml White wine vinegar
Salt & pepper
Sprig of thyme
Clove of garlic

Deep fried celeriac straw

4 celeriac fondants, cut in half
16 slices perigord truffle
8 edible flowers

METHOD

Celeriac purée

In a saucepan sweat the onions, celery and salt with the butter, add the milk, chicken stock and water then the celeriac and pepper. Bring to the boil and reduce to a simmer. Cook for 30 minutes and then allow to cool. Drain through a colander and then place into a Robot Coupe (food processor) and blend until fine. Remove from the Robot Coupe and then place into a blender and blend to a very fine purée.

Soy & truffle vinaigrette

Sweat the shallots in 30ml of the olive oil, add a pinch of salt and lightly colour.

Add the mushrooms and thyme and sweat for a further 2 minutes. Add the soy sauce and reduce to nothing, then add the truffle juice and reduce by half. Add the veal glace and bring to the boil, place into a blender and blend to a fine purée. Warm 100ml olive oil and add to the pulp followed by the truffle oil. Adjust the seasoning and pass through a fine sieve. Place into a plastic bottle and use at room temperature.

French vinaigrette

Mix all together in a bottle and shake before using.

TO SERVE

Pan fry the scallops in a non-stick pan in olive oil.

Dress some celeriac purée onto the plate, then some soy vinaigrette.

Now place 3 scallops and 2½ celeriac fondants onto the plate. Top with the salad flowers and chives dressed in French vinaigrette then add the truffle slices and celeriac straw.

Braised Veal Cheek with a Fricassee of Handrolled Macaroni, Cauliflower and Truffle

Serves 8

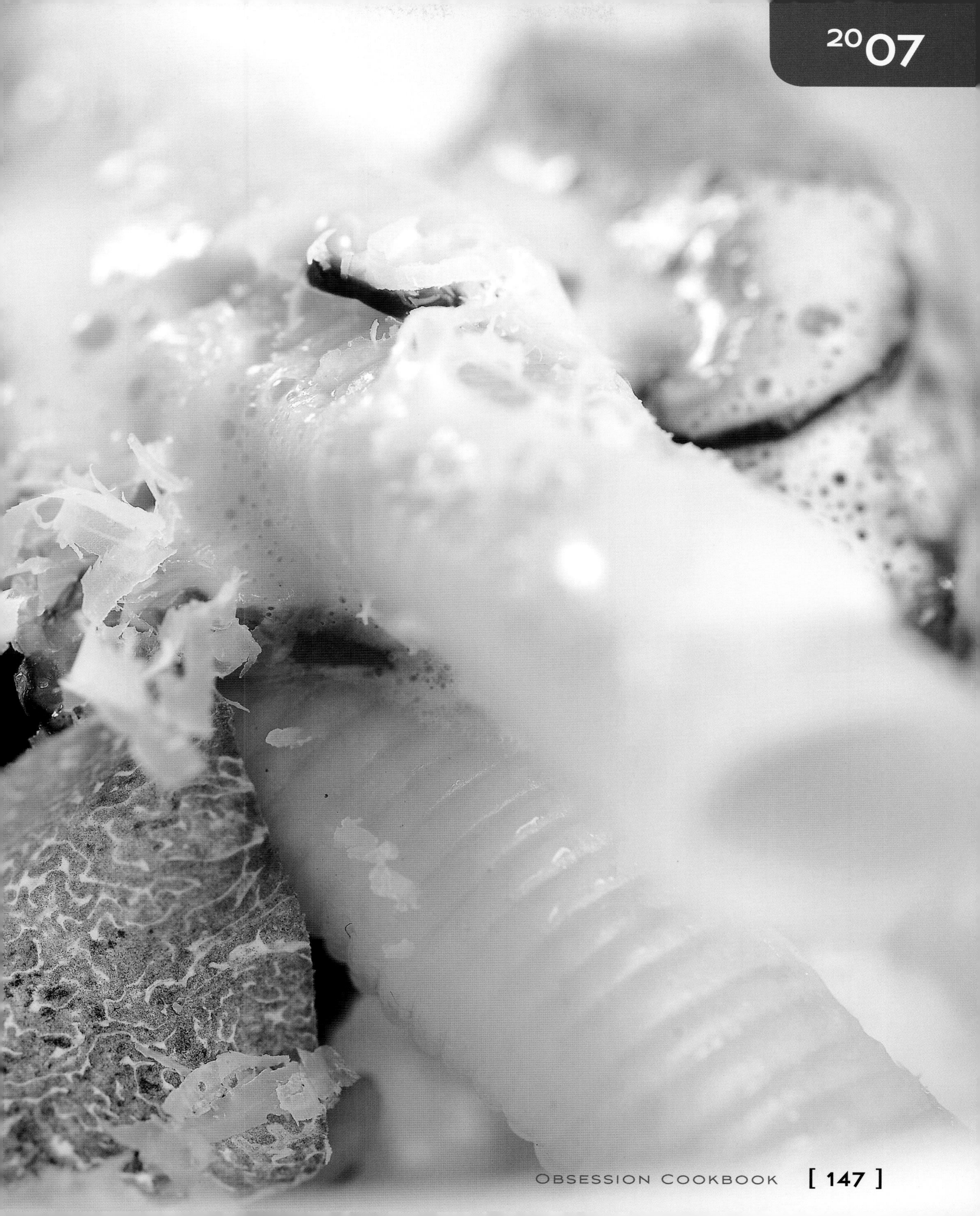

Braised Veal Cheek with a Fricassee of Handrolled Macaroni, Cauliflower and Truffle

Serves 8

INGREDIENTS

Veal
16 Veal cheeks
Salt & pepper
100g Plain flour, on a plate
100ml Grapeseed oil
100g Butter
500ml Veal stock
1 Onion, peeled and quartered
1 Carrot, peeled and quartered
1 Leek, peeled and quartered
1 Celery stick, peeled and quartered
250g Button mushrooms, washed and cut in half
1 Calf's foot – split in half lengthways
1 Bay leaf
10 Peppercorns
2 Stems of thyme

Macaroni
2 Eggs
6 Yolks
Splash of olive oil
300g '00' pasta flour
Salt
Couscous
50ml Grapeseed oil

Cauliflower cheese
1 Onion, finely sliced
1 leek, finely sliced
70g Butter
Salt
450ml Milk
1 Bay leaf
1 Large, firm, luxury cauliflower
80g Flour
50g Beaufort cheese, grated
50g Parmesan, grated

To finish the sauce
2 Shallots, finely sliced
150g Button mushrooms, washed and finely sliced
50g Butter
Salt
100ml White wine

Vegetables/other ingredients
8 Salsify pieces, 10cm long
8 Swiss chard leaves
1 Perigord truffle, finely grated on a microplane.
100ml Crème fraîche

METHOD

Veal
The back bone of flavour in a braised dish comes from the initial caramelisation of the meat and vegetables. The extent to which you do this varies from dish to dish but it is a critical point, the importance of which can not be underestimated.

Place a hot, large, heavy based, oven proof dish on the stove over a high heat and leave for 5 minutes. Trim any skin and membrane off the cheeks and dry them on a cloth. Transfer to a plate, season with salt and pepper, and press each side onto the flour.

Pour grapeseed oil into the pan and add the cheeks. Veal goes a rich golden colour when browned. Do not take it past this point. Turn the cheeks and at the point when the second side is just golden add the butter. Turn the cheeks over a couple more times to ensure a thorough colouring is achieved. If at any stage it looks like the butter is going to burn, turn down the heat.

Remove the cheeks from the pan, add all the vegetables, a pinch of salt and, while stirring occasionally, caramelise them until lightly coloured all over. Return the meat to the pan, add the calf's foot, the bay leaf, peppercorns and thyme and cover with water. Bring to the boil, skim off any scum and tick over for 5 minutes. Skim.

Add the veal stock, cover with a lid or disc of parchment paper and cook in an oven at 110°C/225°F/gas mark ¼ for an hour. Check the veal at this point. It should feel supple and tender. Check two or three pieces. If it is still firm, place back in the oven and check every 15 minutes, until you feel the meat 'give'. While it should have some bite to it, it must be tender.

Remove from the oven and allow to cool to room temperature. Carefully lift out the 16 cheeks, season with a pinch of salt and cover with cling film. Drain the stock through a colander, discard the vegetables, and pass the stock through a fine sieve. It can be chilled at this point or processed into the finished sauce (see below).

Macaroni

The hand-rolled macaroni are a fantastic refinement, but bought macaroni would more than suffice. Make a firm pasta dough in a food processor by adding the eggs, yolks and olive oil to the flour and salt. Rest, well wrapped, for 2 hours.

Roll it out into sheets 2mm thick. Now cut this sheet quickly so it does not dry, into rectangles 2x5cm and cover with cling film. You will need 80 pieces.

At this point recruit a partner to put the pasta through the machine while you roll them into tubes – this will save both time and excessive ageing! Place the long edge of the rectangle between the rollers of the pasta machine, set 1 notch finer than when you rolled the sheets. Now roll it through, short side first, at the finest setting. Each piece will vary slightly but you are aiming to make these pasta sheets 10x5cm.

Now dip a pencil into a bowl of flour to completely coat with a film of flour. Have the rectangles of pasta horizontally in front of you, sitting on a wooden butter ball pat. Place the pencil on the long edge closest to you and in one move roll the pasta sheet into a tube. Slip it off the pencil and place on a tray covered in a layer of couscous. This will stop the pasta from sticking and ensure it dries easily. As with all pasta work, there is a knack to this. Work as a pair and do not let the pasta dry out. When you have finished, blanch them all in boiled salted water for 1 minute, drain through a colander, toss in the grapeseed oil and store, covered in the fridge.

Cauliflower cheese

Sweat the onion and leek in 50g of butter and a pinch of salt for 2-3 minutes, until softened. Add the milk and the bay leaf, bring to the boil, simmer for 10 minutes, allow to cool for 15 minutes, pass through a sieve and set aside.

Break the cauliflower down into large florets and boil in a large pan of salted water for 5 minutes. Drain and place in an ovenproof dish.

Melt 20g butter over a high heat and, at the point where it starts to smell nutty, add the flour and cook, stirring constantly, for 2 minutes. Now, gradually add the set-aside milk, stirring all the time, until you have a smooth white sauce. Return to the boil and cook for 1 minute. Add the Beaufort and Parmesan and stir until smooth. Spoon generously over the cauliflower and bake, covered with foil, in an oven at 160°C/325°F/gas mark 3 for 25 minutes, removing the foil for the last 5 minutes. Remove from the oven and leave to cool to room temperature.

Finishing the sauce

Sweat the shallots and button mushrooms in butter with a pinch of salt over a medium heat in a heavy based pan. After 2-3 minutes add the white wine and continue to cook until it has completely evaporated. Add the cheek braising liquor, bring to the boil, skim and reduce by half.

Pass through a fine sieve, return to the heat and taste the sauce. The sauce should have a beautiful rounded flavour and enough body to coat the back of a spoon. If it lacks body, make a paste with 1 teaspoon of cornflour and 1 tablespoon of water and add, bit by bit, to the sauce until it has the desired consistency. Set aside

Vegetables

If you have a professional waterbath refer to the cooking times and temperatures for the salsify and swiss chard. If not, whisk 25g of plain flour into 50ml water and pour into a large pan containing 6l of cold water. This is called a blanc and will keep the salsify and chard white during cooking. Season with salt and bring to the boil.

Peel the salsify and place it in a bowl of water with the juice of half a lemon. Remove the green top from the swiss chard by snapping at the top and remove any 'strings' from the stem in the process. Cut into pieces approximately 10x3cm. Place the salsify in the blanc, turn the heat right down and cook until just tender, approximately 10-15 minutes. Lift out the salsify and allow to cool to room temperature. Similarly cook the swiss chard. Once the vegetables are cooked, cut the chard across into 3mm pieces and the salsify into little rounds about 3mm thick. Set aside in the fridge.

TO SERVE

Reheat the veal by putting all but 200ml of the sauce into an ovenproof pan, adding the cheeks, covering with a lid and placing in an oven at 110°C/225°F/gas mark ¼ sfor 30 minutes. Turn the cheeks from time to time. Reheat the cauliflower cheese in the same oven. When hot, remove from the oven and, using a fork lightly crush the cauliflower to give rise to a coarse, textured mix. Cover with foil and keep hot in the oven.

Reheat the macaroni by plunging them for 15 seconds into boiling salted water. Transfer them to a large pan and add the remaining 200ml of sauce, crème fraîche and grated truffle. Stir carefully to coat the pasta. Taste and adjust the seasoning if necessary. Add the salsify and swiss chard.

Into each of 8 large preheated bowls, place a spoon of the cauliflower. Cover with some of the macaroni mix. Place two cheeks on top of this and coat generously with sauce. Serve immediately.

Warm Loin of Herdwick Mutton, Jerusalem Artichokes, Honey and Mint Dressing
Serves 4

INGREDIENTS

250g Boneless loin of mutton
(silverskin removed and trimmed)
Salt
4g Mint leaves, finely shredded
10g Mutton ham, finely diced
10g Pickled red cabbage
Artichoke purée (see below)
Artichoke crisps (see below)
Honey & mint dressing (see below)

Artichoke purée
100g Jerusalem artichokes, peeled
2g Butter
Salt to taste
100ml Whipping cream

Artichoke crisps
1 x 100g Large artichoke, peeled

Honey and mint dressing
50ml L'Estornell vinegar
1 tsp English heather honey
12g Shallots, finely chopped
1 dstspn Shredded mint
40ml Extra virgin olive oil
Salt & pepper

METHOD

Mutton
Season the loin of mutton with salt then roll the mutton in the mint, completely covering it. Wrap the loin tightly in cling film. Steam for 8 minutes, allow to rest (serve pink and keep warm).

Artichoke purée
Finely slice the artichokes on a mandolin.
In a medium pan, melt the butter then add the sliced artichokes, season with salt and cook for 3-4 minutes without colouring. Add the cream, cling film the pan and cook for a further 10-15 minutes until the artichokes are tender. Once tender place into a Thermomix and blend until smooth. Pass through a fine sieve, check the seasoning, leave to cool and reserve.

Artichoke crisps
Slice the artichoke lengthways as thinly as possible on a mandolin. Deep fry at 160°C until golden and crispy. Remove from the fryer and season with salt.

Honey and mint dressing
Bring the L'Estornell vinegar, honey and shallots to the boil, add the mint and olive oil, season with salt and pepper and allow to cool.

TO SERVE

Take a deep bowl and place a good spoonful of artichoke purée in the middle. Remove the mutton from the cling film and carve into 6 pieces per person. Put the mutton ham on top of the artichoke purée and pour over a spoonful of honey and mint dressing. Place the warm mutton loin carefully on the artichoke purée, garnish with red cabbage and spoon over a little more dressing. Finally, put the crisps on top and serve.

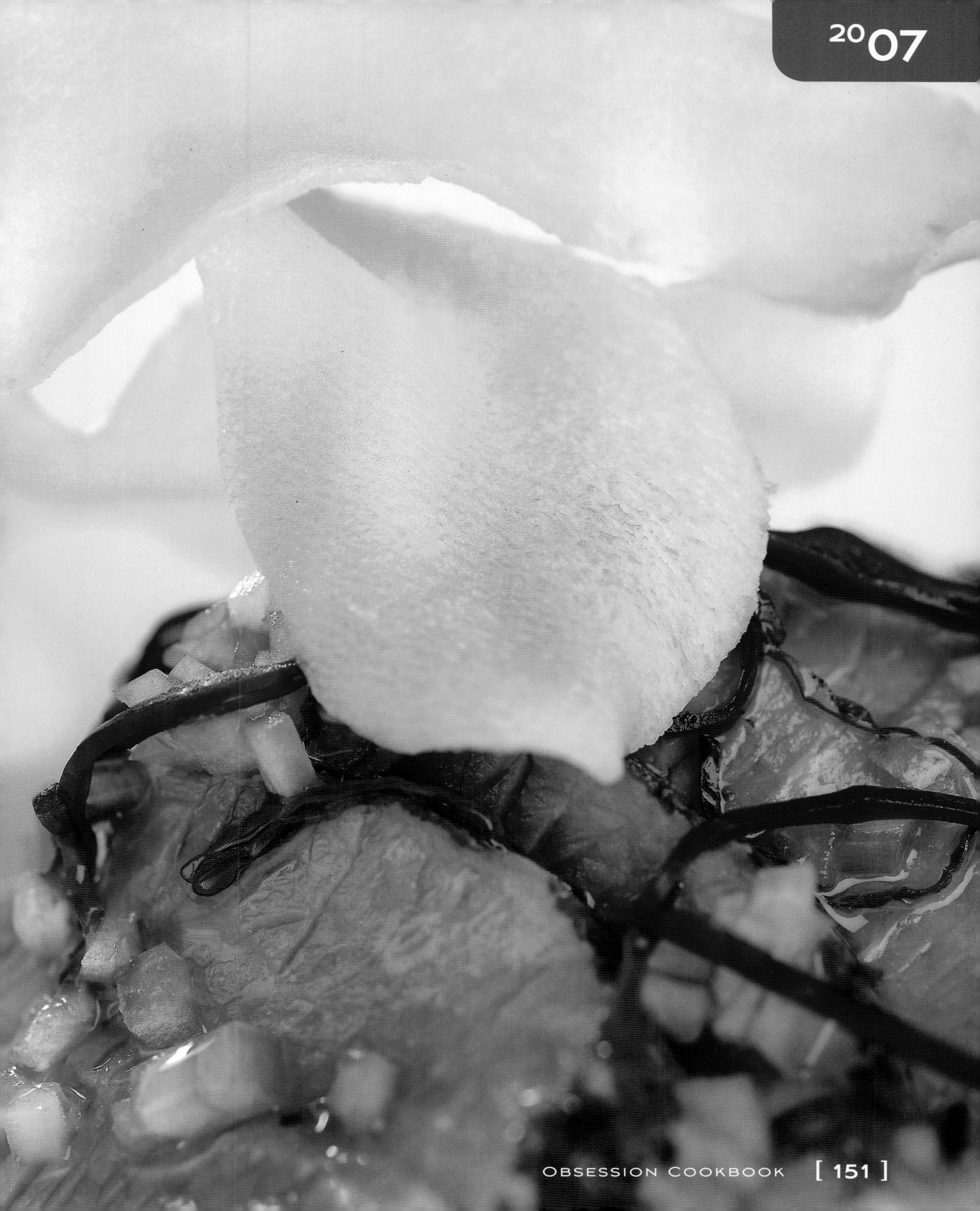

OBSESSION

20O6

This was the year of the infamous game pie, when Phil Howard chose to cook individual game pies. The story goes that this was a simple dish but – two days later – at 7.18pm, minutes before service, we were still making game pies. Claude Bosi stormed in with typical French passion, he started the festival with the delicacy of baked potato soup and melilot flower; the precision of the monkfish and complexity of the venison with his combination of marmalade, chocolate and chicken liver pâté blew everyone away.

David Thompson arrived in with partner Tanongsak Yordwai and the extraordinary flavours he conjured from his time spent in Thailand had to be tasted to be believed – the red curry of duck with santol made with Reggie's Goosnargh cornfed ducks was exceptional and the lobster braised with sugar cane and steamed curried scallops were not to be missed.

Fergus Henderson arrived bringing the flavours of St John, a simple dish of shrimps and cabbage, the famous roast marrow bone and parsley salad, finishing with St John's Eccles cake and Lancashire cheese, a real taste of British heritage. He was absolutely fantastic and his mum and dad came to support him and were very proud of a brilliant evening full of northern appreciation. Fergus is a great character, charming and modest who has championed the best of British throughout his career, wise and thoughtful who certainly liked a tipple of Fernet Branca in the early hours.

Andoni Luis Aduriz arrived with his team of six and everyone had a bespoke job – one was even in charge of looking after garden products. Andoni's very special food was so interesting and stimulating, I don't think the Northcote clientele really knew what to expect. Particularly striking was the vegetable coal, which was yucca plant cooked with aubergine skin to make the flesh go deep purple, to imitate charcoal. His cod and tripe stew even for Lancastrians was challenging and he finished the menu with his version of pain perdu served with raw sheep's milk ice cream – brillante!

I remember they had a late night after service where they sat around the roaring log fire in the bar on a late January morning (2 am). I asked them if they wanted something to eat and their eyes lit up. So I went and knocked up a few rounds of rare roast beef butties and two pots of tea, a real culture change with real British comfort food and they absolutely loved it – wholesome British fare for the team from molecular Mugaritz. This Spanish invasion would not have been possible without the patient help and translation of my great friend and fellow foodie, Alain Mols, who flew from Spain to Northcote at the drop of a hat after we realised that Andoni and his team did not speak English. Alain passed away in October of 2006 and is sadly missed. Mark cooked razor clams and wild garlic, a marriage made in heaven. He also reintroduced us to Carlings – not the lager but those wonderful peas that we all ate around bonfires with a splash of vinegar in the depth of winter in our youth. Nevertheless we had a couple of late nights with Mark (or Hixy, as I like to call him); he doesn't know how to go to bed and it's very difficult to get him away from the bar. He is a true legend in every sense.

Bruce Poole biked up from Wandsworth having accepted my invitation during the Young Chef of the Year in the northern heats. Bruce loves northern hospitality and his football – he is yet another foreign Manchester United supporter. He cooked some truly wonderful dishes, turbot on tartar sauce with the largest turbots to grace the Northcote kitchens and a pithivier of quail, the essence of simplicity.

The Sunday morning was a very cold, crisp day in Lancashire and Paul Heathcote popped by in his running gear. He'd been at Northcote on Bruce's evening as a guest of Reggie Johnson the night before and had left his car, and decided just to jog over (nine miles) and pick it up, as you do! Andy Lynes the journalist couldn't get over the fact he'd just popped in for a bacon butty. That evening while Phil was preparing his chicken wings, I was still rolling out the game pies and the pastry was getting harder, my arms were dropping off. For the first time on that Sunday evening I saw a twinkle of fear in Phil's eyes that we might not get there. He certainly didn't go out for a run that year, which, as far as I can remember, was the first year ever. To add to our problems Aunty Sandra (Craig's adopted aunty) and regular supporter was reluctant to leave the restaurant after lunch. So we couldn't lay up the restaurant for dinner – this all culminated in us promising to never, ever do lunch again throughout the festival, which just made things so much easier from then on in.

MARK HIX

"I grew up on the coast with a good ethic of home-cooking ingredients that were on our doorstep. I remember my gran cooking my mackerel straight out of the water, and eating my grandfather's tomatoes fresh from the greenhouse with Sarson's malt vinegar. I think if you work in, own or run restaurants and kitchens you need to be slightly obsessed with food or it just ain't worth doing."

OBSESSION
FESTIVAL

PHIL HOWARD

"I aged as many years as I spent days at Northcote that year! I made many poor decisions – stuffing chicken wings, making 100 pies and 10 cheesecakes. I went down like a bag of crap! The problem with these events is that the menu is always prized out of me mid December, when The Square is so busy and I don't give it the attention I should – not in terms of quality but more in terms of practicality. I got it all horribly wrong this year but for once, I saw Nigel roll up his sleeves and bail me out!"

NIGEL HAWORTH

"To be obsessed with creativity has no boundaries, a brush stroke to infinity."

CLAUDE BOSI

"Food and cooking has been part of my life for as long as I can remember. There are no boundaries with food, meaning you can always develop and evolve existing dishes, while creating others. You have to be passionate about this industry especially, as positive results only come from hard work and determination."

ANDONI LUIS ADURIZ

"Obsession is the transformation of an apparently unnecessary, or not so unnecessary, idea into a priority need.

Nourishment is not exactly superfluous, although what can be superfluous is the mandatory consumption of culture, practices, styles and original and private visions in addition to nutrients, which is what comprises the essence of gastronomy today.

Strip life of poetics, inspiration and curious gazes and you'll succeed in suppressing passion; but you'll also put an end to the human being."

DAVID THOMPSON

"Food is a happy and wholesome diversion. When I was about twenty-one I became obsessed, it was as if a genetic time bomb went off. I read and ate voraciously, anything and everything to do with food enthralled me. It was during this time I first went to Thailand and it all fell together: the food, the culture and the people. I have been a captive ever since."

FERGUS HENDERSON

"I've always been a gutsy soul and a big believer in the table and white tablecloths. They've held my family together through thick and thin and we all still gather at the table. The power of eating is extraordinary. I trained to be an architect, but all my buildings became feasts and my course was otherwise destined. Genius loci expresses the magic of the moment and place, and never is this stronger than in restaurants – those two moments in the day when wonderful organised chaos takes place. There's something very magical and special about restaurants that's hard to put your finger on, but that's why I like them."

BRUCE POOLE

"I am obsessed with all aspects of running a restaurant in which, naturally, the food plays a major part. I have strong views about what makes a meal enjoyable, or even great, and striving to achieve the latter while in practice having to settle for the former is what moves us onwards as chefs. I wish there were more skilled cooks attempting to simplify their food by taking ingredients away, rather than adding them."

Meadowsweet Panna Cotta, Golden Delicious Purée and Shortbread

Serves 6 - 8

INGREDIENTS

Meadowsweet panna cotta
600g Whipping cream
200g Full fat milk
8g Meadowsweet
120g Caster sugar
2.5 Gelatine leaves

Shortbread
(Makes 15-20 biscuits)
150g Butter
150g T55 flour
75g Cornflour
38g Caster sugar
1 Egg yolk

Golden delicious purée
12 Golden delicious apples

METHOD

Meadowsweet panna cotta
Combine the milk and cream in a saucepan, and bring gently to the boil. Pour over the meadowsweet and infuse for one hour.

Soak the gelatine in cold water until it becomes soft. Strain the milk and cream and add the sugar. Bring back to the boil and cool slightly. Add the soaked gelatine and pass through a sieve.

Pour into glasses and place in the fridge to set overnight.

Shortbread
Mix all the dry ingredients then slowly add the egg yolks.

Roll until level, with a 1cm height. Use a circular cutter to portion. Place on a baking tray and cook at 180°C/350°F/gas mark 4 for 15 minutes. When cool dust with icing sugar.

Golden delicious puréé
Cook the apples over a medium heat, with no added sugar or liquid, until soft. This will take 10-15 minutes. Take them out and purée them. Each serving should be 40g per person. Spoon on top of the panna cotta and serve with the shortbread.

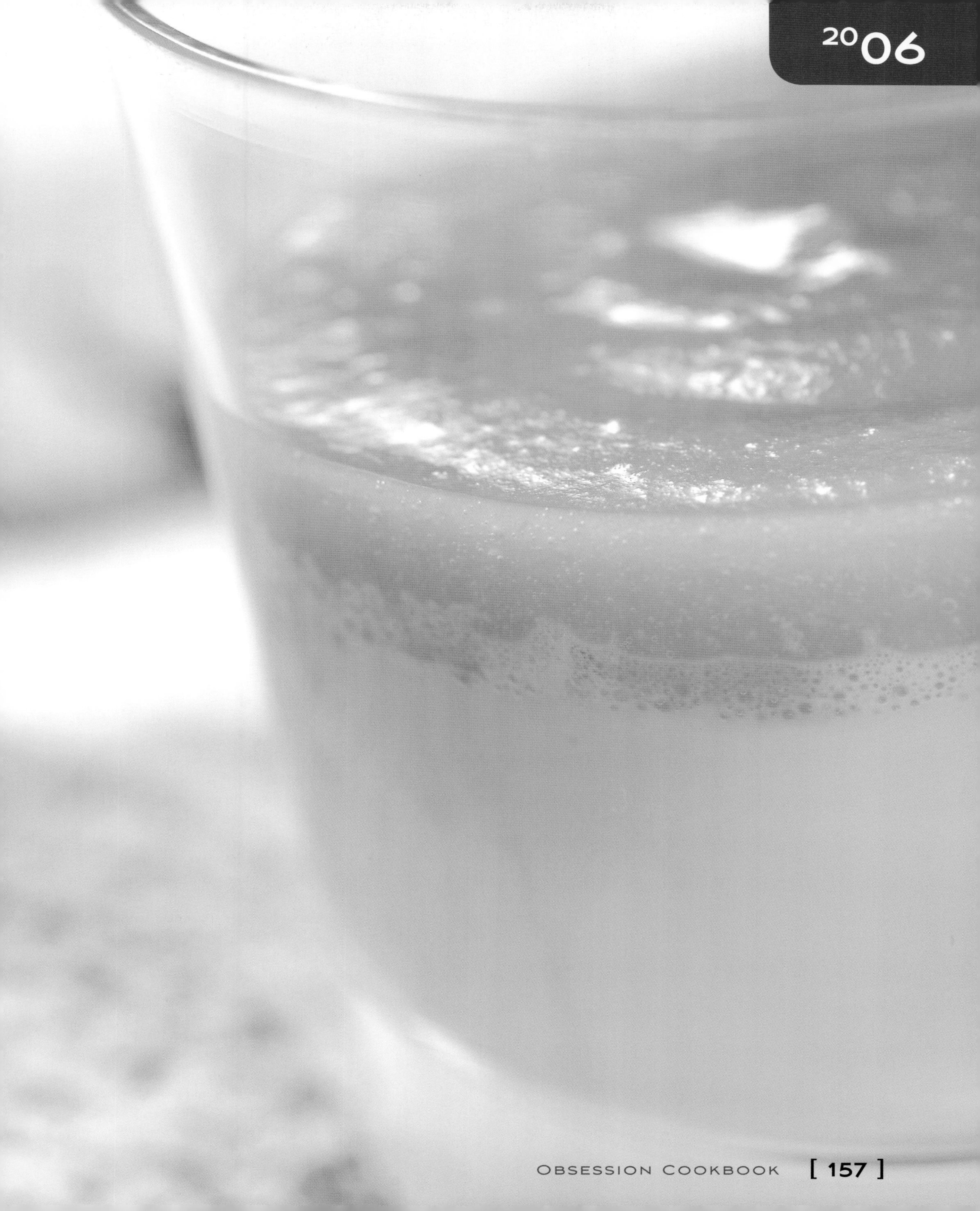

RED CURRY OF DUCK WITH SANTOL

Serves 2 with rice or more if there are other dishes

INGREDIENTS

Curry paste
8 Dried long red chillies, deseeded, soaked and drained
Large pinch of salt
1 tbsp Chopped galangal
4 tbsp Chopped lemongrass
1 tsp Finely chopped kaffir lime zest
1 tsp Scraped and chopped coriander roots
3 tbsp Chopped red shallots
3 tbsp Chopped garlic
A little gapi (optional)
4 Pla salit (salted fish from Thailand)

Duck and santol
1 Large santol (tropical fruit from southeast Asia, available from specialist suppliers)
Salt
2 Duck breasts

Fish sauce
1 cup Separated coconut cream
2 tbsp Palm sugar
1-2 tbsp Fish sauce (to taste)
1 tbsp Tamarind water
3 Kaffir lime leaves, torn
118ml Coconut milk or stock
2 Large red or green chillies, halved

METHOD

Curry paste
First, make the paste by grinding all the ingredients apart from the pla salit together in a pestle and mortar or blender. Lightly grill the pla salit, fillet, skin and grind before adding to the paste.

Duck and santol, and fish sauce
Clean the santol, score the skin and steep in salted water. Trim the duck breast and marinate briefly in the fish sauce. Grill the duck breast to medium then rest.

Meanwhile, heat the coconut cream over a medium heat, add 3 tablespoons of the paste and fry until the paste is smoky and fragrant from the fish. Season the curry with palm sugar, fish sauce – not too much – and then the tamarind water. Do not cook the paste for more than a minute or so after adding the tamarind or it will burn. Squeeze the santol to extract as much water as possible and add to the curry with the kaffir lime leaves before moistening with coconut milk or stock and simmer for a few minutes until the santol has softened. Remove the seeds.

Slice the duck breast finely then add to the curry but do not simmer, remove the curry from the heat. Add the chillies and check the seasoning – it may need more fish sauce. The curry should be reasonably light, salty, smoky, sweet and sour.

ROAST BONE MARROW AND PARSLEY SALAD

Serves 4

INGREDIENTS

7-8cm Pieces of middle veal marrowbone (available from any good butcher)
Healthy bunch of flat parsley, picked from its stems
2 Shallots, peeled and very thinly sliced
Modest handful of capers (extra fine if possible)

Dressing

Juice of 1 lemon
Extra virgin olive oil
Pinch of sea salt & pepper
Good supply of toast to serve
Coarse sea salt to serve

METHOD

Put the bone marrow in an ovenproof frying pan and place in a hot oven. The roasting process should take about 20 minutes depending on the thickness of the bone. You are looking for the marrow to be loose and giving, but not melted away, which it will do if left too long (traditionally the ends would be covered to prevent any seepage, but I like the colouring and crispness at the end).

Meanwhile, lightly chop the parsley, just enough to discipline it, mix it with the shallots and capers, and at the last moment dress it with the lemon juice, extra virgin olive oil, sea salt and pepper.

Using a teaspoon or long thin implement scrape the marrow out of the bone onto the toast and season with coarse sea salt. Put a pinch of parsley salad on top and eat.

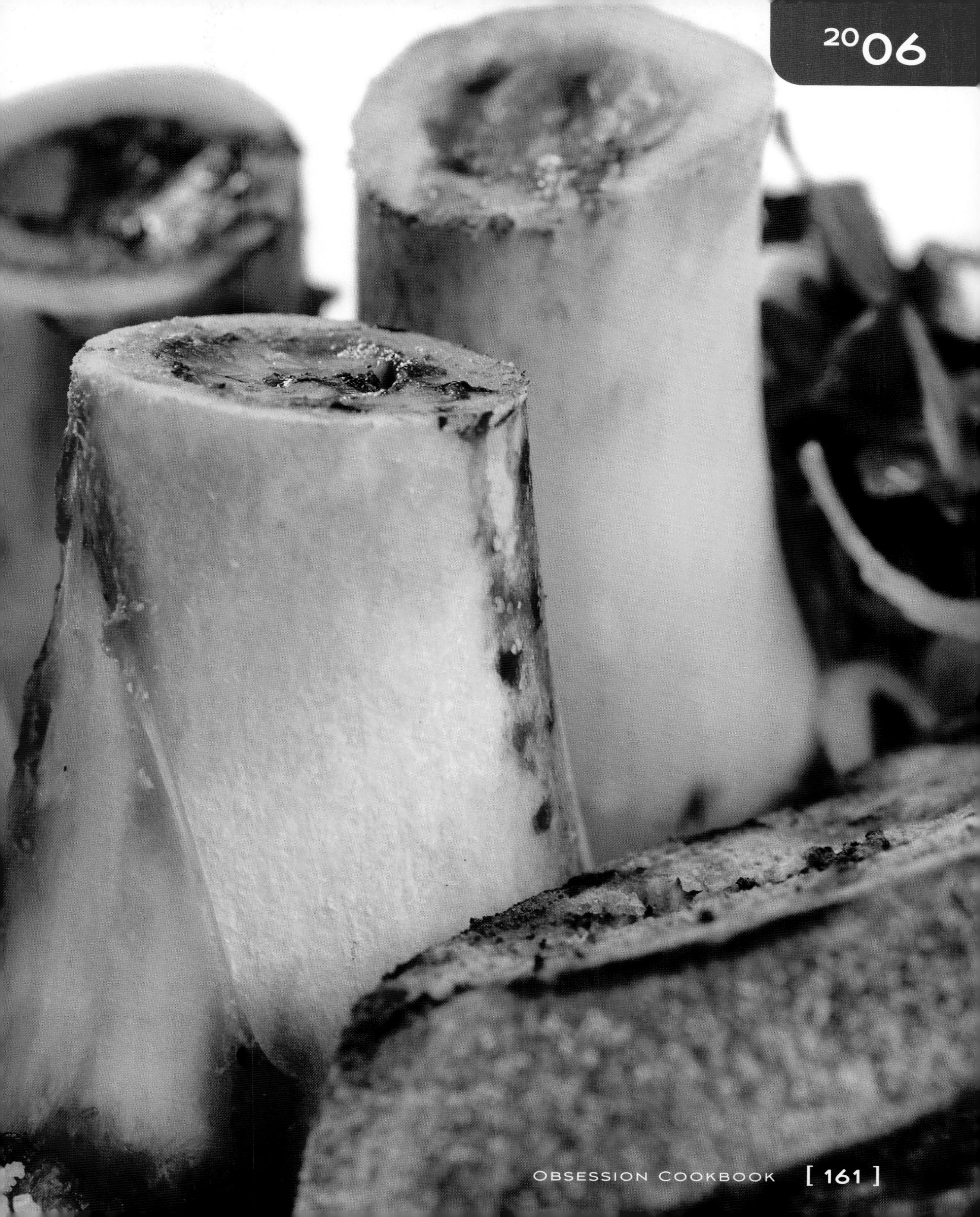

FRENCH TOAST SOAKED IN EGG YOLK, SAUTÉ BROWNED AND CARAMELISED ACCOMPANIED BY AN ICE CREAM HANDMADE WITH RAW SHEEP'S MILK
Serves 4

A homemade brioche is not absolutely essential for this recipe. Brioche may purchased at a good bakery, however, it must be made with butter.

FRENCH TOAST SOAKED IN EGG YOLK, SAUTÉ BROWNED AND CARAMELISED ACCOMPANIED BY AN ICE CREAM HANDMADE WITH RAW SHEEP'S MILK

Serves

INGREDIENTS

Confectioner's custard
250ml Milk
25g Cornflour
40g Sugar
60g Egg yolks
25g Butter, cubed

Almond custard
125g Butter
1 Egg
1 Egg yolk
150g Confectioner's custard
125g Ground almonds
1 Capful of rum
1 Vanilla pod

Brioche
250g Flour
4 Eggs
10g Yeast
190g Butter
25g Sugar
5g Salt

French toast marinade
720g Liquid eggs
440g Sugar
2 ltr Milk
2 ltr Cream

To marinade the Torrija French toast
1 Brioche
1 Batch French toast marinade

Sheep's milk ice cream
1.3 ltr Sheep's milk
200g Sugar
60g Powdered glucose
20g Invert sugar
35g Powdered milk
7g Anti-crystallising agent
Salt

Lemon zest confit
Rind of ½ lemon
100ml Water
100g Sugar

To finish
50g Butter
100g Sugar
Apricot jelly

METHOD

Confectioner's custard

Boil 150ml milk in a saucepan.

In a separate bowl, mix the cornflour, sugar and the remaining milk.

Once the milk has boiled, combine it with the milk mixture and cook for 15 minutes.

In a separate bowl, beat the egg yolks and add a little of the cooked mixture to the beaten egg yolks. Mix quickly and pour over the mixture in the saucepan. Once everything is blended well, remove from heat. Allow the temperature to go down to 60°C and add the cubed butter. Spread out the mixture on a baking sheet. Cover with plastic wrap, ensuring that the plastic touches the custard, to prevent it from forming a skin.

Almond custard

Soften the butter by leaving it out at room temperature or whipping it with a whisk or spatula until creamy. Mix in the rest of the ingredients. Cover and refrigerate. Because this recipe is prepared with raw eggs, it cannot be stored for long and must be used quickly.

Brioche

Combine all the ingredients except for the butter, to form a dough. Knead the dough for approximately 10 minutes, until it no longer sticks to the sides of the bowl. Next, gradually add the butter, only as fast as the dough can absorb it. Once all of the butter has been added, knead the dough until you can form a very fine film with your hand, measuring approximately 20cm (there should be fine lines on the film). A 'dough starter' may be added to this dough if necessary.

Place the dough in a bowl with cellophane at a lukewarm temperature for half an hour and then transfer to the refrigerator for 3 to 4 hours more. Next, knead the dough, shape it and allow it to ferment very slowly for 3 hours in a warm place, between 25°C and 30°C. Once the dough has risen, place in the oven at 180°C for 15 to 20 minutes. If the baking tin is small, bake at 220-230°C/425-450°F/gas mark 7-8 for 6 to 7 minutes.

French toast marinade

Carefully break the eggs and mix them with the sugar. Add in the milk and the cream.

Beat until the liquid is smooth. Strain the mixture through a fine sieve or mesh.

To marinade the Torrija French toast. Cut the brioche into 60g slices. Submerge the slices in the marinade and allow them to soak for at least 4 to 6 hours.

Sheep's milk ice cream

Prepare a cold double boiler with water and ice cubes, and a saucepan with a strainer inside. Boil the sheep's milk in a saucepan if it is home produced and cool immediately. Reheat the milk to 40°C and add the sugar, the powdered glucose and the anti-crystallising agent. Use a whisk to dissolve the mixture completely. Add the invert sugar and the powdered milk and mix again. Heat the entire mixture to 85°C. At this time, strain the contents of the saucepan into the other saucepan, where you have set up the double boiler with the strainer. Shake and cool the ice cream base.

Lemon zest confit

Use a vegetable peeler to remove the rind from the lemon. Remove all excess skin and the inner white pith. Cut the lemon rind into fine julienne strips. Place the lemon rind strips into a saucepan with cold water, and bring to the boil. Strain the strips and repeat the process two more times.

In another saucepan, mix the water with the sugar and bring to a boil. Once the mixture has cooled, add in the lemon rind strips which you have already blanched three times, and bring to a boil one last time. Store in its own syrup in the refrigerator.

TO SERVE

Use an ice cream maker to whip up the ice cream, following the manufacturer's instructions. Store the ice cream in a freezer at approximately -13°C.

Cut the butter into cubes. Melt the cubed butter in a skillet until it is golden brown in colour. At this time, strain the marinated brioche slices, coating each side with sugar, and sauté them until golden brown on both sides. Once fried, ensure that the crust retains the liquid inside the brioche, keeping it moist while still hot.

In a safe place, prepare a blow torch or similar gadget.

Heat the brioche slices in the oven for several minutes and spread the almond cream on one side of each. With a spoon, sprinkle sugar on the surface with the almond cream, until completely covered. Quickly and carefully, torch the sugar. The sugar will burn slowly as it turns to caramel.

Streak a cool flat plate with the apricot jelly. Place the hot brioche Torrija on top of the jelly, with the caramelised side face up. Spoon a ball of the ewe's milk ice cream onto the plate, next to the brioche slice. Finish by placing a strand of the lemon zest confit on top.

Baked Razor Clams with Chorizo and Wild Garlic

Serves 4

INGREDIENTS

1kg Live razor clams
½ Glass dry white wine
Few sprigs of thyme
3 Wild garlic cloves
1 tsp Salt
1 tbsp Chopped parsley, reserving the stalks
250g Broad beans
4 tbsp Olive oil
115g Cooking chorizo. sliced
60g Butter
Pepper

METHOD

Rinse the razor clams in cold running water for about 10 minutes, discarding any that don't close when handled.

Put them in a pot with the wine, thyme, garlic, salt and parsley stalks. Cover with a lid and cook over a high heat for a few minutes, stirring occasionally until all the shells open. Drain in a colander and leave to cool.

Preheat the oven to 150°C/300°F/gas mark 2. Carefully remove the clams from the shells, keeping the shell intact (discard any that haven't opened). Cut away the central dark-looking intestinal sac and discard. Cut each clam into 4 or 5 pieces, place back in the shell and arrange the shells on a baking tray. Keep warm in the low oven.

Meanwhile, cook the broad beans in boiling salted water for 2 minutes, then drain in a colander.

Heat the olive oil in a pan and cook the chorizo on a low heat for 1-2 minutes. Add the broad beans, butter and chopped parsley, season lightly with salt and pepper.

Put the clams in their shells on warmed serving plates and spoon the chorizo mixture over.

Deep Fried Turbot with Tartare Sauce

Serves 4 generously as a starter or as a light main course

This dish is simple but very special indeed. However, the cost of turbot may well put you off which is a great pity, as prepared in this way, it is a blindingly good thing to eat. Cheaper white fish such as lemon sole or plaice will substitute well, but for that added luxury, you simply can't beat turbot – it is in my opinion the king of fish.

INGREDIENTS

1 small (900g) Fresh turbot, filleted and skinned to make 4 fillets
Plain flour
4 Eggs, beaten
Half a loaf of white slice bread turned into coarse breadcrumbs.
Enough vegetable or sunflower oil to half fill a pan big enough to deep fry the fish. You will need more than you think – depending on the size of your pan, at least one litre – and the oil can be filtered and re-used. Remember that the more oil you start with, the easier and quicker it will be to fry the fish.

Tartare sauce

1 heaped tsp Dijon mustard
1 tsp White wine vinegar
2 Egg yolks
Half a pint of vegetable or sunflower oil
Salt & pepper
Fresh lemon juice to taste
1 dstspn Chopped capers
1 heaped dstspn Chopped cornichons
A small handful of chopped fresh parsley
Lemon wedges, to serve

METHOD

Cut the turbot fillets into long even strips about 1cm wide. This cut is called a goujon. Fill three separate, roomy containers with the flour, beaten eggs and breadcrumbs. Toss the goujons in the flour, shake off the excess and add a few at a time to the egg. Completely submerge in the egg, again shake off the excess egg and finally add to the breadcrumbs. This is a messy and rather enjoyable process – you could make it into the kind of cookery lesson kids love. Make sure the goujons are thoroughly and generously coated in the breadcrumbs and leave the fish in with the crumbs. This can be done an hour or two (but no longer) in advance of cooking. Now wash your hands!

Tartare sauce

Make a mayonnaise in the normal way. Add the mustard and vinegar to the egg yolks. Slowly beat in the oil and taste for seasoning adding salt, pepper and lemon juice. Stir in the capers, cornichons and parsley. Add more of any of these ingredients if you like – I like a lot of cornichons in my tartare sauce (minced anchovies are another welcome addition if you like them).

Bring up a large pan of oil to about 180°C. A sugar thermometer is useful here, or simply test the temperature of the oil by dropping in one goujon which will sizzle and float pleasingly when the oil is at the right temperature. Please take great care when deep frying food – on no account should the oil become smokingly hot and never leave the pan unattended. Fry all the goujons, but take care not to overcrowd the pan or the temperature of the oil will drop quickly and significantly and the fish will not fry to a beautiful, golden crispness.

Drain the goujons on paper towels and reserve in a warm place if frying in batches. Divide the goujons onto four plates and serve with the tartare sauce and lemon wedges.

GLAZED CHICKEN WINGS WITH PARMESAN GNOCCHI, FIELD MUSHROOM PURÉE AND BLACK TRUFFLE JELLY

Serves 8

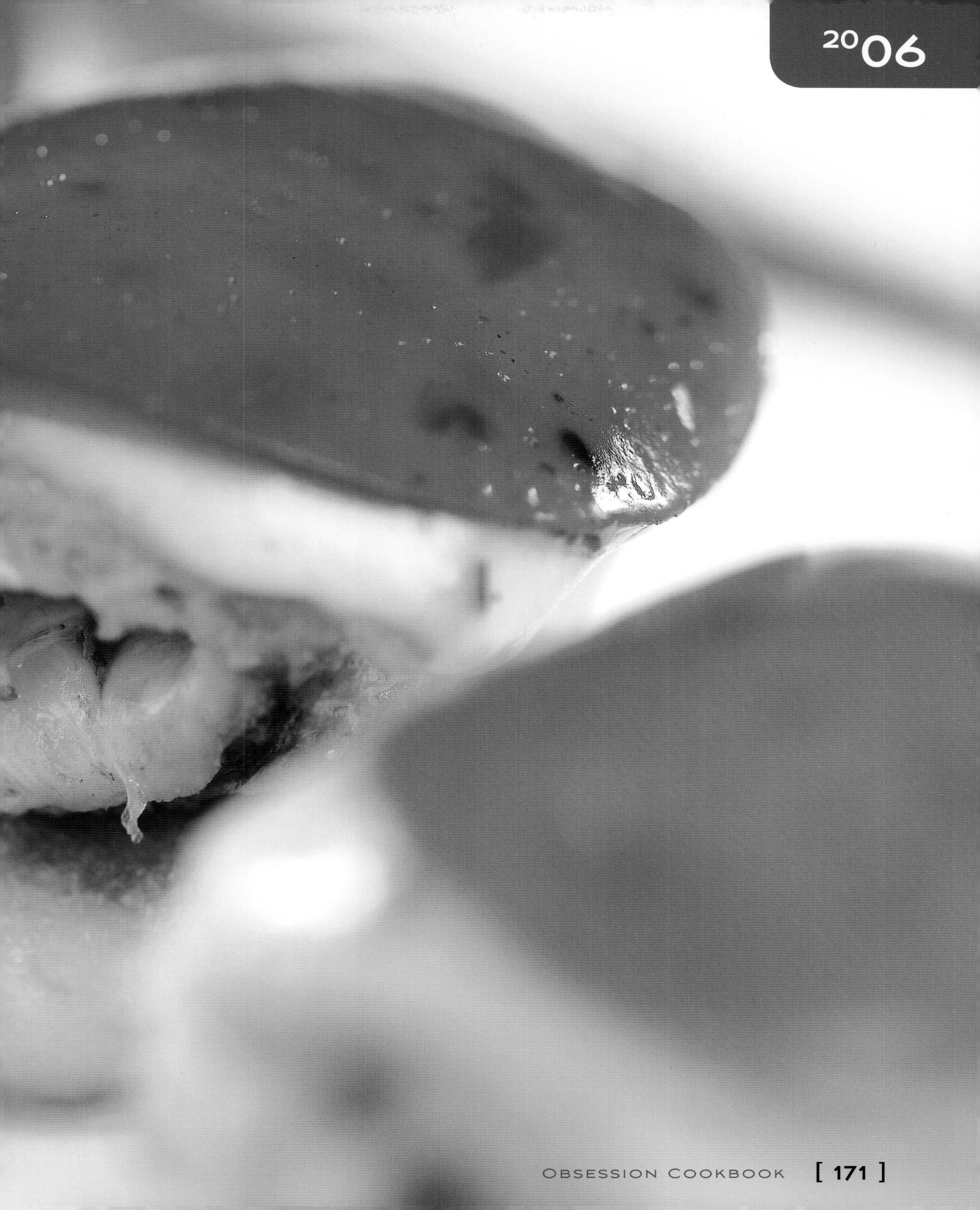

Glazed Chicken Wings with Parmesan Gnocchi, Field Mushroom Purée and Black Truffle Jelly

Serves 8

INGREDIENTS

24 Chicken wings
1 tbsp Grapeseed oil
Salt & pepper
50g Butter
4 Shallots, finely sliced
10 Button mushrooms, sliced
1 Bay leaf
600ml Chicken stock
150g Chicken breast, chilled and trimmed of all sinew
1 Egg
150ml Double cream
1 Sprig of tarragon
3g Sosa elastic gel or agar
1 Small black truffle, finely chopped
½ tsp Cornflour
1 tbsp Water
100g Butter
50g Trompettes de la mort (horn of plenty mushroom)
3 tbsp Olive oil

Gnocchi

3 Large baking potatoes
250g Rock salt
70g '00' pasta flour
1 Egg
10g Parmesan, finely grated
Salt & pepper

Field mushroom purée

50g Butter
1 White onion, finely sliced
Salt
6 Large field mushrooms, finely sliced
250ml Double cream

METHOD

Prepare the chicken wings by trimming the wing tip and first bone away from the prime middle bone. Heat a heavy based pan over a medium heat, add 1 tablespoon of grapeseed oil, season the chicken wings and place them in the pan in a single layer. Brown the first side, turn the wings, add 50g butter and brown the second side. Remove the wings from the pan, add the shallots, button mushrooms and bay leaf and a pinch of salt. Gently cook until all the moisture has evaporated then return the wings to the pan. Add the chicken stock, cover with a lid and cook in an oven preheated to 110°C/225°F/gas mark ¼ for 1 hour.

Remove from the oven, allow to rest for half an hour, lift out the wings, pass the stock through a fine sieve. Remove the prime middle bone from each wing by pulling it out carefully.

Place the chicken breast in a food processor with a generous pinch of salt and blend until thoroughly puréed. Add the egg and briefly blend again. Transfer to a round bottomed bowl, sit over iced water and vigorously beat in 150ml of double cream, adding it gradually. Pick, wash and chop the tarragon leaves and add to the mix. Transfer to a piping bag with a fine nozzle and carefully pipe the chicken mousse into the chicken wings (where the bone was).

Now place each chicken wing on a piece of cling film approximately 20cm x 10cm, roll it up tightly and tie a knot at each end of the wing. Steam the wings for 8 minutes, refresh in iced water, chill for half an hour, unwrap and set aside, covered, in the fridge.

You should have about 400ml of stock left from the cooking of the chicken wings. Divide this in two and check the seasoning. Add 2.5g of Sosa elastic gel or agar to one half, whisk thoroughly, bring to the boil, add half the truffle and tip onto a flat baking sheet or surface. It will set quickly. Using a 2cm diameter pastry cutter, cut 24 small discs and lift off the sheet and set aside in the fridge.

To the other half of the stock add a paste of the cornflour mixed with a tablespoon of water and bring to the boil. Whisk 25g of potato into this until thoroughly combined. Then whisk in 100g of butter and add the remaining truffle. You should have a delicious, rich, coating truffle butter emulsion. Reserve warm.

Sauté the trompettes in 1 tablespoon of olive oil. Season and set aside.

Gnocchi

Bake the potatoes on a bed of rock salt until completely cooked, in an oven at 160°C/325°F/gas mark 3.

Scoop the potato out of the skin and pass through a fine ricer or drum sieve. You will need 300g for the gnocchi and 25g for the sauce. Place 300g into a large bowl, add the flour, 1 egg, parmesan, salt, pepper and knead briefly into a homogenous dough. Turn out onto a floured surface and roll into a long sausage. Cut 24 2.5cm lengths, lightly press down on each one with a fork and transfer to a tray lined with parchment paper. Bring a large pan of salted water to the boil and cook the gnocchi for 2 minutes. Drain, refresh in iced water and set aside in the fridge on a tray lined with a tea towel.

Field mushroom purée

To make the field mushroom purée, place a heavy based pan over a medium heat, add 50g of butter and allow it to melt, add the onions, a pinch of salt and sweat until soft and translucent. Add the field mushrooms and cook until any moisture has evaporated. Add the 250ml double cream, bring to the boil, cover with a lid and cook gently for 10 minutes. Transfer to a blender, purée until smooth and pass through a fine sieve. Check the seasoning and set aside in the fridge.

TO SERVE

Place two large non-stick pans on the stove over a medium heat. Add s1 tablespoon of olive oil to each. Place the chicken wings into one and the gnocchi into the other and gently brown on both sides. Warm the purée, sauce and trompettes de la mort.

Onto each of 8 preheated plates place a spoon of purée, dragging it swiftly across the plate. Place three gnocchi onto each plate, top each with a chicken wing. Spoon a small quantity of sauce over each wing, top with a disc of jelly and finish with a couple of trompettes. Serve immediately.

SEARED DEXTER BEEF, WILD HERB AND SALSIFY SALAD, LIME CARAMEL, ROAST MARROWBONE

Serves 4

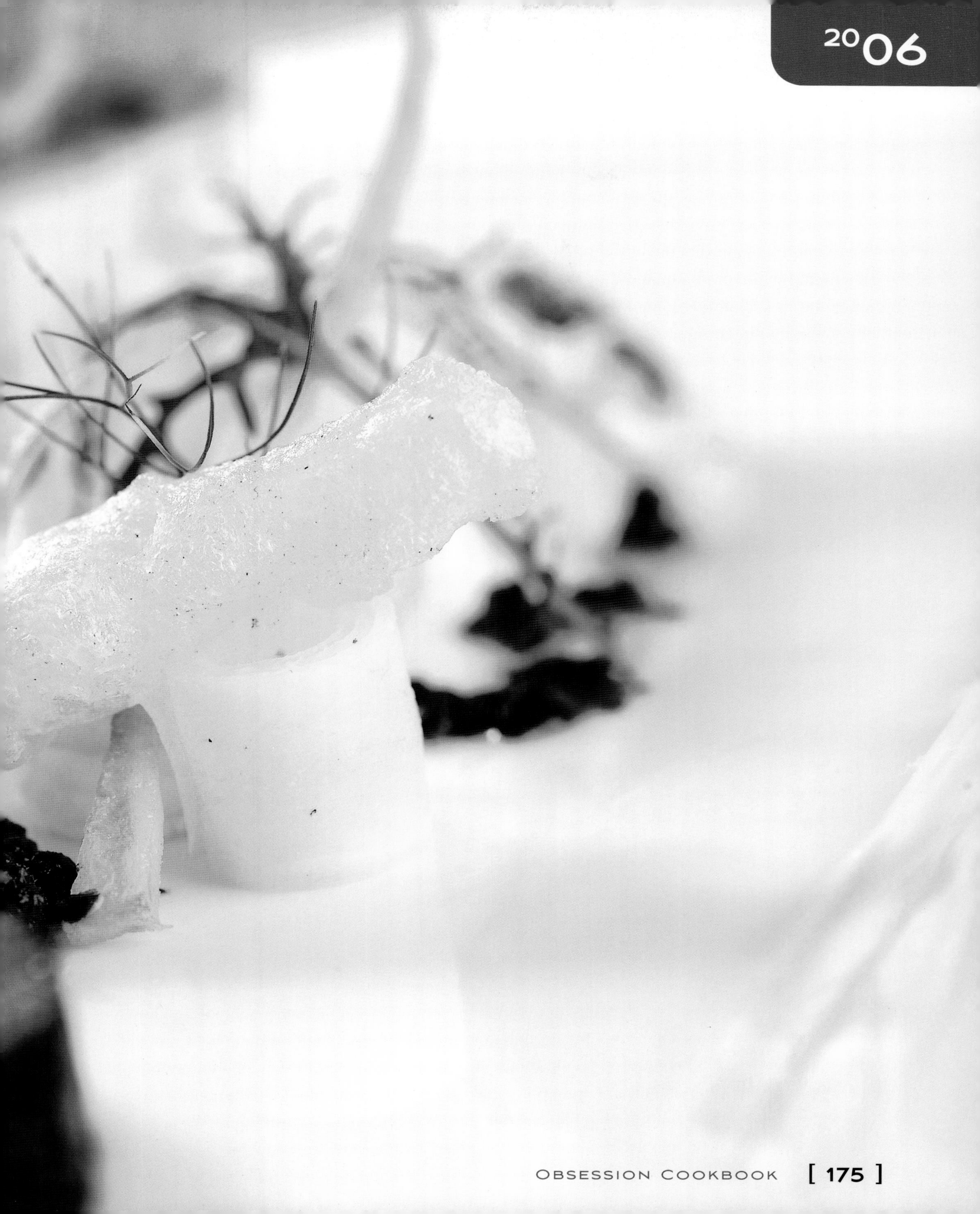

Seared Dexter Beef, Wild Herb and Salsify Salad, Lime Caramel, Roast Marrowbone

Serves 4

INGREDIENTS

Beef
400g Sliced sirloin of Dexter beef
5g Salt
Black pepper
10g Icing sugar

Roast marrowbone and toast
1 Slice of white bread 1.25cm thick
50ml Clarified butter
Salt
4 Middle cut marrowbones (soaked for 24 hours in cold water to remove all the blood – refresh the water regularly)
8 Shallot rings
2 tsp English curly parsley, finely chopped

Lime and caramel syrup
Juice of ½ lemon
Juice of 2 limes
50g Sugar

Herb dressing
15g Parsley, chopped
½ Egg yolk
¼ tsp English mustard
25ml Sunflower oil
25ml Olive oil
5g Chives, chopped
5g Tarragon, chopped Chervil
5g Basil, chopped
2.5g Parmesan cheese
Salt, to taste

Pickled salsify
1 Stick of salsify

300ml Water
Salt, to taste
3 Drops of lemon juice

Pickling liquor
50ml White wine vinegar
25g Sugar
25ml Water

Deep-fried salsify
Stick of salsify

Salsify fritter
2 x 80g Salsify sticks, washed and peeled
5g Butter
1g Lemon juice
2g Salt

Tempura
40g Fecule
40g Self raising flour
40g Cornflour
150ml Sparkling water
2g Salt

Celeriac and horseradish purée
10g Butter
100g Small diced celeriac
15g Small diced fresh horseradish
100ml Cream
Salt to taste

Salad garnish
Bronze fennel
Ruby red streak cress
Garden chervil

METHOD

Beef

To get the 400g piece of beef for this dish you need to strip a sirloin of all its fat, remove all sinew, cut in half across the sirloin then in half lengthways. You will then have 4 fillet-like pieces which you can cut again depending on the amount of meat you require.

Take the 400g piece of Dexter beef, cling film it tight and place into a vacuum pack bag and seal tightly. Put into a water bath at 60°C for 1 hour. Remove from the bath and place in a blast chiller. Once cool, remove from the vacuum pack and wrap in cling film. Dry on absorbent kitchen roll then dust with salt, black pepper and icing sugar.

Seal straight on to the stove top to get a deep dark crust all around the beef, allow to cool then cling film tightly and chill.

Slice the Dexter beef 2cm thick on a slicing machine. Serve at room temperature.

Roast marrowbone and toast

Remove the crust from the slice of bread, cut the bread to a square 9x9cm, place it in the chiller to semi freeze. Once semi frozen cut the bread into fingers 1cm thick, repeating this 8 times to get 8 fingers. In a small pan heat the clarified butter and shallow fry the fingers for 3-4 minutes until golden. Remove from the pan on to absorbent kitchen paper, season with salt and keep warm.

Scrape clean the marrowbones to remove any excess sinew. Put in the oven at 190°C/375°F/gas mark 5 for 8-10 minutes until the marrowbone is soft. Remove from the oven.

Serve hot with two shallot rings mixed with the finely chopped parsley on the top of each marrowbone with two warm fingers of toast.

Lime and caramel syrup

In a heavy bottomed pan add the lemon juice, lime juice and sugar then reduce on a gentle heat until a syrup is able to coat the back of the spoon. Leave to cool. Once cool place into a squeezy bottle.

Herb dressing

In a Thermomix blitz the parsley, egg yolk, English mustard, sunflower oil and olive oil to make a rustic purée. Remove the purée and put it into a bowl, add the chopped chives, tarragon, chervil, basil, parmesan, mix well and season.

Pickled salsify

Peel the stick of salsify and cut into 8cm long sticks, then slice lengthways on a mandolin, as thinly as possible – try to make them look transparent. Bring the water, salt and lemon juice to the boil, add the salsify and cook until tender, then refresh in iced water and drain well.

5 minutes before serving marinate the salsify in the pickling liquor.

Pickling liquor

In a small pan bring all the ingredients to the boil. Remove from the heat and cool. Reserve for the pickled salsify.

Deep-fried salsify

Peel and cut the salsify into 2 batons 8cm long. Slice the salsify long ways on a mandolin 1mm thick, so that they become matchstick size. Deep fry at 180°C for 1-2 minutes until golden. Remove from the fryer and place onto a sheet of absorbent paper and season with salt.

Salsify fritter

Cut the salsify into 4 batons 3cm long, cutting each end at a slight angle. Place into a small pan and just cover with water. Add the butter, lemon juice and salt and bring to the boil. Cook the salsify until tender, remove from the boiling liquor and place into a blast chiller to immediately cool. Once cool reserve for the batter.

Tempura

Mix together all the ingredients and place into a iSi gun and charge with 3 canisters. Take the 4 pieces of salsify and flour lightly. Eject the batter into a bowl, place the salsify into the batter and cover completely. Fry at 180°C for 2 minutes until light and crispy. Keep warm.

Celeriac and horseradish purée

In a medium pan melt the butter, add the celeriac and horseradish, cook for 3-4 minutes without colouring. Add the cream and cling film the top of the pan and simmer until soft. Place into a Thermomix, blitz until smooth and pass through a fine chinoise. Check the seasoning and cool. Once cooled, place into a piping bag and reserve.

TO SERVE

Place a slice of beef onto the plate, pipe on 3 cones of celeriac and horseradish purée and a dessertspoon of herb dressing. Place on the pickled salsify and salsify fritter. Garnish with salad leaves and deep-fried salsify, finish with a small amount of lime and caramel syrup. Place the warm marrowbone and toast onto a side plate and serve.

20O5

We had another great line up for 2005. Eric Chavot started off the festival with Sat Bains and Dieter Koschina – is it possible to start a festival with three bigger characters? Two two stars and a one star. Dieter came to us from Vila Joya in the Algarve through a family connection with Craig, whose cousin Zoe is married to Bruce Hawker who edits Essential Algarve magazine and is bon viveur and great gastronome of some reputation. Bruce introduced us to Joy and Gebhard whose family owns Vila Joya. They asked Dieter if he would cook at the festival. Dieter was so inspired by the event he started his own festival in Portugal that is now a great event in its own right.

A great start with Eric, a man who I have known and eaten with throughout his career in his many venues, always cooking with precision and flair. Eric's sea bass on the confit of lemon and tomatoes was very special and his more-than-spectacular chocolate and orange pudding was a great finish.

I managed to get hold of Sat Bains through judging the Catey Awards prior to the festival. When I asked him if he would be willing to cook at the festival he accepted without hesitation. Then there was Mr Bains' 12-hour slow cooked beef, which proved really interesting from a customer point of view. He also did langoustines with back fat and passion fruit which was so memorable.

Dieter's sauces – which he'd laboriously worked through the night to reduce down – had incredible flavours and you could see how he'd built up his reputation through this kind of cooking. That was a long night. All Dieter's dishes were outstanding, none more so than the ravioli of black sausage and goose liver, and the lobster dish. Then, at four in the morning, he decided to make fillet steak and foie gras butties, which after lots of wine,

went down decidedly well among the other chefs.

Dieter's quote of the festival was his characteristically Austrian "Full Power!" catchphrase, which Eric Chavot also picked up on. The following morning I took him to the Three Fishes and he developed a liking for the Thwaites beer there, and it turned out to be a long and fascinating lunch.

Roy Brett, Rick Stein's executive chef, arrived from Padstow – we'd met when taking my son Kirk down to Rick Stein's for a stagiaire. Roy cooked a truly memorable meal of fish, fish and more fish. He did langoustines, sea bass, brill, smoked salmon and a shellfish soup among other things, which showcased his incredible flair for cooking seafood.

Phil Howard made a delightful Mediterranean dish with red mullet sardine chantilly and anchovies which, with the Pera Manca Blanco, was a marriage made in heaven. His pud was the best rice pud ever with raisins and tangerines – yet another great Howard night.

Richard Corrigan made two superb dishes, a butter poached haddock with caviar, langoustine and champ followed by a spectacular crubeens with Jabuga ham and woodland salad which was characteristically robust yet refined, Irish style rivalling any French imitation. Richard who is forever a true Irish gent certainly had a few drinks that night.

It was my first introduction to Farmer Sharp's mutton which I cooked with Ascroft's yellow beets, infamously known as Lancashire pineapple; mutton is a truly great British product. To finish the evening I chose Queen of pudding soufflé with a lemon and crème fraîche ice cream, reminding me of influences from Granny Ish, a true cook of her generation.

Bravura

ERIC CHAVOT

"This is what I do.
I wish I could turn it
off but I just can't."

OBSESSION
FESTIVAL

DIETER KOSCHINA

"Cooking and food are so important for me because of
having this endless possibility of being creative, and the
creativity goes hand in hand with the enjoying. First comes
the pleasure of being creative, second the joy of finalising
the creation and third the delight with all the human
senses. We chefs have the gratification of being able to
satisfy all the senses of the guests with one single dish.
My biggest Obsession with food is to find the best products
to create the perfect dish. This sounds easy, but is maybe
the most difficult challenge in my life."

"To be Obsessed with
regionality is to love
your roots and express
your belonging."

NIGEL HAWORTH

SAT BAINS

"At first it was a flirtation; then seduction; after that a passion which led to Obsession ... my accidental journey into gastronomy."

"Like everyone who has entered the hospitality profession, in order to stay in it you need to be obsessed and quite possibly mad. I'm both."

RICHARD CORRIGAN

PHIL HOWARD

"2005 was the high octane year with some of the country's most flamboyant cooks descending on Northcote. Eric, Sat, Dieter and Richard set the place alight with cracking banter. In fact, my son still takes the mick out of Dieter who launched into service with yet another glass of fizz shouting "full power, full power – I drink champagne all night and go – crazy!!" Mad man, fantastic food."

ROY BRETT

"When you open a restaurant at 41 you have to be driven to go back to the 16-hour days. It's a never-ending journey, and you can never be bored. It's a privilege to be able to work with the produce we work with and I never feel it's a chore. The day you do is the day you should stop cooking."

GIANDUJA AND ORANGE CRUMBLE WITH ICED NOUGAT

Serves 8

INGREDIENTS

Nougat glace
125g Acacia honey
25g Caster sugar
25g Liquid glucose
120g Egg whites
20g Caster sugar
500ml UHT cream
125g Caramelised hazelnuts
100g Marmalade

Crumble
50g Caster sugar
50g Ground almonds
50g Butter
50g Flour
3g Maldon salt
150g Orange zest

Feuillantine (chocolate thins)
100g Praline paste
150g Tanariva chocolate
10g Cocoa butter
150g Eclats d'or

Orange coulis
200g Orange juice
20g Mango purée
20g Orange concentrate
30g Caster sugar
15g Vitpris (pectin)

Gianduja mousse
250ml Milk
25g Caster sugar
80g Egg yolks
15g Cornflour
½ sheet/2g Gelatine

300g Gianduja noir (a finely ground smooth mixture of chocolate and nut butter, such as hazelnut, almond or pistachio eg. Nutella)
200g Praline
260ml + 60ml UHT cream at room temperature
Dried orange, to decorate

METHOD

Nougat glacé
Whisk the cream and refrigerate.
   Boil the honey, glucose and 25g sugar to 121°C. Pour on to the egg whites. Whisk up to a thick meringue and whisk slowly until cool. Fold in the rest of the ingredients and cream. Pipe into moulds and freeze.

Crumble
Mix the zest with the sugar and then the rest of the ingredients and form the mix into little nuggets. Bake in the oven at 170°C until golden brown.

Feuillantine (chocolate thins)
Melt the cocoa butter and tanariva and incorporate the praline paste and éclats d'or. Roll out between sheets of greaseproof paper to the desired thickness and freeze. Break to required size.

Orange coulis
In a pan warm the orange juice, mango purée and orange concentrate then add the vitpris (pectin) and sugar. Cook for 2 minutes and pass through a fine sieve. Cool down.

Gianduja mousse
Soften the gelatine in ice cold water. Whip 260g cream slowly to a soft peak. Melt the Gianduja and keep at 35°C. Make a crème pâtissière with the milk, sugar, egg yolks and the cornflour. Add the gelatine to 200g pâtissière. Add that mix to the melted Gianduja and the praline. Beat in a blender using the paddle until it reaches 28°C and incorporate slowly the 60g of cream as if you are making mayonnaise. When the mix is smooth, fold the whipped cream in gently.

TO SERVE

Swirl some orange coulis on a plate. Loosen each nougat glacé from its mould and place on the plate. Add the crumble nuggets, feuillantine, mousse and dried orange as pictured.

Dry Aged Scotch Beef, "Textures" of the Onion Family

Serves 4

INGREDIENTS

Braised oxtail
1kg Chopped oxtail
2pt Guinness
6 Sprigs thyme
6 Peppercorns
6 Juniper berries
236ml Brown chicken stock
Salt and pepper
Olive oil

Caramelised shallot purée
8 Chopped shallots
25g Butter
25g Olive oil
Salt
Brown chicken stock

Braised baby onions
12 Peeled baby onions
Salt
Sprig of thyme
15ml Olive oil
Emulsion (25g butter, salt,
200g white chicken stock)

Roast shallots
4 peeled shallots
Salt
Sprig of thyme
15ml Olive oil plus a little extra
for re-heating
Butter

Crispy onion rings
1 Shallot cut into rings about
0.5cm thick
Plain flour
Egg wash
Panko breadcrumbs

Raw shallot salad
1 Shallot sliced wafer thin
Pickling juice (50g white wine vinegar,
25g sugar, pinch of salt)

Spring onions
4 Large spring onions
Olive oil
Butter
Salt

METHOD

Marinade the oxtail in the Guinness
and aromats (thyme, peppercorns
and juniper berries) for 7 days,
strain and pan roast the oxtail
until browned all over, reduce the
Guinness down by half and add the
brown chicken stock, season. Place
the oxtail and the sauce in a pressure
cooker, bring up to full pressure and
cook for 45 minutes. Allow to cool
slightly and then pick off the meat,
discarding the bones. Fold in the
sauce and roll into cylinders, allow
to set. To reheat the oxtail place in a
pan of olive oil, fry both sides of the
cylinder and finish off in the oven at
180°C/350°F/gas mark 4 for
6-8 minutes.

Caramelised shallot purée
Start sweating off the shallots in
the butter and olive oil; when all
the moisture has evaporated lower
the heat and gently caramelise, this
should take around 2 hours. When
caramelised, deglaze the pan with a
little brown chicken stock and blend
to a purée. Season if necessary.

Braised baby onions
Place the onions in a sous vide bag
along with the rest of the ingredients,
place in a pan of boiling water until
soft and then into a tub of iced water.
Reheat in the emulsion.

Roast shallots
Place the shallots in a sous vide bag
along with the salt, sprig of thyme
and olive oil, place in a pan of boiling
water until soft and then into a
tub of iced water. When reheating
caramelise the shallots in a little
butter and olive oil and warm through
in the oven.

Crispy onion rings
Dip the shallot rings in the flour
followed by the egg wash and the
breadcrumbs, fry at 180°C until crispy
and golden brown.

Raw shallot salad
Season the shallot with the pickling
juice just before serving.

Spring onions
Blanch the spring onions in boiling
salted water until soft. Reheat in a
little olive oil and butter then season
with salt.

TO SERVE

Assemble the dish as illustrated.

Medallions of Lobster with Mashed Potatoes and Ceps
Serves 4

INGREDIENTS

2 x 500g Lobsters
300g Potatoes, peeled
20g Chives
250ml Fish nage
8 Ceps
Salt & Pepper
Olive Oil
Lemon Juice

Fish nage
250ml White wine
125ml Noilly Prat
125ml White dry port wine
500ml Chicken soup clear
250ml Clear fish soup
400ml Cream
Salted butter

METHOD

Fish nage
Reduce white wine, Noilly Prat and port wine to a third. Reduce chicken and fish soup to a third. You should cook them in two different pots very slowly to achieve this. When the reductions are done, put the white wine, Noilly Prat and port wine into the soup. You should have around 400ml of that mixture. Put the same amount of cream into it and bind with a little salted butter.

Lobsters
Put the lobsters in water heated to 60°C for 8 to 10 minutes. Remove the pincers and return the lobster without the pincers to the water for another 6 minutes. Remove the lobster from the water and peel it. Cut into 1cm slices, cover with foil and keep warm.

Clean the ceps, cut them in a half and roast with olive oil.

Cook the potatoes in salted water. When they are well cooked mash with a fork. Mix in the chives, lemon juice, salt and some fish nage.

TO SERVE

Put the mash on a plate, place the warm lobster slices on top. Heat the rest of the fish nage then pour it over the lobster.

FISH AND SHELLFISH SOUP WITH ROUILLE AND PARMESAN

Serves 12

INGREDIENTS

Fish soup

50ml Olive oil
50g Butter
1 Red pepper, finely chopped
1 Orange, zest removed, remainder chopped
1 Onion, finely chopped
100g Celery, finely chopped
100g Leeks
20g Chopped garlic
1 Bay leaf
Sprig of thyme
250g Atlantic prawns
50g Tomato purée
½ ltr Reduced fish stock
1 Pinch saffron
400g Tinned tomatoes
1kg Pollock, diced
1 Pinch smoked paprika
Seasoning

Rouille

12 Roasted red peppers
2 tsp Tomato purée
2 tsp Ground coriander
1 Pinch saffron
1 Red chilli, finely chopped
10 tsp Cayenne pepper
Seasoning
25g Crusty white bread
100ml Fish stock
4 tsp Harissa paste
2 Egg yolks
2 Garlic cloves, peeled and finely chopped
200ml Olive oil

Garlic croutons

250g Baguette, sliced into rounds
100g Clarified butter
1 Garlic clove, peeled
Seasoning
Grated parmesan, to serve

METHOD

Fish soup

Heat the oil and butter in the pan, add the mirepoix (red pepper, orange zest and chopped pieces, onion, celery, leeks, garlic, bay leaf and thyme) and cook for 10 minutes. Add the prawns and tomato purée, and cook with the mirepoix for a further 10 minutes. Then add half the fish stock along with the saffron and tinned tomatoes. Bring to simmer for 5 to 10 minutes before adding the pollock. Simmer for a further 5 minutes then liquidise, adding the smoked paprika. Season to taste.

Rouille

Mix the roasted red peppers, tomato purée, ground coriander, saffron, chilli, cayenne pepper and seasoning, and blend until smooth.

Soak the bread in fish stock, then squeeze out the excess. Put the bread in a processor with the harissa paste, egg yolks, garlic and seasoning. Blend again until smooth. Finally, add the olive oil to make a mayonnaise.

Garlic croutons

Heat up the clarified butter in a pan. Cook the croutons until golden brown in small batches. Season well and rub with a little garlic.

TO SERVE

Serve the soup with the rouille, croutons and parmesan.

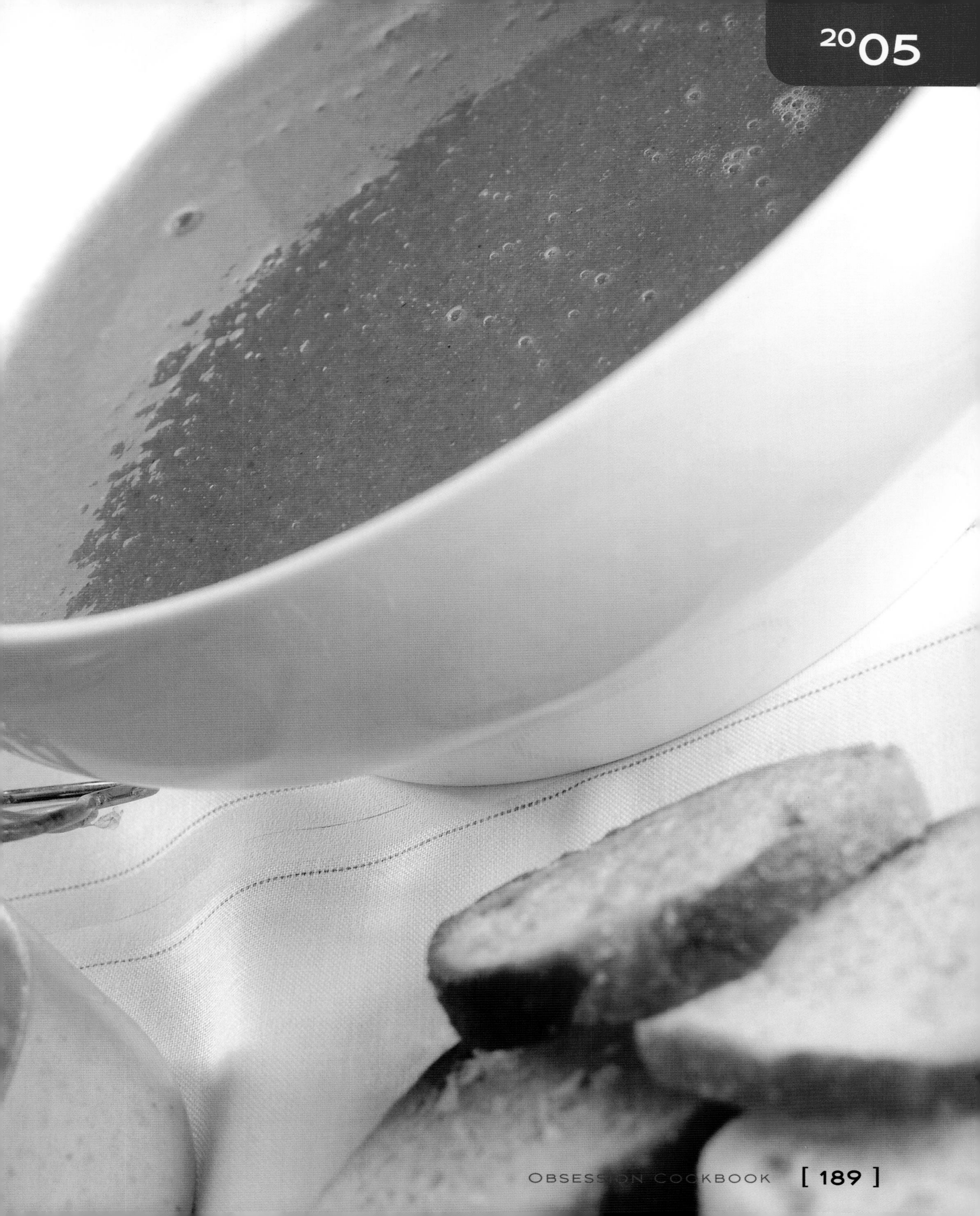

ESCABECHE OF RED MULLET WITH SARDINE CHANTILLY AND ANCHOVIES

Serves 8

INGREDIENTS

Escabeche

300ml Extra virgin olive oil
2 Large white onions, peeled and finely sliced
2 Large carrots, peeled and finely sliced
1 Leek, finely sliced
2 Sticks of celery, peeled and finely sliced
8 Garlic cloves, finely sliced
4 Star anise
1 tsp Coriander seeds
1 tsp Fennel seeds
1 pinch Saffron
300ml White wine vinegar
100ml Water
2 Strips orange zest
¼ Bunch coriander, picked and washed
Salt & pepper
100g Plain flour
4 x 14oz Red mullet, filleted and pin boned

Sardine chantilly

100ml Olive oil
1 Red onion, finely sliced
2 Garlic cloves, finely sliced
½ Red pepper, finely sliced
Salt & pepper
100ml Tomato passata
4 Plum tomatoes, roughly chopped
Pinch of sugar
50g Flour for the sardines
8 Sardine fillets
100ml Whipping cream
100ml Double cream

Other ingredients

1 Head of fennel, very finely shredded
Zest of ¼ orange
100g Black olive tapenade
16 Top quality anchovies (optional)

METHOD

Escabeche

The idea here is to make a hot 'pickle' with all the vegetables and pour it over sealed but uncooked red mullet. The residual heat will cook the fish and, left to sit for 24 hours, this develops into a phenomenal dish, full of flavour.

Place a large heavy based pan on high heat for 2 minutes. Add half the olive oil, followed by the onions, carrots, leek, celery, garlic, star anise, coriander seeds, fennel seeds and saffron. Cook for 5 minutes, stirring frequently and without seasoning. Adding salt too early will make all the vegetables soften which is not what is wanted. At this point, add the vinegar and cook, still over a high heat, until completely evaporated. If you do not reduce the vinegar away completely, the final product will simply be too sour. You can always add a bit more vinegar at the end if the dish is lacking a 'tang'.

Now add the water, the remaining olive oil, orange zest and the coriander. Bring back to the boil and simmer over a low heat for 5 minutes.

Set aside at room temperature. When it has cooled, season with salt and pepper – this is a key to the dish's success and bear in mind you are seasoning something warm which will be served cold.

Now reheat this mix, flour the mullet fillet on the skin side and fry, skin side down, in a splash of olive oil for 30 seconds, turn over and seal for 5 seconds, then transfer to a shallow dish. Pour the hot vegetable marinade over the fish. Leave to cool and place in the fridge.

Sardine chantilly

Heat a heavy based pan over a medium heat, add half of the olive oil, the onions, garlic and red pepper and a generous pinch of salt. Sweat for 5 minutes, stirring frequently. Once softened, add the tomato passata and fresh tomatoes and a generous pinch of sugar. Cook very gently for a further 5 minutes.

Now flour the sardine fillets, on the skin side, season them with salt and pepper and pan fry, skin side down in olive oil – 1 minute each side will do. Add to the tomato mix, stir gently, cover with a lid or disc of parchment paper and cook in an oven at 110°C/225°F/gas mark ¼ for half an hour.

Remove from the oven, stir briefly and pass through a coarse sieve. This should give rise to a delicious oily, sardine vinaigrette. Adjust the

seasoning if necessary, place in a small container, spoon off any excess oil and chill.

TO SERVE

Remove the mullet from the fridge half an hour before serving. Pour the whipping and double cream into a large bowl, season with salt and pepper and whip until peaks form. Add a tablespoon of the sardine

paste and fold in with a rubber spatula. Whisk further if it is not thick.

Season the fennel, add the orange zest, mix briefly and divide among 8 plates. Place a fillet of red mullet on top, along with plenty of the vegetable marinade. Put 3 small spoons of tapenade on each plate and garnish with a quenelle of sardine chantilly (spoon it onto the plate using a hot dessert spoon) and 2 anchovies, if desired.

CRUBEENS, JABUGA HAM WITH WOODLAND SORREL, BEETROOT AND HORSERADISH REMOULADE

Serves 4

INGREDIENTS

4 Pigs' trotters, soaked in brine overnight
1 Onion, chopped
2 Carrots, chopped
1 Garlic bulb
1 Bouquet garni
1 Ham hock
Mustard
Parsley
Flour
1 Egg (beaten)
Breadcrumbs
40g Parmesan, grated

To serve

Woodland sorrel or watercress
Beetroot and horseradish remoulade
(grated beetroot and horseradish)
Jabuga/Serrano ham

METHOD

Wash brine off pigs' trotters, cover them with water, add chopped onion, chopped carrots, a bulb of garlic and bouquet garni. Bring to the boil and skim. Simmer for 3 hours until the meat falls off the bone. After one hour of cooking add the ham hock (the ham hock will only need cooking for 2 hours).

Remove from the pot, lay all the meat on a tray and separate fat, gristle, meat and bones.

Shred the ham hock off the bone, mix with nuggets of trotter meat, add a little gristle and half of the fat, mustard and parsley.

Line out the four trotter skins and spoon in the ham mix. Roll each trotter into the shape of a ballotine and refrigerate.

When cold cut each ballotine into quarters length ways, then cut into even-sized pieces, the size of a thumb nail.

Dip into flour, beaten egg and breadcrumbs.

Deep fry until crispy and serve with beetroot and horseradish remoulade, woodland sorrel/ watercress, Jabuga/Serrano ham and sprinkle with the parmesan.

GOOSNARGH CORNFED DUCKLING BREAST, DUCK STRAWS, SPICY RED CABBAGE, MEAD

Serves 4

GOOSNARGH CORNFED DUCKLING BREAST, DUCK STRAWS, SPICY RED CABBAGE, MEAD

Serves 4

INGREDIENTS

1 x 2.5kg Cornfed Goosnargh duck
50ml Duck fat
Salt & pepper
100ml Duck sauce
4 Duck straws (see below)
4 Baby turnips (see below)
Mead syrup (see below)
Red wine syrup (see below)
Turnip purée (see below)
Spicy red cabbage (see below)

Mead syrup
350ml Mead

Red wine syrup
250ml Shiraz wine
60g Sugar

Duck straws
100g Flaked slow cooked duck
(leg meat)
20g Duck fat
8 Green peppercorns, crushed
Pinch of salt
2 Spring rolls sheets
50g Plain flour with a few drops of
water (to make a thick paste to stick
the pastry down)

Spicy red cabbage
½ headRed cabbage
15g Coarse sea salt
100ml Sesame oil
50g Icing sugar
50ml Sherry
50ml White wine vinegar
1 Red chilli, finely chopped
10g Fresh ginger, grated

Turnip purée
200g Unsalted butter
200g Turnip, peeled and diced
100ml Whipping cream
Pinch of salt

Baby turnips
4 Baby turnips
100ml Water
40g Butter
Salt
Sugar

METHOD

Take the duck and remove the legs (reserve for the slow cooked duck straws). Remove the excess duck fat and break off the undercarriage. Render the duck crown in a medium-size frying pan with the 50ml of duck fat – this should be done slowly until the fat is golden and will take about 10 minutes.

Remove the duck breasts from the crown and allow to cool. Wrap them individually in cling film and then into a vacuum pack bag and seal. Cook off the breasts in a water bath at 68°C for 27 minutes and reserve.

When you are ready to assemble the dish, place the duck breasts skin side down in a little of the remaining duck fat and fry the duck breasts carefully until golden brown and crispy. Season with salt and pepper. Remove from the pan and allow to rest on a cooling rack for at least 2 minutes.

Mead syrup

Reduce down to approximately 50ml. Pour into a small pipette bottle and allow to cool.

Red wine syrup

Reduce the ingredients down to 50ml, place into a small pipette bottle and allow to cool.

Duck straws

In a mixing bowl add the duck, duck fat, green peppercorns and pinch of salt. Mix all the ingredients together carefully until a rough mixture is formed, then roll the duck into pencil thickness strips approximately 18cm long.

Cut the spring roll sheets into half lengthways and then brush each sheet down the sides and along one end with the paste.

Place the rolled duck on the opposite end, roll the pastry tightly around the duck mix and crimp at both ends, Repeat with the other straws. When you are ready, fry in a deep fat fryer at 180°C for 2-3 minutes until golden. Remove from the fryer and reserve (cut off one end on a slant before serving).

Spicy red cabbage

Finely slice the red cabbage and mix with sea salt, leave for 4 hours. Wash off all the salt thoroughly and drain well.

Preheat a large heavy bottom pan, add the sesame oil and quickly fry off the cabbage without colour for a few minutes. Push the cabbage to one side of the pan, sprinkle the other side with icing sugar, allow to caramelise then add the sherry, white wine vinegar, ginger and chilli, mix the red cabbage in well and continue to fry for approximately 2 minutes. Remove from the pan and reserve.

Turnip purée

Melt the butter in a thick bottom pan, sweat off the turnips carefully without colour, add the cream and reduce until the cream almost splits. Blitz in a Thermomix until it makes a smooth purée, season with salt, pass through a fine sieve and then place into a piping bag ready for use.

Baby turnips

Cook the turnips in the water and butter, add a pinch of salt and a large pinch of sugar. Boil carefully and leave al dente.

TO SERVE

Reheat the duck sauce, red cabbage, turnip purée and baby turnips. Deep fry the duck straws. Reserve. Place the red cabbage in the middle of the plate, remove the fillet from the duck and place to the side of the cabbage. Carve the duck breast in half lengthways and place onto the cabbage. Garnish with the duck straws, turnip purée and baby turnips, then sauce over with the duck sauce and finish with the two syrups.

20O4

Year four: Peter Gordon came in short long pants. John Campbell kicked all the staff out of the kitchen, his usual focused self. Rowley Leigh wasn't happy with Craig's wines, and changed some of them on the day. Darina Allen arrived from Ireland and promptly sent us out for Kerrygold butter, a taste of home and some decent organic cider vinegar because she said that ours was too harsh.

Peter Gordon's flavours in the smoky coconut and tamarind laska were just incredible and to finish – a stunning chocolate cake with cranberry and rose-water compote. John's menu was technically astute, executing some excellent dishes none better than the turbot braised with oxtail and slow cooked veal cheeks – the mandarin parfait and espuma was a knock-out.

Rowley Leigh cooked a favourite of ours with his partridge with pigs' trotters, chestnuts and lentils, a dish with influences from France; he also brought a fantastic truffle brie which was sensational.

It was an honour to have Darina Allen cooking with all the flair of the Irish dynasty of Ballymaloe, ably assisted by a former student Breda Murphy, who now runs Food by Breda Murphy Deli Bistro in Whalley, Lancashire.

Her potato, parsley and chorizo soup with her famous soda bread was simplicity itself. Darina's husband Timmy spent the whole day preparing the breads and cheese biscuits alongside our own team, sharing his knowledge which we still use today.

Phil Howard pulled the rabbit out of the hat with a great monkfish dish that was on the bone. I can't imagine anyone else cooking monkfish on the bone like that – especially not for 90 people.

This was the year Giorgio Locatelli walked in to the kitchen with his right-hand man Frederico. Phil and I were getting ready for the evening service at the side of the fish corner when suddenly we noticed a large presence. Giorgio walked in wearing a full-length moleskin coat, trilby and all. The Italian mafia had arrived. A man of great presence, Giorgio brought his family and it was a joy to have Plaxy and his daughter Margherita so involved in the festival. Margherita was a little star full of fun and mischief – she stole the show in many ways.

Giorgio cooked risotto with Barolo wine and he finished the dish with Castelmagno cheese. He told an epic story about this cheese, which was a mark of his roots from his home village where it had been hung and dried for three years: the story lasted for days and was long and passionate.

This was the year I made treacle salmon for the first time. I was looking to do a regional salmon dish, which I marinated and cured with treacle. I used to tell the customers that there was a very famous treacle mine in Sabden – Lancashire legend has it that it was mined by 'The Treacle Miners' – and a surprising amount of people believed me!

DARINA ALLEN

"I've been obsessed with cooking and using really good ingredients since I was a tiny child because I grew up with a kitchen garden, hens and a house cow. But now as a grandma my main Obsession is passing on the skills to my grandchildren to cook and sow seed and grow things so that they can grow their own ingredients. It's getting more difficult to source really good fresh produce – and that's what good health and good food are based on."

OBSESSION
FESTIVAL
2004

ROWLEY LEIGH

"My Obsession with food comes partly from the fact that I'm very greedy and I like food. I always grew up with good food and I always thought it rather mattered what you put in your mouth. I just love the business of transforming ingredients into something delicious."

NIGEL HAWORTH

"In detail there is an Obsession to harmonise, to balance, to perfect and not to overdo."

JOHN CAMPBELL

"My Obsession started at an early age, about four years old, and I very quickly realised food made people happy and was an emotive part of what we did every day. Later on in my gastronomic infancy, perhaps pre-teens, I was very clear in what I wanted to do for the rest of my life – I wanted to cook and make people smile. Each plate of food is unique and can never be recreated; although consistency plays a huge part in our focus during a busy service, each dish is unique and a one-off.

The very foundation of life relies on food; creating beautiful harmonies from nature's larder is one of the greatest gifts mankind possesses. Food is about bringing people together, it is about comfort and memories; nothing is more powerful or emotive than food glorious food."

PETER GORDON

"I am obsessed by the 'new' of discovering new flavours, tastes and textures from around the world. I can't think of a healthier Obsession as it also encourages exploration of other cultures and an understanding of other people. At the moment I'm obsessed with tapioca and tofu (recurring Obsessions I have to say) and it's a fun Obsession."

PHIL HOWARD

"I just remember meeting some great people this year. John Campbell, for one, has become a great friend over the years. I have dipped into Darina Allen's cookbook many times and I am reminded of how important this "cross pollination" of ideas that happens at The Festival is. The phenomenal local produce is showcased once again with the use of Lancashire venison."

GIORGIO LOCATELLI

"Food for me is a way of life – the rhythm of the restaurant has dictated the rhythm of my life from when I was a young boy.

Creating the perfect sense of conviviality day in, day out, is the most gratifying thing in my career and is what is behind the passion I have for food."

CHOCOLATE CAKE WITH SALTED ALMOND CREAM AND CRANBERRY ROSEWATER COMPOTE

Serves 10

This flourless cake is always a winner – rich and mousse-like, you don't need too large a portion. I team it with a lovely fragrant cranberry compote and give it an edge with the salted Marcona almond cream. These are the best almonds in the world and the saltiness really brings the dish together.

INGREDIENTS

Chocolate mousse cake
300g Dark chocolate (minimum 65% cocoa butter)
150g Unsalted butter
6 Eggs
60g Caster sugar

Cranberry rosewater compote
100g Caster sugar
30ml Lemon juice
2 Strips lemon peel
½ tsp Pure vanilla extract
200g Fresh cranberries
20ml Rosewater

Almond cream
100ml Double cream
50g Mascarpone
1 tsp Caster sugar
12 Salted Marcona almonds, crushed

METHOD

Chocolate mousse cake
Preheat the oven to 180°C/350°F/gas mark 4.

Wrap tin foil around the base of 10 ring moulds and sit on a baking tray lined with a sil-pat or baking parchment.

Melt the chocolate and butter in a double boiler over simmering water. Once it's almost completely melted, separate your eggs. Add all but 2 tablespoons of the sugar to the whites, the remainder to the yolks. Beat the whites to a soft meringue.

Whisk the yolks and sugar for 20 seconds, then mix in the melted chocolate. Stir one-third of the meringue into this, then gently fold in the remainder. Fill your ring moulds and bake for 9 minutes. Remove from the oven and leave to cool for at least 3 hours before serving.

Cranberry rosewater compote
Place the sugar, lemon juice and peel in a small pan and slowly bring to the boil. Once the sugar has dissolved add the cranberries and cook gently, stirring frequently, until they begin to bleed their juice into the syrup and burst. Stir in the vanilla then take off the heat. Gently stir in the rosewater, cover tightly and leave to cool. If upon tasting the compote the rosewater isn't pronounced enough, add some more to taste.

Almond cream
Lightly whip everything except the almonds to a soft peak. Mix in all but 1 teaspoon of the almonds and whip to a firm peak.

TO SERVE

Simply dollop the cream on to the cake and sprinkle the reserved crushed almonds on top, then spoon the compote around the cake.

"MANDARIN" PARFAIT, E'SPUMA, GRANITA

Serves 12

"MANDARIN" PARFAIT, E'SPUMA, GRANITA

Serves 12

INGREDIENTS

Malt swipe
100g Liquid malt extract
50g Water
1.5g Agar

Mandarin e'spuma
400g Reduced mandarin purée (1kg slowly reduced to 400g)
400g Natural yoghurt
2 Leaves of gelatine

Mandarin granita
500g Fresh mandarin juice
120g Sugar
250g Water
400g Reduced mandarin purée (1kg slowly reduced to 400g)
3 Leaves of gelatine

Mandarin parfait
15 Egg yolks
250g Caster sugar
5 Leaves of gelatine
300g Double cream
250g Mandarin reduction (1kg slowly reduced to 400g)
100g Mandarin juice

Chocolate spray
300g Dark chocolate
150g Cocoa butter

Hobnob biscuit crumbs
300g Plain flour
300g Oats
395g Demerara sugar
450g Butter
15g Baking powder
15g Salt

Spiced jelly
50g Light brown sugar
50g Madeira
50g Marsala
75g Port
1/2 Vanilla pod
1 Clove
½ Star anise
2 Leaves of gelatine

METHOD

Malt swipe

Boil all the ingredients together and allow to cool to room temperature. The mixture will set firm. Blitz for 5 minutes in a Thermomix until smooth and reserve.

Mandarin e'spuma

Soak the gelatine in cold water. Warm the purée and add the softened gelatine. Mix well, whisk into the yoghurt and then pour into a 1 litre iSi cream whipper. Charge with two n20 gas canisters. Place in a fridge until required.

Mandarin granita

Soak the gelatine in cold water. Place all the other ingredients into a saucepan. Heat this syrup gently to dissolve the sugar, then add the gelatine. Mix well. Pour into a large tray and place in a freezer. Break up using a whisk every 20-30 minutes.

Mandarin parfait

Soak the gelatine in cold water. Whisk the egg yolks for 5 minutes. Boil the sugar to 120°C and pour onto the whisked yolks. Add the gelatine to the hot yolk/sugar mixture. Whisk until it cools to blood temperature. Semi whip the cream and fold half into the yolk/sugar mixture. Gently fold in the mandarin purée and fresh juice. Fold in the rest of the cream,

place into cone-shaped moulds and freeze. Once frozen remove from the moulds and spray with chocolate.

Chocolate spray

Melt both ingredients together to just above blood temperature. Place in a small art paint sprayer.

When the parfaits are frozen place on a small tray with a little space around them to allow easy spraying. The mix will freeze immediately and form a shell. Return to the freezer until needed.

Hobnob biscuit crumbs

Cream the butter and sugar together for 5 minutes. Add the flour, oats, baking powder and salt. Mix gently to form a paste. Roll between greaseproof paper and bake in a pre-heated oven at 180°C/350°F/gas mark 4 for 12-15 minutes until golden brown. Leave to cool and then break up into crumbs. Reserve in an air-tight container.

Spiced jelly

Soak the gelatine in cold water. Place the rest of the ingredients into a pan and reduce to 150g. Leave to cool for 10 minutes, then add the soaked gelatine. Pour into a small container and place in a fridge until set.

TO SERVE

Take a rectangular plate and place ½ tablespoon of the malt swipe in the bottom left corner. Using the back of a spoon and following the shape of an arc, drag the swipe mixture to the bottom right corner of the plate.

Place the parfait in the middle of the plate, towards the left. Add two spoons of hobnob biscuit crumbs to the right of the parfait. At the top of the plate, in the middle, place a large scoop of the spiced jelly at an angle.

Next, in the bottom of a tall shot glass, place a little hobnob biscuit crumb. On top of this fill the glass halfway up with the mandarin granita. Place the glass at the top of the plate towards the right-hand side. Fill the glass to the top with the mandarin e'spuma.

Serve immediately.

PARTRIDGE WITH PIGS' TROTTERS AND LENTILS

Serves 4

INGREDIENTS

2 Pigs' trotters
2 Onions, 1 sliced, 1 whole
1 Carrot, chopped
Thyme sprigs
Bay leaves
12 Peppercorns
100g Green lentils
8 Cloves
1 Chilli
4 French (red-legged partridges
Salt & pepper
25g Butter
1 tbsp Cooking oil
1 Glass dry white wine
100ml Chicken stock
16 Braised chestnuts

METHOD

Split the trotters (or ask your butcher to!) in half and rinse them in cold water. Put them in a pan with a sliced onion and carrot, thyme, bay leaves and the peppercorns. Bring to a boil, skim well and poach very gently for three hours. Leave to cool overnight.

Rinse the lentils and cover with cold water, adding an onion studded with 8 cloves, 2 bay leaves, a sprig of thyme and a chilli. Bring to a simmer and cook gently until the lentils begin to soften. Allow to cool.

Season the partridges very well with salt and pepper. Heat a heavy frying pan and melt a third of the butter together with the tablespoon of cooking oil. Brown the partridges in this fat on a steady heat, turning them three ways so that they are evenly coloured. Place the partridges, breast side up, on a deep roasting tray and place in a hot oven (230°C/450°F/gas mark 8) for 12 to 14 minutes. Remove the birds from the oven: they should still be slightly pink, but feel firm to the touch. Place the partridges on a plate in a warm place and leave to rest for 15 minutes.

With a small sharp knife, carefully remove the bones from the trotters and cut the meat into 2cm squares. Heat a knob of butter in a skillet and colour the trotter meat gently before adding the lentils, minus the onion and chilli.

Pour the wine into the pan in which the partridges were cooked and scrape up the juices before adding the chicken stock. Reduce these together to half their volume before whisking in a knob of butter. Strain into a gravy jug.

To dress, place the lentils in the centre of the plate and arrange the partridge, trotters and chestnuts around. Sauce over.

POTATO, CHORIZO AND FLAT PARSLEY SOUP
Serves 6

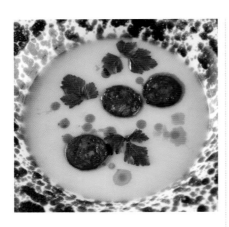

Most people have potatoes and onions in the house even if the cupboard is otherwise bare so you could make this simply delicious soup at a moment's notice. While the vegetables are sweating, pop a few white soda scones or cheddar cheese scones into the oven and wow, won't they be impressed.

INGREDIENTS

50g Butter
550g Peeled diced potatoes, 1cm dice
110g Diced onions, 1cm dice
Salt and freshly ground pepper
1 ltr Homemade chicken stock or vegetable stock
100ml Creamy milk
18 Slices of chorizo
Snipped flat parsley sprigs

METHOD

Melt the butter in a heavy saucepan. When it foams, add the potatoes and onions and toss them in the butter until well coated. Sprinkle with salt and a few grinds of pepper. Cover with a butter wrapper or paper lid and the lid of the saucepan. Sweat on a gentle heat for approximately 10 minutes. Meanwhile bring the stock to the boil; when the vegetables are soft but not coloured add the stock and continue to cook until the vegetables are soft. Purée the soup in a blender or food processor. Taste and adjust seasoning. Thin with creamy milk to the required consistency.

Just before serving cook the slices of chorizo for a minute or two on each side in a non-stick pan – oil will render out of the chorizo.

Serve three slices of chorizo on top of each bowl, sprinkle a few flat parsley sprigs on top, drizzle a little chorizo oil haphazardly over the soup and serve immediately.

SAUTÉ OF TIGER PRAWNS WITH A TART FINE OF ONION AND THYME
Serves 8

INGREDIENTS

175g Unsalted butter
8 Large white onions, sliced
Salt & pepper
1 tsp Thyme leaves
250g Ceps
250ml Whipping cream
300g Puff pastry
40 Medium-sized, raw Tiger prawns
6 Garlic cloves, 5 finely sliced, 1 crushed

METHOD

Onions

In a large heavy based pan melt 75g of the butter and sweat the onions. This process is key. Start the onions over a high heat and without salt. If you add the salt too early it will turn to a mush. Let the onions start to soften and release their moisture. Cover with a lid, if it seems too dry, but stir every half a minute.

After about 5 minutes, by which time you should have a soft mix, add the salt and a twist or two of pepper, turn the heat down and continue to sweat until you have a pale golden, soft, sweet fondue of onions. Stir in half the thyme leaves, remove from the heat and drain in a colander. Chill.

Cep purée

Melt 50g of butter in a heavy based pan. Finely slice the ceps and add to the pan with a generous pinch of salt. Sweat until softened, add the cream, cover and cook for 10 minutes over a low heat. Blend to a smooth purée, pass through a fine sieve, transfer to a small pan, cover and reserve. This will make more than you need, but any excess can be thinned down with chicken stock and milk to make a delicious soup.

Tart fine

Roll out the puff pastry on a cold surface to a neat 30x12cm rectangle. Prick with a fork. Spread the onion mix evenly over the pastry, leaving a ½ cm gap along the long sides. Bake in a hot oven at 200°C/400°F/gas mark 6 until the pastry is crisp and golden – about 20 minutes. Remove from the oven, place on a cooling rack and allow to rest for 5 minutes.

TO SERVE

Melt the remaining 50g butter in a large heavy based frying pan. Just at the point where it starts to smell nutty throw in the prawns and season. Sauté over a high heat for 2 minutes – turning the prawns half way. Add the garlic and remaining thyme leaves, toss once more and tip onto a serving dish.

Warm through the cep purée and place half a teaspoon in the centre of 8 plates. Cut the tart fine into 8 slices and sit one on each plate on the cep purée.

Now place a generous spoon of purée onto each plate and finish by placing 4 prawns on each piece of tart. Drizzle the pan juices around and serve immediately.

OXTAIL RAVIOLI

Serves 4

OXTAIL RAVIOLI
Serves 4

INGREDIENTS

3 tbsp Extra-virgin olive oil
1 Oxtail
4 Chopped garlic cloves
2 Carrots cut into large dice
2 Banana shallots (or 4 small ones) cut into large dice
1 Bouquet garni, made with a sprig of rosemary and a small bunch of sage
70g Pork belly
2 ltrs Chicken stock
350ml Dry white wine
50g Tomato paste
40g Grated parmesan cheese
1 Egg
20g Unsalted butter
1 Carrot, finely diced

Pasta
500g 00 (doppio zero) flour, sieved
3 Large eggs plus 2 extra (large) egg yolks (all at room temperature)
Pinch of salt

METHOD

Filling and sauce

To make the filling, cut the oxtail into 4 or 5 pieces, rinse, put in a large pot, cover with cold water and bring to the boil, then skim, drain and set aside. Put the extra-virgin olive oil in another pan big enough to hold the oxtail, with the chopped garlic cloves, the carrots and the banana shallots, and cook gently for about 10 minutes, then add the bouquet garni, the pork belly and the oxtail. Cook gently for 5-6 minutes, then add the white wine and continue to cook until the wine evaporates.

Next add the tomato paste and the chicken stock, bring to the boil, skim, then turn down the heat and simmer for 45-60 minutes, until the meat falls apart. Separate the meat and vegetables into two different bowls. Put the remaining cooking liquid through a fine sieve into a clean pan and put back on the heat and simmer until it thickens to a sauce-like consistency.

Flake the oxtail meat with your fingers, breaking the meat down as much as possible, discard the bones and any fatty parts (don't chop with the knife or you will lose the nice 'stringiness'). Mix in half of the reserved vegetables, put into a food processor and whizz to a rough paste. Add the grated parmesan cheese, taste and season, then add the egg and mix together – the mixture should come together easily in soft balls, but if it seems too dry, mix in a little of the sauce.

Pasta

Preferably make the pasta by hand – especially if you are making a relatively small quantity like this, which will be difficult for a food processor to mix well. Sieve the flour into a clean bowl, then turn it out into a mound on a clean surface and make a well in the middle (in Italy we call this the fontana di farina 'fountain of flour'). Sprinkle the salt into the well and then crack in the eggs.

Have a bowl of water on one side so you can dip your hands into it and wet them, to help bring the dough together if it is being stubborn towards the end of kneading. To begin, break the yolks with the fingertips of one hand, and then begin to move your fingers in a circular motion, gradually incorporating the flour, until you have worked in enough to start bringing it together in a ball. Then you can start to work the ball of dough by pushing it with the heel of your hand, then folding the top back on itself, turning it a little clockwise, and repeating, again and again, for about 10 minutes, wetting your hands if it helps, until the dough is springy, but still feels quite firm and difficult to work.

Don't worry that the dough feels hard; after it has relaxed for a while it will be perfect.

Divide the dough into 2 balls, wrap each in a damp cloth and rest for about an hour before using.

Roll the first ball of dough with a rolling pin (keep the rest covered in the damp cloth) – until it is about 1cm thick and will go through the pasta machine comfortably (if it is too thick, the pasta machine will have to use so much force to make it go through that it will damage the machine and squeeze out too much moisture in the process, so the pasta will be dry). There isn't an exact number of times you will need to feed the pasta through the machine – each time you make it might be slightly different (and not every pasta machine has the same number of settings), but use the next few steps as a guide, and after a while you will get the hang of rolling the pasta and feel your own way.

Put the machine on the first (thickest) setting to start with, then feed the piece of pasta through the machine turning the handle with one hand, and supporting the dough as it comes through with the other. Then change to the second setting, and put it through again. Repeat another 2-3 times, taking the setting down one each time. Don't worry if the pasta appears slightly streaky, this should disappear as you carry on rolling it.

Next, fold the strip of pasta back on itself, put the machine back onto the first setting and put the pasta through again. Repeat 3-4 more times, again taking the setting down one each time and you will see that the pasta begins to take on a sheen. As it begins to get longer, you will find that you have to pull it very gently, so that it doesn't begin to concertina. You shouldn't need to dust it with flour, unless you feel it is too soft and likely to stick and stretch too much.

Now you need to cut your strip in half. Keep one half covered in a damp cloth, then fold the length of the other strip into three, bringing one end in and the other over the top of that, so that the pasta is the same width as the machine. Roll it with the rolling pin, so it is no more than 0.5cm thick, then put the machine back onto the first setting and feed the pasta through – the opposite way this time, i.e. widthways, not lengthways. The idea of changing direction is to put equal elasticity and strength throughout the pasta. Keep feeding it through this way, taking it down two or three settings as you go.

Finally, fold the pasta back on itself, then put the machine back onto the first setting, and take it down again through the settings until it is about 1.5mm thick.

Repeat with the other half strip, then the other ball of dough.

Ravioli

To make the ravioli mark the halfway point of your first strip of pasta and brush one half with beaten egg, then place little mounds of filling (about a teaspoonful to make a round mound with a circumference of about 4cm) two abreast on the half that is brushed with egg, leaving a space of about 3-4cm between each mound. You should have enough to make around 30-32 so each person will get 7 to 8 ravioli each.

Fold the other half of the pasta over the top, carefully matching the long edges down one side and pressing them together, then doing the same the other side. Gently press down around each raviolo (don't worry if you compress the filling a little as you go).

Using a fluted ring cutter about 1cm bigger in circumference than the filling, cut out each raviolo and discard all the trimmings. Now you need to seal each one and press out any air trapped inside, so take each raviolo and carefully, with your thumbs, pinch around the outside. If you hold each raviolo up to the light, you can see where the filling is, and whether or not you have smoothed out all the air pockets.

Bring a large pan of water to the boil for the pasta.

Melt the butter in a large sauté pan and, when the butter begins to foam, add the finely diced carrots and about 2-3 ladlefuls of the sauce.

Put the ravioli into the boiling water and cook for 3-4 minutes, then drain using a slotted spoon or a spider and transfer to the pan containing the sauce. Toss gently for a couple of minutes or so and serve.

TREACLE SALMON, SCALLOPS, PICKLED GINGER

Serves 4

INGREDIENTS

1 Piece of treacle marinated salmon (see below)
4 King scallops
Salt
1 Lemon
Few drops of sunflower oil

Salmon marinade
350g Middle cut salmon (skin on scale)
60g Fine sea salt
60g Caster sugar
6g Chopped chili (hot, with seeds)
10g Chopped lemongrass
15g Coriander
40g Root ginger, peeled and grated
125g Treacle (at room temperature)
200ml Dark soy sauce (at room temperature)

Salmon sauce
50ml Rice vinegar
50ml Soy sauce
50ml Oyster sauce

Garnish for the salmon
12 Thin slices of pickled ginger
20g Spring onions, sliced
40g Beansprouts
1 Punnet mustard cress
16 Sprigs coriander
Maldon sea salt

METHOD

Heat a medium-sized non-stick pan and add a small amount of oil. Lightly season the scallops with salt. Place the scallops into the pan, press slightly, cook for 1-2 minutes until golden on one side. Then turn the scallops over and cook for a further minute, add a squeeze of lemon juice. Then immediately remove from the pan onto a piece of absorbent paper. Season with Maldon salt and place on top of the treacle salmon.

Salmon marinade
Carefully score the skin side of the salmon with a sharp knife. In a Thermomix add the salt, sugar, chilli, lemongrass, coriander and root ginger, blitz to make a paste. Remove from the Thermomix and rub the paste evenly onto both sides of the salmon. Place the salmon into a vacuum pack bag, add the treacle and soy sauce, vac pac tight and leave to marinate for 12 hours. After 12 hours wash off the marinade and pat dry.

With a small amount of salmon sauce (see below) glaze the flesh side – this should be a nice dark colour.

Salmon sauce
Mix all the ingredients together and place into a small pan, reduce by half to make a syrup that holds when cold. Leave to cool, then place into a squeezy bottle.

TO SERVE

Cut the salmon into 3mm thick slices, remove the skin and the brown flesh – this gives 60g of salmon per portion. Place a number 80 cutter (round cutter 80mm in diameter) into the centre of the plate, line the cutter with 60g of treacle salmon, the glazed flesh to the outside. Put the pickled ginger, spring onions, beansprouts and an even layer of mustard cress on top. To finish put 10 dots of sauce evenly around the plate, 1 warm scallop on top, coriander and a few flakes of Maldon sea salt.

20O3

This was the first year of seven nights, and the year of many things. It was the year that Kaye got lost driving Christian Olsson back from Manchester airport, and ended up halfway to Wales before Christian noticed that they were heading in the opposite direction to Northcote.

And it was the year of late nights with the Galvin brothers. One night we'd certainly had quite a bit to drink and Jeff and Chris were up for a really good night. Then they became hungry at about 4.30am, and the only thing we had which was convenient to cook in the fridges were the staff meat and potato pies left over from lunch, so Chris and Jeff quickly set about heating them up in the microwave, and tucking in. I couldn't keep my eyes open any longer so I had to leave them to it. The rest is history.

The Galvins did an incredible smoked quail consommé with a pithivier of quail which was absolutely stunning and great ravioli of sea scallops and langoustine. The milk-fed Pyrenean lamb they made was very interesting – they're very influenced by France, and they made a beautiful Sauternes soaked Forme d'Ambre with dried Muscat grapes, which was wonderful.

This was also the year of Heston's football match. Northcote played The Fat Duck in a game of football on what used to be the old tennis courts (which we won). He also fed Craig's children with his chocolate and caviar dish and snail porridge, which was greatly appreciated by the little Bancrofts. The funniest thing about Heston's night was getting the nitrogen from BOAC in Manchester. It was an absolute nightmare. They thought we were international terrorists or something – we had to get three tanks of this stuff for 50 people. At this point Heston was just on the cusp of greatness; The Fat Duck crew had to train Craig and the team to go around all the tables doing the famous nitro-poached green tea and lime mousses. Heston also made an orange and beetroot reverse jelly, which had a wonderful quirky simplicity.

One of the things that really hit home was the delice of chocolate with a cumin caramel – it was the first time anyone had touched cracking candy since childhood.

We then had probably the liveliest night of the festival, with Heston, Ashley and his pastry chef Jockey, who told many tales which were incredibly funny, but not for the pages of this cookbook.

Phil Howard's snails never arrived and he got lost on one of his famous runs. Phil used to go running every time he came up and this time he got lost between York Village and Rishton, and ended up by Blackburn Royal Hospital, which is about seven miles away. He had to get to a phone box to find out how to get home, and he ran back quite exhausted. Phil did an outstanding sweet and sour belly pork, but his pièce de résistance was a banana soufflé with chocolate ice cream, which was very dapper and a truly classy Howard dish.

Highlights of the food that year were Christian Olsson's seafood escabeche: scallop, lobster and octopus with garlic and parsley foam which was pretty special and a forward-looking dish for 2003. They use a lot of cloudberries in Scandinavia and he made a cloudberry granita with a little shot of lemonade, which was memorable.

Neil Wigglesworth flew in from Twin Farms in Vermont for our first chef visiting from America. Interestingly, Neil used to run a restaurant called Tiffany's in Great Harwood which at its height had eight in the Good Food Guide. It was in Tiffany's that I got to know Neil and where we had many a night with lashings of good food, wine and fun. I first discovered it after crashing my old Morris Ital (the worst designed car in the world) into a lamp-post nearby. He used to do a fabulous dish of sea bass on wilted lettuce with a julienne of vegetables and seafood veloute with chives, and it was always memorable. Then he married an American and moved to Vermont.

HESTON BLUMENTHAL

"I love the fact that food and cooking have the ability to stimulate social interaction and produce emotions in people. And eating is the only thing that we do that uses all of the five senses at the same time: the way that sound, sight, touch, taste and smell all interact during such a simple everyday process is fascinating to me."

OBSESSION
FESTIVAL
2003

NEIL WIGGLESWORTH

"You would have to have an Obsession to open a high quality restaurant in Great Harwood on the site of the Old Launderette, which is exactly what I did. Tiffany's was certainly my Obsession all those years ago — it had passion, it had flair and fun which was a success but maybe not the huge success I would have wanted it to be. So we went overseas sto follow our Obsession where food was a principal part of a fantastic journey, to come back from the USA to cook with an old friend alongside great names and show my talents was a great honour and of course much fun, thanks Nigel. "

PHIL HOWARD

"I remember Neil Wigglesworth impressing me with a cooking technique involving a toilet roll — it was clever but that has long since been forgotten. Heston was here to work his magic and certainly didn't disappoint. My third year and I've still not learnt to avoid the bloody soufflés! It is beginning to become evident that modern cooking techniques are spreading far and wide."

CHRIS AND JEFF GALVIN

"My passion for cooking was inspired by our childhood holidays driving through France. We would stop off at the most wonderful food markets brimming with locally grown produce, ingredients that I had not seen in the UK at that time (40 years ago!). I love to create food that makes people happy; even now cooking for family, friends and our diners at the restaurants is a pleasure that has never diminished.

Chris Galvin

My Obsession was partly due to seeing the passion and enthusiasm my brother Chris had for cooking and ingredients. I was lucky enough to have the best training possible under the tutelage of Anton Edelmann at the Savoy. This is an ever-evolving industry and it is impossible not to live and breathe cooking, you never have a chance to become bored and my enthusiasm for it never wanes."

Jeff Galvin

NIGEL HAWORTH

"To be obsessed with the theatre of kitchen is comforting, almost womb-like."

CHRISTIAN OLSSON

"I'm obsessed with food because I have an ongoing craving to make today's food better tomorrow. What drives that passion is my imagination and also that I constantly surround myself with interesting and professional people in my kitchen."

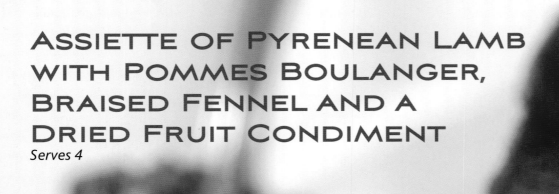

ASSIETTE OF PYRENEAN LAMB WITH POMMES BOULANGER, BRAISED FENNEL AND A DRIED FRUIT CONDIMENT

Serves 4

ASSIETTE OF PYRENEAN LAMB WITH POMMES BOULANGER, BRAISED FENNEL AND A DRIED FRUIT CONDIMENT

Serves 4

INGREDIENTS

1 Rack of baby suckling lamb
1 Saddle of baby suckling lamb
1 Orange
200ml Lamb juice

Dried fruit condiment
2 Fillets of salted anchovies
10 White raisins
8 Fresh almonds
2 Dried apricots
1 Branch rosemary
4 Garlic cloves
Butter
1 tsp Sugar
2 tbsp Dried breadcrumbs
Sherry vinegar

Lamb juice
1kg Chopped lamb bones
200g Lamb fat
2Carrots
1 Onion
1 White leek
1 Head fennel
Olive oil
Half bottle dry white wine
2 Sprigs of thyme
2 Sprigs of rosemary
1 Garlic bulb
200g Deseeded tomatoes
3 ltrs Water

Pommes boulanger
1 Baby lamb shoulder
2 White onions, very finely sliced
1 Garlic bulb, halved

5 Large desiree potatoes
1l Lamb juice (see above)

Braised fennel
2 Large bulbs of fennel
Olive oil
400ml Water
2 Garlic cloves
Pinch fennel seeds
Salt & pepper

To serve
4 Whole fresh ceps
Olive oil
1 dstspn Butter

METHOD

Trim the rack and saddle leaving a little fat on the back of the meat. Wash the orange, peel off a little peel and keep; juice the orange through a strainer into a pan, add the lamb juice and reduce over a medium heat until syrupy, add the peel and cool. Brush all over the lamb and set in the fridge to marinate.

Dried fruit condiment

Rinse the anchovies and let them soak for 2 hours, drain and dry, then crush with the back of a fork and set aside. Soak the raisins in hot water for 1 hour, then drain, open the fresh almonds, peel and cut in two. Slice the dried apricots into strips, chop the rosemary very finely and set aside in a bowl. Peel and quarter the cloves of garlic, take out the centre germ, sauté in some hot butter until golden, sprinkle with the sugar and let them caramelise, then set aside. Toast the breadcrumbs in some more hot butter and drain.

In a pan heat a dash of olive oil, add the raisins, almonds, apricots, garlic and rosemary, add a few drops of sherry vinegar, sprinkle on the toasted breadcrumbs and mix to dry out, spoon in the anchovies and season.

Lamb juice

Roast the bones in a hot oven at 150°C/300°F/gas mark 2 until brown. Chop all the vegetables roughly and caramelise in a deep pan in a little olive oil. Place in the lamb bones, wine, herbs and tomatoes, cover with the water and place the pan with no lid into the oven at 150°C/300°F/gas mark 2 with the fat for around 4 hours, remove and let it cool and settle for 1 hour. Then pour through a cheese cloth and set aside for later use.

Pommes boulanger

Place the lamb shoulder in a deep ovenproof dish, peel and slice the onion very fine, cut the garlic in half and cover the lamb. Put a lid on the dish and place in a medium oven for 4 hours, 150°C/300°F/gas mark 2.

Cool the lamb for 1 hour; pick all the meat off the bone, shred into smaller pieces with your fingers, being careful not to have too much fat incorporated, then set aside. Peel the potatoes and slice very finely on a Japanese mandolin, layer the potatoes up in a shallow ovenproof dish; when half-way up place the meat in a thin layer, finish with layers of potato to the top. Heat the lamb juice and pour over, place into a medium oven 150°C/300°F/gas mark 2 for approximately 1½ hours, press down half way through with a palette knife to help colour on top. When done the potato should be dry, well coloured and a knife should pass through easily. Leave to cool.

Braised fennel

Trim and peel the fennel, cut in half, heat a pan with a dash of olive oil, colour the fennel all around until golden and place in a deep pan. Heat the water, add the garlic and fennel seed, season and poach very lightly until tender.

TO SERVE

Heat a large sauté pan and cook the cuts of lamb in a little olive oil for 12 minutes, turning frequently. When done place on a warm grill to rest for 10 minutes.

While the lamb is resting, cut your potato into a shape to suit, place in a hot oven at 200°C/400°F/gas mark 6 to warm.

Slice the fennel into equal wedges and keep warm.

Take 4 whole fresh ceps, trim and clean then sauté in a little hot olive oil, finish with butter to glaze, keep warm.

Take 4 serving plates, place the potato in the centre, cut the lamb into portions and arrange with the fennel and ceps around the potato, sprinkle over some fruit condiment and serve the rest on the side.

Pour around a little more reduced lamb juice.

SMOKED QUAIL CONSOMMÉ, PITHIVER OF QUAIL
Serves 4

INGREDIENTS

5 Jumbo quails
10 Quail carcasses (to be smoked then used in clarification)
200g Cherry wood chips for smoking

Clarification
100g Chicken breast
4 Smoked quail breasts
10 Smoked quail carcasses
50g Onion, peeled
80g Carrot, peeled
50g Leek, washed
50g Celery, washed
2 Egg whites
Sprig of tarragon
2 ltrs Brown chicken stock

Pithiver
2 Quail breasts
6 Quail legs, boned
4 Quail legs, slow cooked
50g Italian lardo (pork fat)
50g Chicken breasts
20g Fresh white breadcrumbs
1 Egg yolk
1 tsp Chopped parsley
Salt & pepper
200g All butter puff pastry (rolled 3mm thick)
Egg yolk for egg wash
Garnish
4 Quail breasts
4 Soft poached quail eggs
1 Plum tomato, diced
4 Blades of truffle cut into julienne (straw like)
Chervil, to garnish
Few drops of black truffle oil

METHOD

Clean the quails and remove the wish bone and legs. Reserve 6 legs for the pithiver and bone them for mincing; the other 4 should be slow cooked in duck fat (see pithiver recipe).

The breasts should all be smoked on the crown, along with the carcasses. 4 breasts are for the garnish, two are for the pithiver and the rest go into the clarification.

To hot smoke
In a small roasting tray heat the cherry wood chips until they are smoking, place a wire rack over the chips and place both the quails and the quail carcasses on top. Smoke constantly for 10 minutes then remove the quail and allow to cool. Remove all the breasts off the bone and reserve. The breasts should be nice and pink at this stage.

Clarification
Place all the clarification ingredients, except the chicken stock, into a Robot Coupe (food processor) and blitz for a minute or two. Whisk on to the cold chicken stock and bring to the boil, stirring every few minutes to form a pad (a pad is what forms when the proteins rise to the top and the liquid clarifies) then simmer gently for 20 minutes. Pass through a muslin cloth.

Pithiver
Mince the quail breasts, meat from the boned quail legs, chicken breast and pork fat together. Add the breadcrumbs, egg yolk and parsley. Check the seasoning, mould in to a 2cm cutter. Remove the thigh bone and skin from the slow-cooked quail legs and put them on top of the mince fillings. Cut the puff pastry into 8 discs and use them to make the pithiver, leaving the bone sticking out of the top. Egg wash twice then score the pattern on the top. Rest for at least an hour then bake for 8 minutes at 180°C/350°F/gas mark 4.

Consommé and garnish
Warm the quail breasts and quail eggs and place in the consommé cups. Add the tomato dice, truffle and chervil then pour in the boiling consommé, drizzle on a few drops of truffle oil and serve with the warm pithiver.

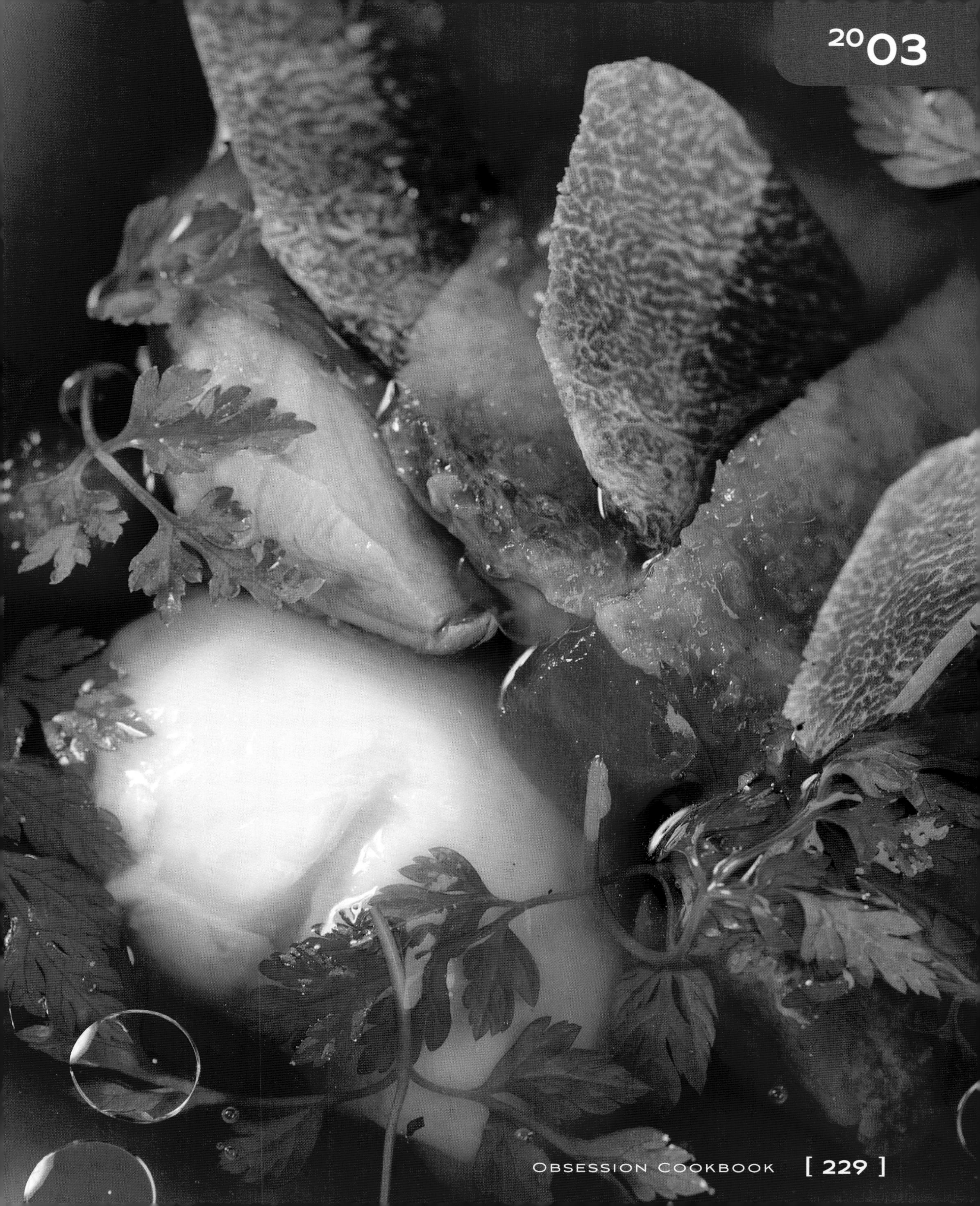

SEAFOOD ESCABECHE, SCALLOP, LOBSTER, OCTOPUS, GARLIC PARSLEY FOAM

Serves 4

INGREDIENTS

10 Ripe (preferably Sicilian) tomatoes
3 Garlic cloves
5 Sprigs of thyme
1 tbsp Sugar
1 tbsp Coarse sea salt
1 tbsp Olive oil
½ Cucumber
½ tbsp Spanish pimento powder
1 pinch Spanish saffron
Juice from 1 lime
1 Red chilli pepper, chopped
Garlic oil
Salt & pepper
1 Bunch coriander, chopped
(including the stems)

Parsley and garlic foam
50ml Parsley and garlic infused oil
(put 200ml oil, 1 garlic clove and a
bunch of fresh Italian parsley in a
blender until the oil is hot then strain
through a filter)
50ml Whipping cream
1 tbsp Champagne vinegar
Salt

Seafood
1 Scottish lobster, cooked and
separated
4 Scallops
1 Baby octopus, cooked and
char grilled

Vegetables and fruit
4 Baby artichokes cooked 'au
barigoule' (parboiled in salted water,
cooled and leaves removed)
100g Sweet watermelon, cubed
1 Grilled red bell pepper, sliced
1cm Square avocado terrine (made
with avocado, agar agar, chilli, salt
and lemon)
Spring onions, thinly sliced to garnish
Nori, finely chopped to garnish

METHOD

Cut the tomatoes in half and place
in a baking pan. Crush some garlic
cloves and put in the pan along with
the thyme, salt, sugar and olive oil.
Place in the oven at 200°C/400°F/gas
mark 6 for about 10 minutes. Remove
from the oven, cover with cling film
and leave to rest for 15 minutes.
Strain slowly and carefully through
a chinoise (sieve) – don't push it
through.

Roast the pimento powder in a
small pot, add a little water to make a
paste and then add saffron and mix.

Peel and blend the cucumber;
let it strain by itself slowly through a
chinoise.

Mix a little of the tomato water
with the paste so there are no lumps.

Then season with the cucumber juice,
lime juice, sherry vinegar, garlic oil,
chopped red chilli, salt and pepper,
sugar and chopped coriander.

Let it sit for an hour before
serving then strain.

Parsley and garlic foam
Put the oil, cream and vinegar in a
bowl, season with salt and blend
carefully before pouring it into a
siphon. Charge with two cream
chargers and shake the siphon very
carefully, continually testing the
mixture until it is the consistency of
shaving foam.

Keep cool but not too cold.

TO SERVE

Place a little of the strained tomato
liquid in a dish. Assemble the lobster,
scallops and baby octopus on top
with the baby artichoke, sweet
watermelon, baby tomatoes, red
pepper and avocado terrine. Scatter
with a little puffed wild rice, spring
onions and nori.

Banana Soufflé with Chocolate Ice cream
Serves 8

INGREDIENTS

10	Large bananas
500ml	Milk
6	Egg yolks
280g	Sugar
25g	Cocoa powder
100g	Valrhona 70% chocolate
125g	Mascarpone
20g	Cornflour
100ml	Banana liqueur
100g	Softened butter
100g	Dried banana bread, blended into a fine crumb
360ml	Egg whites
Icing sugar, to serve	

METHOD

Bake 8 of the bananas in their skins in an oven at 160°C/325°F/gas mark 3 for 20 minutes – they will turn black.

Meanwhile, bring the milk to the boil in a heavy based pan. Whisk the egg yolks with 100g sugar and the cocoa powder. Pour on the milk, whisk briefly to incorporate the yolks, return to the heat and cook, stirring continuously, until the custard coats the back of a wooden spoon (84°C). Remove from the heat, add the chocolate and mascarpone and whisk until homogeneous. Chill and churn in an ice cream machine until set. Store in a freezer.

Remove the bananas from the oven, allow to rest for 10 minutes. Remove the pulp and transfer to a large bowl. Discard the skins. Fork through the banana to create a rough purée.

Mix the cornflour with 40ml of the banana liqueur, add to the banana and transfer to a heavy based pan. Bring this mix to the boil and cook out, beating vigorously, for 3 minutes. Transfer to a blender and purée until smooth. Reserve at room temperature.

TO SERVE

Carefully brush the soufflé moulds (10x5cm) with butter, using vertical brush strokes. Coat each mould with banana breadcrumbs by pouring the crumbs into a buttered mould and tipping into the next while rotating.

Transfer the ice cream from the freezer to the fridge 20 minutes prior to serving.

Peel the two remaining bananas and mash with a fork. Add the banana mix equally then add the 30ml of banana liqueur to each. You will need to make the soufflés in two batches if using a standard-sized electric mixer.

Place 180g egg whites into the mixer and turn onto the lightest setting. Once lightly aerated, gradually add 90g sugar and beat until stiff. Add a large spoon of mix to one of the bowls and whisk briefly. Then incorporate the rest of the mix for that batch carefully with a rubber spatula.

Repeat the same process with the second batch of whites.

Spoon the finished mix into the soufflé moulds, gently tapping on the work surface. Using a large palette knife, smooth off the surface of each soufflé. Run the tip of your thumb round the inside of the rim by pinching with your thumb and forefinger and rotating the mould. This will prevent them from sticking.

Place the soufflés in an oven, preheated to 170°C/340°F/gas mark 3½. Make sure there is at least an 8cm clearance! They will take 8-10 minutes. Turn the tray after 5 minutes. If they have risen at least 3-4cm after 8 minutes, remove the soufflés carefully, dust with icing sugar and serve immediately. Drop a ball of ice cream into the middle of each soufflé.

Snail Porridge, Jabugo Ham

Serves 2

SNAIL PORRIDGE, JABUGO HAM

Serves 2

INGREDIENTS

Duck ham
1 Bay leaf
15g Black peppercorns
15g Coriander seeds
50g Sel gris (grey salt)
5g Sprigs of thyme
5 Gressingham duck breasts, fat scored

Parsley butter
550g Unsalted butter
85g Garlic, minced
10g Lemon juice
50g Dijon mustard
40g Ground almonds
15g Table salt
240g Curly leaf parsley
Clarified butter
40g Ceps, cut into 1cm dice
60g Shallots, cut into brunoise (2mm squares)
80g Reserved duck ham, cut into brunoise (2mm squares)

Chicken bouillon
3kg Chicken (2 good-sized chickens)
250g Carrots, peeled and finely sliced
250g Onions, finely sliced
100g Celery, finely sliced
75g Leeks, white and pale green parts only, finely sliced
10g Garlic, crushed
3 Cloves
10g Black peppercorns
50g Sprigs of thyme
20g Parsley leaves and stems
3g Bay leaves

Braised snails
100g Helix pomatia snails (shelled weight)
2 Cloves
120g Onion, cut in half
40g Carrot, cut in half
90g Leeks, cut in half
2 Sticks of celery
30g Garlic bulb, cut in half
2 Bay leaves
50g Sprigs of rosemary
50g Sprigs of thyme
120g Water
250g Dry white wine
50g Parsley leaves and stems

Walnut vinaigrette
75g Walnut vinegar
145g Grapeseed oil
5g Dijon mustard

Snail porridge
10g Fennel, shaved paper-thin
Reserved walnut vinaigrette
Table salt
Black pepper
Fleur de sel
30g Unsalted butter
12 Reserved braised snails
30g Reserved chicken bouillon
10g Porridge oats, sieved to remove the powdery bits
30g Reserved parsley butter, at room temperature
20g Jabugo ham, cut into chiffonade (long, thin strips)
Pinch of micro parsley and micro coriander to garnish.

METHOD

Duck ham

Snip the bay leaf into 8 pieces. Grind the peppercorns and coriander, combine with the sel gris, thyme and bay leaf. Spread a layer of this mixture over the bottom of a roasting tray and place the duck breasts on top. Cover completely with the remaining salt mixture, then refrigerate for 24 hours.

Brush the salt cure from the breasts, wrap them in muslin and tie securely with string. Hang in a cellar or other cool place for at least 20 days. Remove the duck from the muslin and refrigerate until needed.

Parsley butter

Melt 50g of the unsalted butter in a pan, add the garlic and sauté until pale gold and fragrant. Add the lemon juice to the pan, then transfer the mixture to a Pacojet beaker along with the mustard, ground almonds, salt and the remaining 500g unsalted butter.

Chop the parsley, sprinkle on top of the butter mixture and run the beaker through the Pacojet machine. Remove the beaker and freeze the mixture until completely solid. Run the frozen mixture through the Pacojet, then freeze solid again. Repeat this process until all trace of the parsley has disappeared. After the final use of the Pacojet, at which point the mixture will have an ice cream consistency, set aside the butter at room temperature until needed.

Heat some clarified butter in a pan, add the ceps and sauté until caramelised.

Strain and set aside.

Wipe the pan clean, then heat some more clarified butter in it. Add the shallots and cook over a very low heat for 30–40 minutes, until very soft and translucent.

Fold the caramelised ceps, the cooked shallots and the duck brunoise into the reserved parsley butter. Refrigerate or freeze until needed.

Chicken bouillon

Place the chickens in a large pan and cover with cold water. Bring to the boil, then carefully remove them and discard the water. Rinse the chickens under cold running water to remove any scum.

Put the chickens in a pressure cooker and add just enough cold water to cover them. Bring to a simmer, skimming off any scum on the surface. Add the vegetables, cloves and freshly crushed peppercorns to the pan. Put the lid on, bring to full pressure and cook for 30 minutes.

Remove the pan from the heat, allow to depressurise, then remove the lid. Add the thyme, parsley and bay leaves and leave to infuse for 30 minutes. Strain the bouillon through a fine sieve lined with several layers of damp muslin. Refrigerate or freeze until needed.

Braised snails

Rinse the snails in several changes of water to remove any grit. Preheat the oven to 120°C/250°F/gas mark ½.

Press a clove into each half of the onion, then place in an ovenproof casserole with all the other ingredients, apart from the snails and parsley, and bring to a simmer on the hob.

Add the snails, cover with a cartouche (circle of paper to stop a skin forming) and place in the oven for 3–4 hours. Remove the casserole from the oven, add the parsley and set aside to cool.

Drain the snails from the liquid and trim away their intestines and white sac.

Refrigerate until needed.

Walnut vinaigrette

Combine all the ingredients, mix thoroughly and set aside until needed.

Snail porridge

Dress the fennel with the vinaigrette, season with table salt, freshly ground pepper and fleur de sel and set aside.

Heat 20g of the butter until foaming, then sauté the snails and season with table salt and freshly ground pepper. Add the remaining butter to the snails, then remove from the heat and keep warm.

Heat the chicken bouillon in a small saucepan. When hot, stir in the oats. Once they have absorbed the liquid, add the parsley butter and season to taste with table salt and freshly ground pepper. Adjust the consistency of the porridge with chicken bouillon if necessary until it resembles wet rice pudding. (It is important not to overcook the oats or else they will become starchy and lose their texture.)

TO SERVE

Divide the porridge between 2 warm plates and cover with the Jabugo ham. Place the warm snails on top, add the dressed fennel and micro salads to serve.

Heather-Fed Bowland Lamb, Morecambe Bay Shrimp, Dry-Cured Ham and Herb Polenta, Tomato Lamb jus
Serves 4

INGREDIENTS

2 Short loins of heather-fed Bowland lamb (silverskin removed and trimmed)
Salt
Butter
Herb polenta (see below)
80g Morecambe Bay shrimps (warmed and seasoned)
Tomato lamb jus (see below)
Paprika, to dust

Dry-cured ham and herb polenta
30g Butter
100g Fine polenta
Salt, to taste
300g Chicken stock
40g Double cream
40g Dry-cured ham, cut into small dice
2g Chopped chives
2g Chopped parsley
2g Chopped tarragon
20g Grated parmesan

Tomato lamb jus
150g Chopped onion
40g Butter
100g Sliced tomatoes
150ml Madeira
500ml Lamb stock
500ml Chicken stock
1 tsp Fecule (potato flour) mixed with a few drops of water before adding to sauce to thicken (or cornflour)

METHOD

Roll the loin of lamb in cling film, put in a vacuum pack bag and seal tight. Cook the lamb in a water bath at 68°C for 14 minutes. Allow to rest for 5 minutes. Remove from the vacuum pack bag and season with salt.

In a non-stick hot frying pan, seal the lamb for 2-3 minutes, basting in butter. Remove from the pan and carve into 8 slices.

Dry-cured ham and herb polenta
Bring the chicken stock to the boil. Meanwhile, in a medium pan, melt the butter then add the polenta with a pinch of salt. Add the boiling chicken stock and bring back to the boil. Cover and simmer for 5-10 minutes. Once cooked add the cream, dry-cured ham and chopped herbs, check the seasoning.

Tomato lamb jus
Sweat off the onions in the butter until they caramelise, add the tomatoes and cook for a further 3-4 minutes. Add the Madeira and reduce by two-thirds. Add the lamb and chicken stocks and reduce to approximately 300ml then lightly thicken with fecule or cornflour. Blitz the sauce with a stick liquidiser for a few seconds and check the seasoning.

TO SERVE

Take a rectangular plate and put 2 dessertspoons of the ham and herb polenta down the centre. Place 4 slices of the lamb on the top, scatter around the shrimps and finish with the jus and paprika.

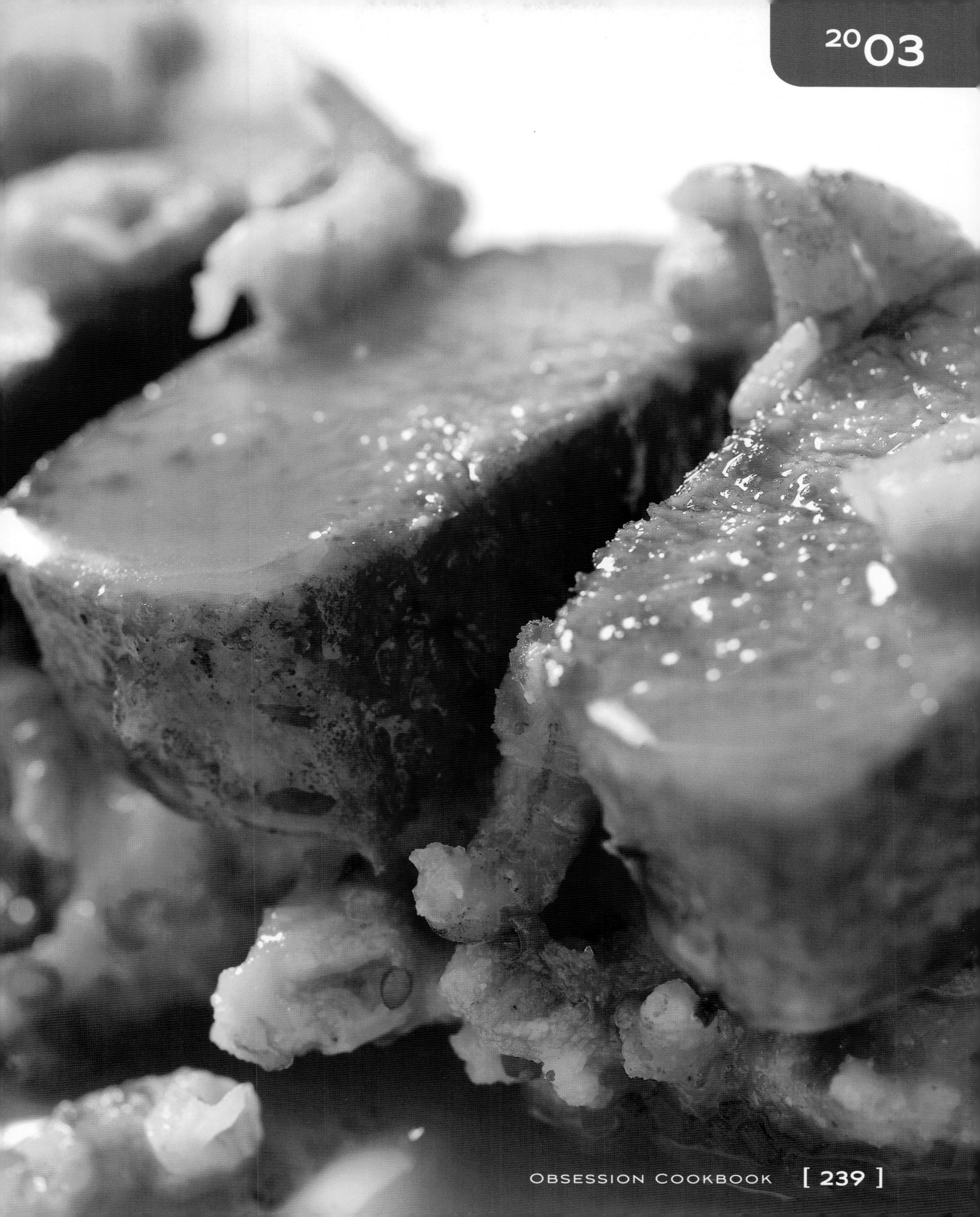

"HINDLE WAKES" GOOSNARGH CHICKEN BROTH FLAVOURED WITH DRIED PLUMS, BROWN RICE, STREAKY BACON AND BASIL

Serves 4

"HINDLE WAKES" GOOSNARGH CHICKEN BROTH FLAVOURED WITH DRIED PLUMS, BROWN RICE, STREAKY BACON AND BASIL

Serves 4

INGREDIENTS

4 Slow-cooked chicken wings (see below)
Chicken mousse (see below)
4 Dried plums (see below)
Brown rice and bacon (see below)
4 Crispy chicken skins – (see below)
4 Chiffonade of basil leaves (long thin strips)

Chicken broth
(makes 10 portions)
500g Ground Goosnargh chicken mince
250g Finely chopped vegetables (onions, carrots, celery and leeks)
2 Parsley stalks/chervil
1 Sprig of thyme
1 Bay leaf
80g Egg whites
5g Chicken bouillon
Salt
6 Crushed black peppercorns
2 ltrs Good white chicken stock

Chicken mousse
200g Chicken breasts, diced
250ml Cream
1 Egg yolk
10g Chives, chopped
5g Chervil, finely chopped
4g Salt

Slow-cooked chicken wings
4 x 300g Chicken wings
2g Thyme, chopped
40g Rock salt
1 Garlic clove, crushed

Dried plums
2 Victoria plums
Salt
Icing sugar, to dust

Brown rice and bacon
40g Brown rice, washed
10g Diced streaky bacon

Crispy skin
Chicken skin from 2 large
chicken breasts
Salt

METHOD

Chicken broth
(makes 10 portions)
Combine the ground chicken,
chopped vegetables, herbs, egg
whites, bouillon and seasoning in a
mixing bowl. Mix well.

Put the chicken stock into a large
heavy bottomed pan. Carefully mix in
the ground chicken mince. Mix well
and check the seasoning. Place the
pan on to the stove and bring to a
simmer over a medium heat, stir the
contents of the pan frequently until
the pad starts to set on the surface
of the stock. Once the pad has risen
give it a final stir and then allow the
pad to set, make a small opening to
the side and allow the broth to boil.
Gently simmer for 1½ hours.

Once the broth is cooked remove
from the heat and carefully strain
through a tammy cloth, being careful
not to disturb the pad too much.
Check the seasoning.

Chicken mousse
Place the diced chicken, 100ml
of cream, egg yolk and salt into a
Pacojet beaker. Freeze to -20°C.
Once frozen, Pacojet three times.

Place into a metal bowl over ice
and beat in the remaining 150ml of
cream until smooth and shiny. Mix
in the chives and chervil, check the
seasoning and put into a piping bag.

Slow-cooked chicken wings
Cut the knuckle and the tip of each
wing off. Place the wings on a
stainless steel tray and sprinkle with
thyme, rock salt and crushed garlic.
Marinate for 4 hours.

Wash off the marinade under cold
running water and then dry. Place the
wings in a vacuum pack bag and seal,
place into a water bath at 75°C for 10
hours.

Remove the wings from the bag,
leave to just cool then remove the
two bones in the wing, being careful
not to tear the wing. Once you have
removed the bones pipe chicken
mousse into each wing then cover
with cling film, sealing the ends tight.
Put the wings into a steamer for 10
minutes, then keep warm.

Dried plums
Cut the plums in half and remove
the stone, being careful not to cause
damage. Lightly season the halves
with salt and a dust of icing sugar. Put
the plum halves skin down, flesh up
on to a tray and place in a dehydrator
at 57°C for 10 hours.

Brown rice and bacon
Place the washed rice into a pan,
season with salt and cover with 2.5cm
of water above the rice. Bring to the
boil on a high heat. Once the water
has nearly evaporated, turn the heat
down low, cover with a lid and allow
the rice to cook completely in the
steam for 13 minutes.

In a non-stick frying pan, fry the
bacon until just crispy. Drain off the
excess fat and mix into the steamed
rice, check seasoning and reserve.

Crispy skin
Cut the skin in half to make 4 pieces.
Lightly season with salt. Place the skin
flat between 2 metal plates and put
into a fryer at 160°C for 6-8 minutes
until the skin is crispy and golden.
Remove from the fryer and leave to
cool.

TO SERVE

Cut the ends off each steamed
chicken wing, place into a bowl, add
the dried plum and a small spoon of
the bacon and brown rice. Pour in the
broth, stand the chicken side up and
finish with a chiffonade of basil.

20O2

This year we'd grown the line-up to six chefs. I'd been chatting to Accrington College senior lecturer and old friend Neil Hogg about an educational link with a Swedish Cookery School, Matpedagogerna. He asked me to cook a six-course regional menu for 60 people at their Hotel School in Stockholm. When I was in Stockholm the senior lecturer, Stefan Brandhoffer, took me to a restaurant called Fredsgatan 12, and there I met the head chef Danyel Couet, who was a key player in the Swedish cookery team that won gold in the "Culinary Olympics" in 2000. I approached Danyel to cook at the 2002 Food Festival; he agreed and became the first of our many starred overseas chefs. That's how I recruited the first of the chefs for 2002.

I had known Brian for several years and cooked with him in Mauritius after winning the Wedgwood Chef and Potter competition in 2000 that led to him joining the bill that year – great to have a Yorkshireman of such note in the Red Rose county, an incredible character who we all have learnt to respect over the years. Everyone loved him red wine and

all! Then Phil Howard said he'd do it again and my very good friend Robbie Millar came on board. I met Robbie at the 1996 Michelin awards, which was the year we got our star. I was sitting with Robbie, Terry Laybourne, Tom Aikens and Eric Chavot and we all got merrily drunk. Robbie and I clicked and he became a very good friend of mine. Tragically, Robbie was killed in a car crash on 13th August 2005.

Germain Schwab opened the food festival; one of his courses being his famous tri-coloured cannelloni with a langoustine and chicken mousse, and sweetcorn sauce, and a beautiful chocolate pavlova with gold leaf to finish. Winteringham Fields was a truly great restaurant and one of only several two stars ever to be awarded in the north; having a two Michelin-starred Swiss chef to cook at Northcote was another great milestone.

Phil Howard got the first of many speeding offences on his way up here in his old Aston Martin. Phil was getting into his stride at that time. He did a roast turbot with hand-rolled macaroni, chanterelles and thyme, an

inspirational dish. One of the memorable incidents that happened that year was a Michelin inspection. It was at lunch service on the Tuesday prior to Phil's evening. We were open as normal for lunch in those days. The pastry chef had forgotten to make any ice cream on that day and, of course, this particular inspector ordered ice cream. So we had to rush around making the ice cream base, and getting it churned in what was a very old Robot Coupe in an incredibly busy kitchen. Funnily enough, after we'd finished the festival and Phil had gone back down to The Square, he phoned to say he'd been inspected on that day too – at dinner time. Sods law.

Robbie Millar did the best dish I think I've ever had with pheasant. It was a fricassée of pheasant with chestnuts and it was really imaginative, and a totally different way of cooking the bird. Instead of roasting it or cooking it whole, he cut the breast into goujons and quickly pan-roasted it off and put them into a chestnutty cream sauce – and it worked really well and went down tremendously. At that time his signature dish was a salad of pancetta and chicken liver with lentils and he did that wonderfully too.

Brian bounced in with classic British food coinciding with the release of his book on his life story *A Yorkshire Lad 'My Life with Recipes* – a tremendous rack of English veal finishing off with a classic English trifle, proving the point that simple things often can be the best.

Danyel did some wonderful dishes including a marinade of scallops with green chilli which went down fantastically well in the restaurant apart from Reg Johnson (The Chicken Man) and the Goosnargh gang. Danyel for his brushetta gourmand required a specific Rougie bloc foie gras which had been overlooked as a specific – we had only got normal foie gras – so we had to send someone all the way down to London to get it for him, which was rather expensive.

I wrapped up the festival for the first time on a Saturday, again matching wines with Charles Metcalfe, and it was the first time we used the ice cream (that later became infamous on The Great British Menu with Oliver Payton's dislike of cheese with desserts) in one of my favourite dishes, apple crumble soufflé with Lancashire cheese ice cream. There's a favourite saying of my business partner Craig that can be applied to this dish. It's an old Lancashire saying that goes "a kiss without a squeeze is like apple pie without the cheese".

We had a couple of late nights this year, particularly with Robbie Millar who was the life and soul of the party. He just wouldn't go to bed, especially when he had a good bottle of wine in his hands. He was the wild man of 2002 and the other guys were comparatively sedate in his wake.

BRIAN TURNER

"I love sitting round a table with friends, so to be able to provide food and drink that tastes good is what drives my passion; and a good old roast is my favourite."

OBSESSION
FESTIVAL
2002

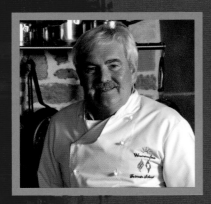

GERMAIN SCHWAB

"Some people are born with a talent: artists, poets, writers etc. I believe it is the same with cooking. You create; discover and satisfy an inner need to please others. From the age of seven I knew I wanted to cook. My grandparents ran a mountain restaurant in the Jura, Switzerland, raising their own livestock for the table; making cheese and cooking to please all who sat at their tables, and this was all I wanted to do. There is no greater joy for a chef than to watch his food being enjoyed and appreciated. If, at the end of the day, the 'great and the good' also like what you do then you can consider it a job well done and grab your five minutes of fame."

NIGEL HAWORTH

"To be obsessed with the quality of the ingredient is to be obsessed with the very essence of flavours."

ROBBIE MILLAR

"Robbie was obsessed with food, wine and restaurants. Shanks in Bangor County Down, which he ran with Shirley from 2004, reflected their eclectic yet contemporary style. He used the best of local ingredients, blended with Mediterranean and Asian influences. Robbie was awarded a Michelin Star in 1996 . He cooked every day and under his leadership Shanks was undoubtedly one of Ireland's finest restaurants. Robbie the man was warm, caring and exciting to be around, he lit up a room whenever he entered, and with Robbie we always had fun. As a chef with food he was intelligent, articulate and precise — he was an exceptional cook. A loving husband, a great family man and a true friend sadly missed."

DANYEL COUET

"My upbringing with a French father gave me a free path into genuine food culture. I have always loved the endless potential that comes with creating innovative courses with unexpected combinations based on the best of traditional cooking. I love the mixture of direct physical action together with an Obsession for the aesthetic output. There is always a new goal to achieve!"

PHIL HOWARD

"I guess this was the year of Robbie Millar — such a great lad and a fantastic cook. He is sadly missed but I had one of the longest, rambling and enjoyable food conversations I can recall with him. Hand rolled macaroni for 100? Second year, second mistake! My second trip to Northcote also enlightened me to the bond and relationship between supplier and chef. In London, it is business, here it appears to be a wholesome partnership. Impressive."

Quasis (Rump) of Venison with Chestnut, Mushrooms and Red Cabbage Compote, Gnocchi and Sauce Grand Veneur

Serves 6

Quasis (Rump) of Venison with Chestnut, Mushrooms and Red Cabbage Compote, Gnocchi and Sauce Grand Veneur

Serves 6

INGREDIENTS

Quasis of venison
1kg (approx 180g pp)
Rump of venison
4 soup spoons Dijon mustard
3 Garlic cloves
2 Garlic cloves, finely chopped
2 Sprigs of thyme
400g Sliced, fresh cep mushrooms
4 tbsp Duck fat
15ml Hare's blood
4g Green peppercorns
200ml Red burgundy wine
50ml Cognac
4 tbsp Redcurrant jelly
Freshly milled salt & pepper

Red cabbage compote
1kg Red cabbage, thinly sliced
2 Large shallots, thinly sliced
2 Cloves garlic, crushed
20 Cooked chestnuts
25ml Malt vinegar
20g Demerara sugar
20g Raisins
100ml Red burgundy wine
1 ltr Chicken stock
Zest and juice of one orange
1 soup spoon Duck fat
1 Bay leaf
1 Cinnamon stick
Pinch grated nutmeg
2 Cloves
4 Juniper berries
Salt & pepper

Potato gnocchi
1kg King Edward potatoes
1 Egg
300g Pasta flour
Salt & pepper
Grated nutmeg
50g Grated parmesan
Double cream
Olive oil

METHOD

Quasis of venison

Season the venison with freshly milled salt and pepper and roll in the Dijon mustard, cover and keep in the fridge overnight.

Preheat the oven to 220°C/425°F/ gas mark 7. In a roasting tray heat the duck fat, place the already seasoned quasis in the hot duck fat, seal and brown. Place into the oven with the sprigs of thyme and 3 whole cloves of garlic, and roast for 20 minutes. Remove from the roasting dish, cover with foil and leave to rest for 10 minutes. Remove all fat from the roasting dish and deglaze with a little water, keeping the juices to one side to finish the sauce later.

Pan fry the sliced ceps in duck fat until golden brown, add the finely chopped garlic cloves, cook for a few more seconds, place in a serving dish and deglaze the pan with half of the Cognac, once again keeping this for the sauce.

To finish the sauce, mix together all the deglazed juices in the pan. Add the red wine, the rest of the Cognac, the green peppercorns and redcurrant jelly. Bring to the boil and reduce slightly. Take off the heat and leave to cool a little; add to this the hare's blood a little at a time – it may not be necessary to use all the blood depending on the reduction already achieved.

Red cabbage compote

Into a heavy-based casserole dish place the duck fat, thinly sliced shallots and crushed cloves of garlic, cook gently until soft but not coloured. To this add the juice of the orange, red wine, vinegar and the chicken stock, keep simmering gently. Then add the raisins, bay leaf, cinnamon stick, nutmeg, cloves, juniper berries, the zest of orange and the sugar. Bring to the boil and cook for 5 minutes, season to taste. Add the thinly sliced red cabbage, cook for 25 minutes. In the last 10 minutes of cooking time add the chestnuts. Remove the cinnamon stick before serving. The cabbage will keep for several days in the fridge (without the added chestnuts).

Potato gnocchi

Preheat the oven to 220°C/425°F/gas mark 7. Wash and bake the potatoes until soft, remove the insides and pass through a fine sieve. Place in a bowl. Season then beat in the egg quickly. Add two handfuls of the pasta flour and bind together until a silky smooth dough is achieved. Place the rest of the flour on to a pastry table, tip out the dough and knead until all the flour is incorporated. Do not overwork the dough. Divide the dough into 4 and roll into long sausage shapes the thickness of your finger, cut at an angle into 2cm long pieces.

Bring a large pan of salted water to the boil and add the gnocchi, reduce to a simmer for 2 to 3 minutes – the gnocchi will rise to the top when cooked. Remove from the pan with a sieve, drain and place in a tray, sprinkle with olive oil. The cooked gnocchi will keep in the fridge for 2 to 3 days.

Place the gnocchi into an ovenproof dish, pour over a little double cream and sprinkle with parmesan, grate over a little nutmeg, cook for 10 minutes until starting to colour.

TO SERVE

Sauce the plates, add a little of the red cabbage, slice the rump and place on top, add the ceps and gnocchi.

MILLE-FEUILLE OF RED MULLET AND AUBERGINES WITH A VINAIGRETTE OF SARDINES AND WILD ROCKET

Serves 8

INGREDIENTS

Sardine vinaigrette
1 Red onion, finely sliced
Salt
200ml Olive oil
12 Sardine fillets
100g Plain flour
6 Garlic cloves, crushed
6 Plum tomatoes, roughly chopped
1 Sprig of basil
Pinch of sugar
250ml Tinned, peeled tomato pulp
or passata
Zests of ¼ lemon and 1/8 orange

Aubergine
4 Round Italian aubergines
Salt & pepper
10ml Extra virgin olive oil
8 Leaves of basil, finely sliced

Mille-feuille
16 Sheets feuille de bric
Olive oil
1 tsp Ground cumin

Mullet
16 Fillets of red mullet from 340g fish
Olive oil
Flour
8 Leaves of basil, finely sliced

Garnish
2 Bunches wild rocket

METHOD

Sardine vinaigrette
In a heavy based ovenproof pan, sweat the red onion with a pinch of salt, in half the olive oil. Dip the sardine fillet, skin side down, into the flour to lightly coat the skin and pan fry, skin side down, in the remaining olive oil. When they are nearly cooked, turn over, add the garlic and swirl the pan for 30 seconds. Tip into the pan with the onions. You may need to do this in two batches. Add the tomatoes, basil, sugar and tomato pulp. Stir briefly, cover with a lid and cook in a slow oven at 110°C/225°F/ gas mark ¼ for half an hour.

Remove from the oven and push, carefully, through a fine sieve. This should give rise to a rich, oily, sardine vinaigrette. Add the zests, stir and reserve at room temperature.

Aubergine
Cut the aubergines in half, season with salt and pepper, brush with some of the extra virgin olive oil, wrap in foil and bake until completely tender at 170°C/335°F/gas mark 3½. This will take about 45 minutes. Carefully scrape out the flesh and drain in a colander for half an hour. Transfer to a bowl, add the remaining extra virgin olive oil, and break down the aubergine with the back of a fork. Adjust the seasoning if necessary and finish with basil leaves. Reserve at room temperature.

Mille-feuille
Lay 8 sheets of feuille de bric out in front of you. Brush sparingly with olive oil, season with the cumin and cover each with a second sheet and press. Out of these, cut 16 ovals measuring 10x5cm and bake until golden between parchment paper, pressed between two baking sheets at 160°C/325°F/gas mark 3. Reserve at room temperature.

TO SERVE

Pan fry the red mullet fillets in olive oil until just cooked. Start them, lightly floured, skin side down and after 1½ minutes turn them for half a minute to finish. Place the fillets on a tray and brush liberally with sardine vinaigrette.

Place a tiny bit of aubergine in the centre of each of 8 plates. Cover with a sheet of feuille de bric. Spoon a small layer of aubergine over this and top with a fillet of red mullet. Repeat for a second layer. Spoon a little bit of sardine vinaigrette around the plate and garnish with a few rocket leaves dressed in olive oil.

Seared Scallops with a Purée of Carrot and Ginger, Crispy Carrots, Chinese Five Spice

Serves 4

INGREDIENTS

12 Medium king scallops
Lemon juice
Carrot and ginger purée (see below)
Carrot crisps (see below)
Watercress purée (see below)
Chinese five spice

Carrot and ginger purée

100g Carrots, sliced thinly
10g Grated root ginger
10g Butter
100g Cream

Watercress purée

40g Parsley
240g Watercress leaves
50ml Cream
2g Roast garlic
3g Salt

Carrot crisps

2 Peeled carrots

METHOD

Place the scallops into a hot non-stick frying pan, press slightly, cook for 2-3 minutes until golden on one side turn the scallops over, add a squeeze of lemon juice and cook for a further minute. Remove from the pan and place onto absorbent paper.

Carrot and ginger purée

Sweat the sliced carrots and ginger with the butter for 3-4 minutes, without colouring them. Season, add the cream and cook for 10-12 minutes until the carrots are soft. Place into a blender and blend until smooth, pass though a fine sieve and check the seasoning.

Watercress purée

Blanch the parsley in boiling water for 2 minutes and the watercress for 1 minute, refresh in iced water. Squeeze the watercress and parsley, removing all the excess water. Place in a Pacojet, add the cream, garlic and seasoning then freeze to -20°C.

Remove from the Pacojet, process, then place in a small pan and gently reheat.

Check seasoning and put into a squeezy bottle.

Carrot crisps

Slice the carrot lengthways, as thinly as possible, ideally on a mandolin. Deep fry at 160°C until golden and crispy. Remove from the fryer and season with salt.

TO SERVE

Put 7 lines of carrot and ginger purée across the plate. Place the 3 scallops in the middle, 6 dots of watercress purée around and finish with the carrot crisps and a dusting of Chinese five spice.

ROAST RACK OF ENGLISH VEAL, BUTTER BRAISED CARROTS AND PARSLEY POTATOES

Serves 6

INGREDIENTS

Small rack of veal (1.3kg with bones)
1 tsp Turmeric
1 tsp Cumin
1 tsp Paprika
1 tsp Oil
57g Butter
24 Even-sized new potatoes
57g Butter
Salt & pepper
1 tbsp Chopped parsley
450g Carrots
Pinch sugar
57g Butter
113g Butter
1 glass Dry white wine
½ glass Madeira
3 Shallots, finely chopped
236ml Chicken stock
1 tbsp Chopped parsley

METHOD

Trim the veal leaving the eye of the meat and the rib bones.

Mix the turmeric, cumin and paprika.

Colour the veal meat side in a hot roasting tray or frying pan then leave to cool.

Rub with the mix and leave to rest for 24 hours.

Heat the oil and 57g butter. Add the veal and roast in a hot oven 200°C/400°F/gas mark 6 for 10 minutes, turn down to 180°C/350°F/gas mark 4 and roast pink to medium, for approximately 30 minutes, take out and leave to rest.

Meanwhile cook the new potatoes in salted water, drain, season, add 57g of butter and the parsley, keep warm.

While the potatoes are cooking cut the carrots and cook in boiling salted water with a pinch of sugar; when cooked drain and add 57g butter, season and keep warm.

Remove the veal from the tray and keep it warm. Pour away any excess fat. Put one-third of the chopped shallots into a roasting tray. Add the white wine and Madeira and reduce by two-thirds.

In a clean pan, sweat off the rest of the shallots in 57g butter. Then add the stock and reduce by half. Strain the wine mixture into this sauce and reduce to desired taste.

TO SERVE

Stir in cold butter to the sauce as desired, re-season, add parsley and serve with the veal, potatoes and carrots.

BRUSCHETTA "GOURMANDE", BLACK TRUFFLE AND FIG

Serves 4

INGREDIENTS

240g Fillet of beef
4 Slices of brioche
200g Terrine of duck liver (foie gras)
2 Figs, peeled and cut into 8 wedges
1 Small black truffle
1 tbsp Mayonnaise
Salt & black pepper
Salad leaves or watercress for garnish
400ml Red port
2 tsp Sherry vinegar
2 tbsp Olive oil

Port vinaigrette
400ml Red port
2 tsp Sherry vinegar
2 tbsp Olive oil

METHOD

Roll the fillet in cling film and freeze lightly. Slice thinly and put on cling film. Grate half of the truffle finely and mix with the mayonnaise. Slice the rest of the truffle and keep for a garnish.

Toast the brioche and allow to cool. Put the terrine of duck liver on top. Place the 4 quarters of fig on the duck liver. Then put the thin slices of the fillet above the terrine and top with the truffle mayonnaise and slices of truffle. Garnish with salad leaves or watercress and serve with the port vinaigrette.

Port vinaigrette
Pour the port into a heated pan and reduce to 100ml. Add the sherry vinegar, salt, black pepper and olive oil. Take the figs and place in a small bowl and macerate for 30 minutes in half of the port reduction.

APPLE CRUMBLE SOUFFLÉ, LANCASHIRE CHEESE ICE CREAM

Serves 4

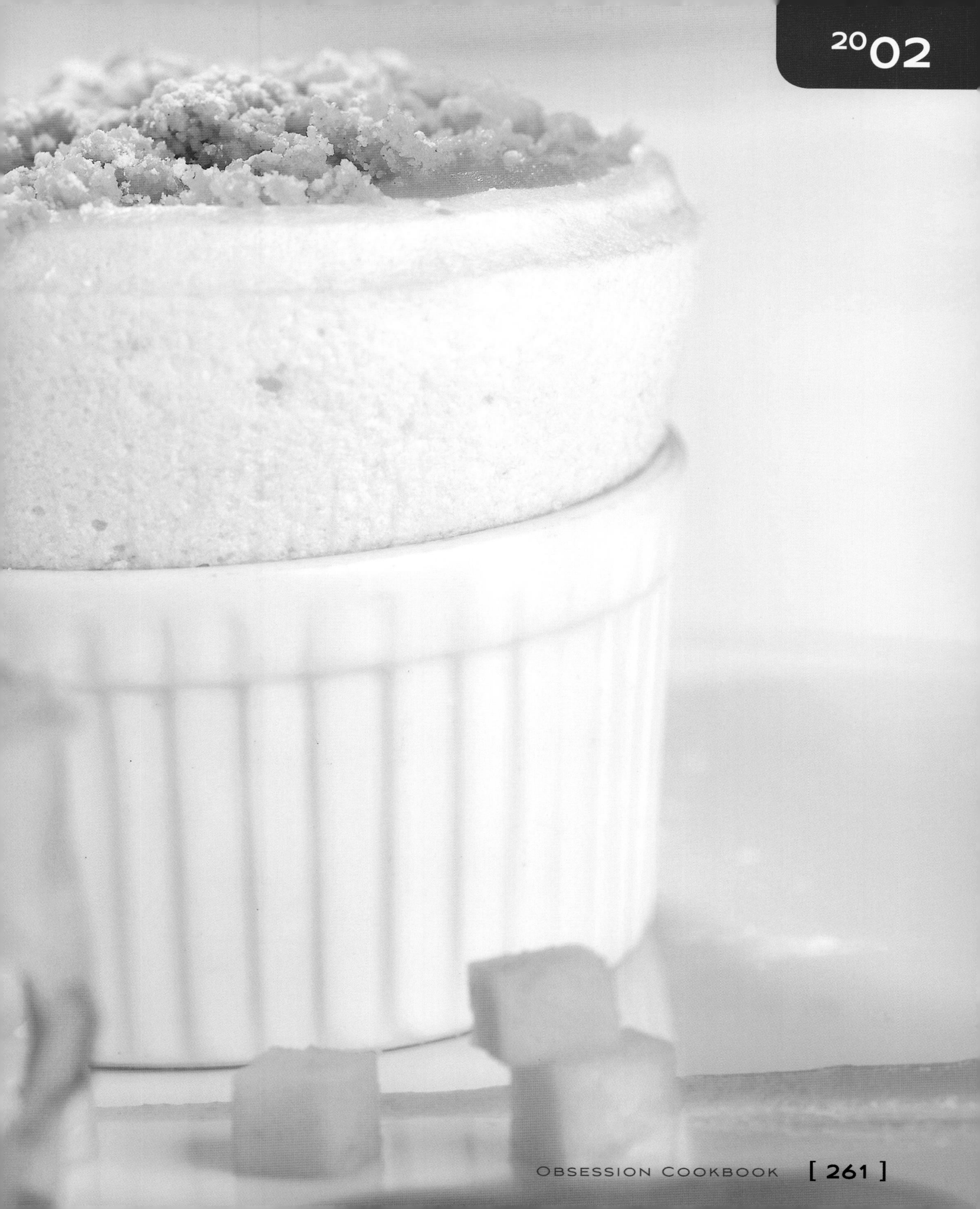

Apple Crumble Soufflé, Lancashire Cheese Ice Cream

Serves 4

INGREDIENTS

Apple soufflé
150g Egg whites
75g Caster sugar
300g Apple purée (see below)
Crumble topping (see below)

Apple purée
500g Bramley apples, cored and thinly sliced
200g Caster sugar

Crumble topping
90g Plain flour
55g Unsalted butter
55g Granulated sugar

Lancashire cheese ice cream
210ml Double cream
210ml Milk
5 Egg yolks
90g Caster sugar
150g Philadelphia cheese
75g Medium Lancashire cheese, grated

Apple compote
Granny Smith apple

Apple baskets
2 Cox's apples, medium size
Caster sugar

METHOD

Apple soufflé

You will need 4 ramekins, twice buttered and lined with sugar.

Whisk the egg whites to soft peaks, then slowly add the sugar until fully incorporated.

Put the apple purée into a clean bowl. Mix in one-third of the egg whites and then carefully fold in the remainder. Place in a piping bag.

Half fill the ramekins with the soufflé mix, put 1 teaspoon of apple purée in the middle, pipe the rest of the mix on top, put 1 more teaspoon of apple purée on top and spread evenly. Tap the bottom of the ramekin then, with the point of a small knife, clean the lip of the ramekin (this stops the soufflé from possibly sticking). Finish with a generous amount of crumble on top and bake at 180°C/350°F/gas mark 4 for 7-8 minutes.

Apple purée

Place the finely sliced apples and sugar in a vacuum pack bag and seal tightly. Cook at 70°C for 15 minutes until the apples are soft. Remove from the vacuum pack bag into the Thermomix and blitz until smooth. Pass through a fine sieve and reserve.

Crumble topping

Rub together the flour and butter to resemble breadcrumbs. Stir in the sugar. Place on a metal tray and bake for 15 minutes at 180°C/350°F/gas mark 4.

Lancashire cheese ice cream

Boil the cream and milk together. Mix together the egg yolks and caster sugar. Add one-third of the cream/milk mixture to the egg yolks and caster sugar. Add the remainder of the milk and cream. Pass through a fine sieve. Allow to cool until the mixture is just warm then blitz in the grated Lancashire cheese and Philadelphia. Churn in an ice cream machine and reserve.

Apple compote

Cut the apple into small diced pieces. Blanch for 10 seconds in sweetened acidulated (with lemon juice added) water. Drain and reserve.

Apple baskets

Slice the apples thinly on a mandolin. Place on a silpat on a flat tray. Sprinkle with caster sugar. Bake at 150°C/300°F/gas mark 2 for approximately 10-15 minutes until golden. Remove from the oven. Place the apple rings in a non-stick dariole mould, overlapping as you go – the mould will take approximately 5 rings. Allow to set and simply remove.

TO SERVE

Put a small amount of apple purée and 4 pieces of diced apple compote onto the plate, followed by an apple basket with a large scoop of Lancashire cheese ice cream and the hot soufflé.

20O1

This was the first ever Festival of Food and Wine (Obsession); it was a daunting prospect and understandably there were a lot of nerves flying about. We produced a really low-key brochure on a very tight budget. I remember talking to all the chefs about the essence of the festival, which was to cook in an environment that was relaxing, professional and above all friendly, trying to bring people together as a gathering of friends actually cooking and relaxing, exchanging views and experiences. In that sort of environment you get to see the real chef, the real person and their families more intimately. Over the years many strong and lasting relationships have been forged, many of the festival chefs have since become great friends.

The festival began its infancy with Terry Laybourne on the Tuesday night, cooking some typically great 21 Queen Street food. Terry is a legend in Newcastle and he started the festival with a warm, set potato terrine with caviar which was outstanding, it was simply wonderful. He also did a tempura lobster with fennel; stunningly crisp and with great flavours.

At the beginning I didn't know whether we'd fill any of the nights and I certainly didn't know if we'd fill mine, which is why we asked Charles Metcalfe, the respected wine critic and great friend to come and join us – we did it as a wine and food night, so that we didn't fall flat on our faces. We were basically

dead in January in those days, so it was very much a suck-it-and-see scenario; that evening I cooked a selection of Spanish tapas as we were doing an evening of Spanish food and wine matching with Charles. I remember I had to bring two extra fryers into the kitchen to cook the king prawn and squid for the Spanish tapas. I also prepared figs in Pedro Ximénez sherry, which was well received.

Then the Thursday was the start of Phil Howard's ten-year pilgrimage to the North, a Two-Star Chef cooking in Lancashire was a real coup. He did his legendary dish of tortellini of crab with herb – which will live with me forever – among many other exciting things that he did on that night. The evening went down an absolute storm to much acclaim from our most discerning guests who now visit The Square in London on a regular basis.

Nick Nairn closed the festival on the Friday and cooked a great array of dishes – one which I'll always remember is the truffled honey with the Cashel Blue and toasted walnut bread, which was just simplicity itself. Of course, one of his signature dishes is the salad of wood pigeon with black pudding, which was wonderful. That wrapped up the first year, and we hadn't a clue whether it had been successful, but we'd managed to fill the nights and laid the foundation stones of success, and it was onwards and upwards to 2002.

Wednesday
24th January

Charles Metcalfe
presents
A Truly Spanish Wine Evening
with genuine Spanish cabaret from the
London-based
Montuno Trio

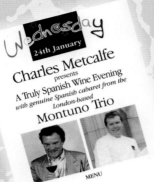

MENU

Tapas –
A selection of Spanish delicacies

✦ ✦ ✦

Confit Shoulder of Lamb studded with
Rosemary and Garlic, Poached Plum Tomatoes,
French Beans, Puree Potatoes

✦ ✦ ✦

Poached Figs in Pedro Ximenez Sherry,
Caramelised Saffron Bread

✦ ✦ ✦

Freshly Ground Coffee and Petit Fours

Friday
26th January

Nick Nairn

MENU

Gateau of Hot Smoked Salmon, Avocado and Mango
Salsa, Langoustine Vinaigrette

✦ ✦ ✦

Warm Salad Wood Pigeon, Stornoway Black Pudding,
Fifeshire Bacon and Cumberland Sauce topped with
Crispy Parsnips

✦ ✦ ✦

Fillet of John Dory,
Cabbage and Bacon, Mini Fondant Potato,
Caviar Butter Sauce, Balsamic Roast Cherry Tomatoes

✦ ✦ ✦

Toasted Walnut Bread, Cashel Blue, Truffled Honey

✦ ✦ ✦

Hot Raspberry Souffle, Raspberry Sorbet

Thursday
25th January

Philip Howard

MENU

Tortellini of Crab with Herbs

✦ ✦ ✦

Ballotine of Foie Gras, Poulet De Bresse
and Artichokes

✦ ✦ ✦

Papillotte of Red Mullet with Cre

✦ ✦ ✦

Herb Crusted Saddle
with Shallot Puree and

✦ ✦ ✦

Date and Honey
Crème Fraiche

✦ ✦ ✦

No

Sunday 27th January

JAZZ BRUNCH
FEATURING KENNY DAVERN
Northcote, Lancashire

MISSISSIPPI RICE BALLS

SHRIMP RISOTTO WITH CUCUMBER
AND JALAPÉNO
Sauvignon Blanc, Marlborough, South Island,
Ponder Estate, 2001

ROAST LEMON PEPPER DUCK,
RED WINE VINEGAR SAUCE
Gigondas, Domaine Bernard Cassan, 1998

PUMPKIN BREAD PUDDING,
CALIFORNIA GRAPEFRUITS
Sauvignon Blanc, Late harvest, Semi-Dulcee,
Bornos, 2000

Tuesday
23rd January

Terry Laybourne MBE

MENU

Potato Terrine with Caviar

✦ ✦ ✦

Celeriac Soup with Black Truffle

✦ ✦ ✦

Tempura of Lobster and Fennel
Asian Cream

✦ ✦ ✦

Reg's Duck – Cooked 5 Ways!

✦ ✦ ✦

Coconut Pannacotta

"Cooking gives me a means of expression, in fact, it's the medium through which I communicate the best. And it continues to challenge me. There's always something new to discover and that's why I enjoy it as much now as I did 25 years ago."

NICK NAIRN

OBSESSION FESTIVAL

"To evolve this Obsession is a journey and an achievement that has no end."

NIGEL HAWORTH

TERRY LAYBOURNE

"My Obsession with food comes from the fact that what we do is effectively in a permanent state of flux. The product today is different from the product tomorrow — food is alive and is constantly changing, which means I have to continually adapt and shift in order to move forward. I like to think I put myself at the service of the food rather than view the food as a medium I then need to manipulate in order to work with — I try to work hard to do as little as possible to the ingredients and let them speak for themselves. "

"I felt I was only there in order to demonstrate that Northcote is an equal opportunity employer — the token southerner! Date soufflé in an unfamiliar kitchen — first year, first mistake. I had never really met Craig and Nigel before but their mark was made. What impressed me most was their display of Lancastrian hospitality."

PHIL HOWARD

Coconut Panna Cotta with Tropical Fruits

Serves 4

INGREDIENTS

Panna cotta
300g Tinned, sweet coconut cream
335ml Whipping cream
4 Gelatine leaves
1 tbsp Malibu

Syrup
1 Clove
¼ tsp Chinese 5 spice
Zest from 1 lime
Zest from 1 orange
Zest from ¼ lemon
1 Vanilla pod, split
1 Bulb lemon grass
½ tsp Grated ginger
2 Coriander seeds
75g Sugar
500ml Water

Tropical fruits
1 Small ripe mango
3 Passion fruits
1 Kiwi fruit
1 Slice pineapple (20mm thick)
1 Orange
2 Mint leaves (finely shredded)
Mango sorbet (to serve)

METHOD

Panna cotta
Soak the gelatine in cold water. Bring the whipping cream to a boil, add the soaked gelatine and pour on to the coconut cream. Pass through a fine chinoise (sieve) and stir in the Malibu. Divide between 4 dariole moulds. Place in a refrigerator for 3-4 hours to set.

Syrup
Mix everything together, bring to a full boil and allow to cool.

Tropical fruits
Peel the mango and cut into neat dice. Scoop out the pulp from the passion fruits, peel the kiwi and pineapple and cut into neat dice. Segment the orange and cut into chunks. Strain the cold syrup over the fruit and chill for 2 hours.

TO SERVE

Turn out the panna cotta into the centre of a chilled dessert plate. Spoon a little of the fruit salad and its syrup around the edge of the plate. Add a spoonful of mango sorbet. Decorate with mint leaves.

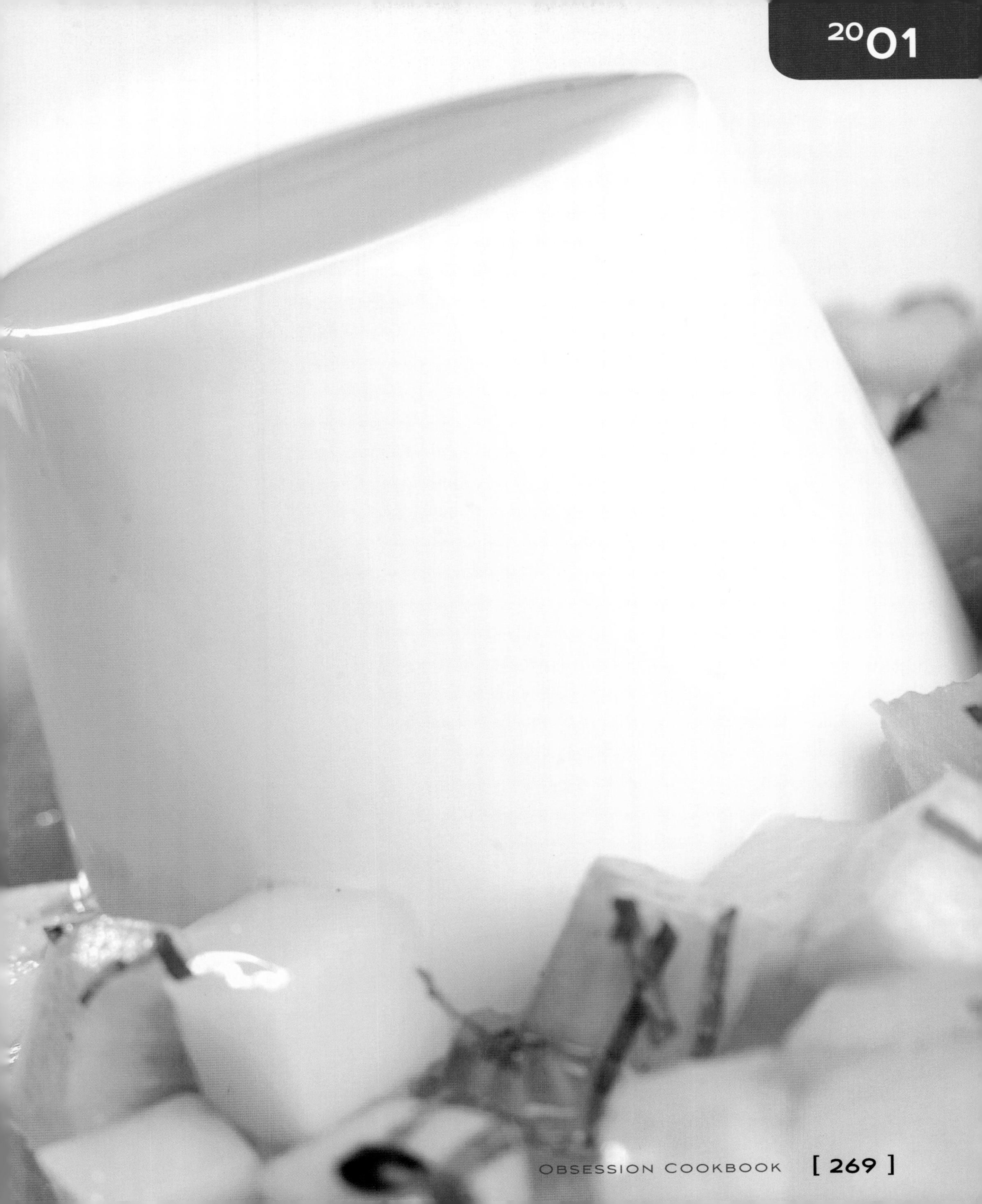

Confit Shoulder of Lamb Studded with Rosemary and Garlic, Poached Plum Tomatoes, French Beans, Purée Potatoes

Serves 10

Confit Shoulder of Lamb Studded with Rosemary and Garlic, Poached Plum Tomatoes, French Beans, Purée Potatoes

Serves 10

INGREDIENTS

2.4kg Boneless shoulder of lamb
110g Coarse sea salt
10g Picked rosemary (small plushes/sprigs)
25g Sliced peeled garlic (cut the cloves into 3, lengthways)
110g Coarse sea salt
Duck fat
Mash potatoes (see below)
500g French beans (see below)
10 Plum tomatoes (see below)
Roast gravy (see below)

Roast gravy

250g Banana shallots, sliced
350ml Madeira
1 ltr Lamb stock
750ml Chicken stock
50g Butter

Mash potatoes

1.6kg Peeled and chopped Maris Piper or desiree potatoes
300ml Milk
100g Butter
Salt

Poached plum tomatoes

10 Medium-size plum tomatoes
100ml White wine
200ml Olive oil
30 Slices of garlic clove
Good handful of rosemary
Good pinch of salt
Few turns of the peppermill

French beans

500g Extra fine French beans (top and tail)
50g Butter
Sea salt
Black pepper

METHOD

Take the shoulder of lamb and salt overnight (approximately 12 hours), wash off the excess salt under cold running water then dry the shoulder thoroughly with a kitchen cloth. Make small incisions on both sides of the shoulder and stud with the rosemary and garlic. Slow cook the shoulder in duck fat for 3-3½ hours at 140°C/275°F/gas mark 1, make sure the lamb is completely covered in the duck fat, then cover with silicon paper and tin foil.

When the lamb is ready remove from the oven and allow to cool a little before removing it from the pan and placing it on to a tray to cool. Allow the shoulder to set, then place onto a carving board and, with a very sharp knife, cut the shoulder into 10 pieces.

When ready to serve the lamb place the shoulder pieces under the bottom of a salamander or in a hot oven 200°C/400°F/gas mark 6 until crispy on the outside.

Roast gravy

Sweat off the shallots lightly to caramelise, add Madeira, reduce by three-quarters, add the lamb and chicken stock. Reduce down to the desired consistency and pass through a tammy cloth, blend in the butter and reserve.

Mash potatoes

Place the potatoes into a pan of water and boil until cooked. Then strain away the water, add the milk, butter and salt and beat until smooth. Put the mash into a piping bag and keep warm.

Poached plum tomatoes

Gently poach the tomatoes in the white wine, olive oil, garlic and rosemary. Season with salt and pepper, reserve when ready.

French beans

Take the French beans and boil in lightly salted water until al dente, take the beans out and refresh in iced water. When the beans are cold pour off the ice and water and keep them on a small tray ready for use. The beans are reheated in a little butter, a few drops of water and seasoned with salt and pepper.

TO SERVE

Take a large white pasta bowl and place a quenelle of hot mash to one side. Put the shoulder of lamb at the side of the mash then add the poached tomato, garlic and rosemary. Put the French beans on top, pour over the gravy and serve.

TORTELLINI OF CRAB WITH HERBS

Serves 8

Tortellini of Crab with Herbs
Serves 8

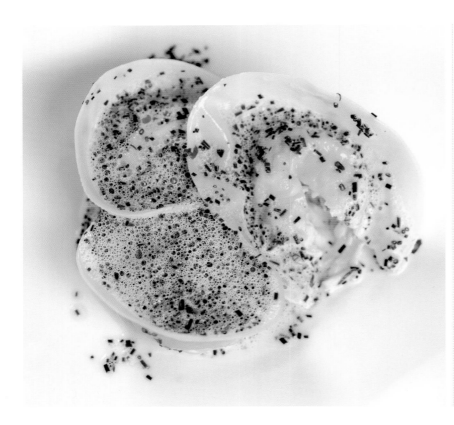

INGREDIENTS

325g '00' pasta flour
12 Eggs
4 Yolks
Salt
1 tbsp Olive oil
200g Scallops, out of the shell, skirts reserved
200ml Double cream
Juice of ½ lemon
400g White crab meat
4 Basil leaves, finely sliced
2 Shallots, finely sliced
½ Head of fennel, finely sliced
1 tbsp Olive oil
1 Star anise
10 Fennel seeds
10 Coriander seeds
250ml Champagne
300ml Water
100g Crème fraîche
20 Tarragon leaves, finely chopped
1 Bunch of chives, finely chopped
½ Bunch chervil, finely chopped

METHOD

To make the pasta dough place the flour, the eggs and 3 yolks in a food processor with a pinch of salt and a tablespoon of olive oil. Blend until the mix turns to a crumb. If it tries to clump into a dough, add a bit more flour. The pasta dough must be firm or making the tortellini will be trying to say the least. Turn the mix onto a work surface, press together firmly and briefly knead into a dough. Wrap tightly and chill.

Crab mix

First of all make the mousse. Blend the scallops in a chilled food processor bowl with a generous pinch of salt. Scrape down the sides of the bowl during this process. Add the remaining egg yolk and blend for 30 seconds. Re-chill in the fridge.

Now place this scallop purée into a decent sized bowl set over ice. With the use of a wooden spoon incorporate the double cream, bit by bit, while beating vigorously. Once all the cream is added season with lemon juice and chill. To confirm you have made a good mousse place half a teaspoon of this mix in a pan of simmering water. Remove from the heat. The mousse should cook – becoming light and springy in texture. If it 'splits' and disperses across the surface you have probably added the cream too fast or not incorporated it with enough vigour. Taste the mousse to check for seasoning. Now mix the mousse with the crab and add the basil. Mix and reserve in the fridge.

Sauce

This is a simple, fresh sauce and should be made quickly. Rub the scallop skirts (the frill running around the shell) with plenty of salt to clean. Rinse under running water. In a shallow heavy based pan sweat the shallots and fennel together in olive oil until soft. Add a pinch of salt, the star anise, fennel seeds and coriander seeds. Cook over a high heat for one minute – do not colour.

Add the scallop skirts. These will release liquid. Reduce until this has all gone. Add the Champagne and similarly reduce. Add 300ml water, bring to the boil and cook gently for 5 minutes. Pass through a fine sieve into a small pan, add the crème fraîche and whisk. Taste and adjust the seasoning if necessary. Reserve in the fridge.

To make the ravioli

Roll out the pasta dough and cut into discs 5cm in diameter and no more than 2mm thick. You will need 24 discs but roll out a few extra! Cover a plate with cling film, place the discs on top, covering immediately so they do not dry out. Place a large pan of water on to boil. Have a large bowl of iced water to refresh the ravioli and a bag of flour to hand and dust the work surface lightly. Divide the crab mix into 24 little spoonfuls on another plate and keep chilled.

Take the first disc, put it through the pasta machine to take it to 1mm thick. Turn the machine now to the penultimate setting to roll the disc once more. You should end up with an oval approximately 12x10cm. Put the crab mix in the centre, fold the disc over and press to seal. Do not have excess flour or the pasta will not stick. Now pick up the half made raviolis in your left hand with the curve of the pasta running above your fingertips. Gently holding one side of this inbetween your thumb and index finger wrap the other end around your thumb and pinch firmly to secure. Keep your hands dusted with flour. Once all 24 are made, blanch them for 2 minutes in the salted water, refresh in the iced water, drain and reserve chilled until required.

TO SERVE

Reheat the tortellini in a large pan of preheated, salted water for 3 minutes. Drain and divide among 8 bowls. Heat up the sauce. Blend with a hand blender to aerate, add the herbs, briefly blend and spoon over the ravioli.

WARM SALAD OF WOOD PIGEON, STORNOWAY BLACK PUDDING, FIFESHIRE BACON AND CUMBERLAND SAUCE, TOPPED WITH CRISPY PARSNIPS

Serves 6

Cooked properly – nicely rosy pink – pigeon (without the rubbery skin) is one of my favourite game birds and available all year round. There are certain flavours that are just made for each other, and the pigeon and black pudding combo is one of them. Although my natural preference is for the fantastic black pudding from Stornoway (comes in a thick log and has no great gobbits of fat in it!), other local black puddings can be used instead. The parsnip crisps can be cut two ways – long and ribbon-like so that they curl around each other, or into rounds like normal crisps. This was something of a signature dish in my Braeval days.

INGREDIENTS

Cumberland sauce
500g Redcurrant jelly
250ml Ruby port
Juice and grated zest of 2 lemons
Juice and grated zest of 2 oranges
1 tsp Ground cinnamon
2 tsp English mustard

Salad
50g Puy lentils, soaked overnight
8 Slices Fifeshire streaky bacon
3 Slices Stornoway black pudding
4 Skinned wood pigeon breasts
Sea salt and freshly ground black pepper
Sunflower oil for deep-frying, plus 1 tbsp
150g Parsnips, thinly sliced lengthways or rounds
150g Mixed washed salad leaves
½ Red onion, sliced paper thin
3 tbsp Extra virgin olive oil
1 tsp Aged sherry vinegar (or more to taste)
2 tbsp Water
1 Shallot, finely diced
Sea salt and freshly ground black pepper

METHOD

Preheat the oven to 220°C/425°F/gas mark 7.

Cumberland sauce
Place all the ingredients into a saucepan and bring to the boil. Skim away the froth and reduce over a medium heat for approximately 30 minutes. Strain through a fine sieve and cool. When cold, it should have the consistency of runny honey. This zingy, fruity sauce keeps sfor up to eight weeks in the fridge. I store mine in a squeezy bottle so that I can easy drizzle it around the plate.

Salad
Drain the lentils and put them in a saucepan with just enough water to cover and cook them very slowly for eight to ten minutes until tender. Drain the lentils again and put them in a bowl.

Lay the sliced bacon and black pudding on a tray lined with baking parchment and pop them into the oven to cook for 3-4 minutes. When the bacon is crisp and the black pudding cooked, remove from the oven, drain the bacon on kitchen paper then crumble to break it up. Cut each slice of black pudding into quarters. Keep warm.

Season the pigeon breasts with salt and pepper. Heat a frying pan until it's very hot, add 1 tbsp sunflower oil and lay the breasts skinned side down. Sear the pigeon

breasts for about two minutes on each side. Remove from the pan to a warm tray and allow to rest in a warm place for at least 10 minutes. Keep hold of the frying pan and do not wash.

While the pigeon is resting, heat the oil to 190°C/375°F/gas mark 5 or until a bread cube turns golden in 20 seconds. Deep-fry the parsnips until golden. Drain and leave them on a sheet of kitchen paper until required. Sprinkle with salt.

Slice the pigeon breasts thinly – about a dozen slices per breast (they should still be very pink inside) – and put in a bowl with the black pudding and bacon. Have the salad leaves mixed with the onion ready in a separate bowl.

TO SERVE

At the very last moment, mix the oil, vinegar, water, chopped shallot and lentils together, season well

and use to deglaze the pigeon pan, heating it through at the same time. Once reduced by half, pour over the leaves and toss gently with your hands to coat. Finally, carefully mix the leaves with the pigeon, black pudding and bacon. Divide between four shallow bowls or plates, drizzle with Cumberland sauce and top each pile with some crispy parsnips. Serve immediately before it all goes soggy!

WINE MAN

Over the 11 years of its term to date, Obsession has been lauded for its sophisticated and innovative cuisine. But one very crucial factor of the event's success is the wine, which, over the years, has become Craig Bancroft's labour of love. For the first year, Craig enlisted the expert help of wine critic Charles Metcalfe, with whom he liaised to choose the appropriate wines for each dish of the festival. But the following year Craig, who considers himself a wine enthusiast rather than an expert, felt he wanted to take on the wine element.

"It started in 2002 with me choosing a flight of wine to go with each chef's menu," he says. "It was very daunting because you have to understand the chef's food in order to pick an accompanying wine, and in terms of actually getting the menus off the chefs, this is usually quite a last minute thing. I'd normally get them just ten days prior to event, so I set myself a difficult task. Sometimes I'd ask Nigel to mock up a dish to help me with the flavours. "

Once Craig has the often-elusive menu from a particular chef in his hands, his next stage is to look at it carefully and think about which flavours would work with which wines. He also talks to that particular chef's sommelier for some guidance, and to get a better steer on the wine. "Every dish is matched by a different wine, to give the diner a better experience," says Craig, who has rarely repeated the same wine twice in any one festival.

Creating a wine list to sate the often exacting standards of each particular chef is a challenge in itself, as Craig found out in 2007, when choosing wines for Raymond Blanc. "I was invited to attended The Champagne Academy of 2005 with his sommelier, Xavier Rousset (now of Texture Restaurant London), then after I'd chosen them I called him and he said they looked good. But when Raymond showed up he wanted to taste them all, and was just about to try and change them when I slipped into conversation that they had partly been chosen by his sommelier."

"Some chefs are precious, and there are some who won't have non-French wines on menu, but most have been good fun. Paul Cunningham made us have a very expensive bottle of wine from a Danish vineyard that I couldn't match with anything, and that no one drank."

So where does Craig's enthusiasm for matching wine with food come from? He puts it down to his love of food and his gourmet upbringing. "My parents were real gourmands," he says. "From a very young age we ate at one, two and three Michelin-starred restaurants all over the world. When you're brought up like that good food and wine becomes a way of life, as it has for me and my children now. It's quite embarrassing when we're in public because even my kids can say where they think a wine is from and occasionally be spot on," he chuckles.

Craig sees his passion for food as an advantage when choosing wines for the festival, and something that gives him the edge over most sommeliers. "My first love is food,

which is good because it means that I look at wine in a different way to most sommeliers. The choices I make are more to do with my food than my wine knowledge," he says. "What I'm looking for is what is going to go best with a certain dish – so I'm searching for flavours that match ingredients. Of course sommeliers are incredibly good at what they do, but many don't tend to eat that much and normally concentrate on the wine rather than the food. For a food and wine matching, you need to be equally enthusiastic."

Within the week of the festival, Craig tries to create intrigue, excitement and surprise. But he goes even further than that to give the diner some variety. "Usually in my flight I try to use a different country in each course unless I am working with the origin of the chef or his restaurant as was the case of Dieter Koschina in 2006 where the wine were in the main Portuguese." Though Northcote dabbled with wine sponsorship for some of the festivals, Craig put a stop to this because he found it too restrictive. "We could have got a lot of financial underpinning for the nights, but I'm not a wine prostitute," he says. "Sometimes with the sponsored nights I couldn't find the wines with the flavour I needed, and I realised that it wasn't helping us give the client the best delivery, so I stopped it."

In terms of wines that have particularly stood out during the festivals, Craig remembers a Pinot Noir he matched with Phil Howard's roasted foie gras with raisin purée pain d'epice and a sweet and sour glaze in 2007. "It was a particularly memorable wine," he says. "A Pinot Noir Beerenauslese – Willi Opitz 2005, which was a seamless match for the foie gras. They were just made to go with each other. The wine's acidity came through to cut the foie gras perfectly, but its sweetness also worked incredibly well with the raisins."

Portuguese wines strike a real chord with Craig, and over the years he's really come to love Portuguese red wine in particular. "Using Portuguese wines has been interesting for our chefs because it's still not something represented that well in restaurants. Over the years we've had some crackers, like the Cartuxa de Evora Reserva, Fundação Eugènio de Almeida, 1999 which went particularly well with Dieter Koschina's saddle of venison and port sauce. Because Dieter's restaurant Vila Joya is in the Algarve in Portugal, I used the opportunity to have all Portuguese wines, except for with the dessert.

"Portuguese wines tend to be robust and full bodied, so they go fantastically well with Nigel's food in particular as he has a real depth of flavour in his cooking – so I can match them quite easily to his food. In 2009 we did a fantastic roast loin of braised shoulder of Herdwick mutton with smoked mash and yellow beets and we served a Portuguese Vinha Pan Beiras Luis Pato 2003 with that."

Choosing wines year in, year out is a challenge, but one Craig enthuses about nonetheless. Does he ever get palette fatigue from all those tastings? He insists not. "There's a lot of tasting but I tend to use my brain as much as my palate. Like if there's a port wine in the sauce then porty style wine will go. It's not rocket science but it's about picking up on nuances of flavour and knowing what works together. After years of eating all over the world, which I've been lucky enough to do with Nigel, you learn what works."

Craig and Nigel would like to thank all those who have given them help and guidance with their wine choices over the years, especially our team of sommeliers who have worked alongside us over the 11 years. Special thanks goes to Julian Kaye from the Wright Wine Company, Guy Cliffe and all the team at Louis Roederer, Charles Metcalfe, Nick Adams MW, Miles Corish and all our wine friends.

HOSPITALITY ACTION

FOR OVER 170 YEARS HOSPITALITY ACTION, THE
HOSPITALITY INDUSTRY BENEVOLENT ORGANISATION,
HAS BEEN AT THE FOREFRONT OF THE INDUSTRY
PROVIDING SPECIALISED SUPPORT TO ALL WHO
WORK, OR HAVE WORKED WITHIN HOSPITALITY IN
THE UK AND WHO, THROUGH NO FAULT OF THEIR
OWN, FIND THEMSELVES IN CRISIS.

Hospitality Action offers vital assistance to those who need it most. The organisation supports people suffering from serious illnesses and helps those experiencing poverty, domestic violence and bereavement. Over 80 per cent of the help given to beneficiaries is due to severe financial hardship or life-changing illness while 74 per cent of those supported are under the age of 60.

The hospitality industry can be a demanding place to work with many employees exposed to drink and drugs. The Ark Foundation, part of Hospitality Action, helps tackle the problems of the excessive effects of these substances via educational seminars. These seminars are carried out by experienced industry professionals who have fallen victim to substance abuse. Since 2001 The Ark has spoken to 40,000 catering students offering advice on how to avoid peer pressure and cope with their heavy workplace demands.

Hospitality Action also issues grants to help with the cost of basic essential items such as food, clothing and central heating and supports those who have worked within the industry, but are now retired. This Family Members Scheme is a great way for beneficiaries to make new friends and catch up at regular lunches. They also receive a newsletter with interesting features and relevant news stories as well as being visited in their own homes by a friendly volunteer. The Volunteer Visitors provide someone to talk to in confidence as well as friendship for this often forgotten about group of individuals.

Hospitality Action hosts numerous exciting fundraising events throughout the year in the UK to raise much needed funds. The organisation is very fortunate to have support from a whole host of fabulous chefs, including Nigel Haworth with the Obsession festival and this cookbook.

For more information and ways to get involved and support the charity please visit the website at: **www. hospitalityaction.org.uk**

Heston Blumenthal.
Three Michelin stars.
Two restaurants.
One breakdown.

If Heston Blumenthal had a breakdown everyone would hear about it. But what if it happened to Sam Green?
Every year hundreds of people in our industry suffer a personal crisis. People you'll never hear about. Thankfully
Hospitality Action is always there to pick up the pieces. To make a donation or to find out more, contact us on
0870 3510160 or log on to www.hospitalityaction.org.uk **You look after others, we look after you.**

Raymond Blanc.
Top of his field.
Lowest point ever.

If Raymond Blanc lost his sight everyone would hear about it. But what if it happened to Mark Johnston?
Every year hundreds of people in our industry suffer from a disabling illness. People you'll never hear about.
Hospitality Action is always there to pick up the pieces. To make a donation or to find out more, contact us on
0870 3510160 or log on to www.hospitalityaction.org.uk **You look after others, we look after you.**

HOSPITALITY

Action

Industry Benevolent Organisation

Registered Charity No. 1101083

OBSESSION RECIPES / CHEFS' RESTAURANTS INDEX

ANDONI LUIS ADURIZ
Mugaritz
Spain
00 943 522 455
www.mugaritz.com
*French Toast Soaked in Egg Yolk,
Sauté Browned and Caramelised
Accompanied by an Ice Cream
Handmade with Raw Sheep's Milk*
page 162

ANDREW FAIRLIE
Restaurant Andrew Fairlie
Gleneagles
Scotland
01764 694431
www.andrewfairlie.com
Cep Tart, Roasted Calf's Sweetbread
page 76

ANDREW PERN
The Star Inn
North Yorkshire
01439 770397
www.thestaratharome.co.uk
*Grilled Black Pudding with
Pan-Fried Foie Gras, Salad of
Pickering Watercress, Apple and
Vanilla Chutney, Scrumpy Reduction*
page 136

ANGELA HARTNETT
Murano, Mayfair
London
020 7592 1222
www.angela-hartnett.com
Braised Halibut with Oxtail Ravioli
page 120

*Seared West Coast Scallops, Pata
Negra and Butternut Squash*
page 64

ANTHONY FLINN
Anthony's Restaurant
Leeds
0113 245 5922
www.anthonysrestaurant.co.uk
*Risotto of White Onion,
Parmesan Air, Espresso*
page 114

ATUL KOCHHAR
Benares Restaurant
London
020 7629 8886
www.benaresrestaurant.com
*Goan Spiced Lobster with Coconut
Sauce and Yoghurt Rice*
page 100

BRETT GRAHAM
The Ledbury
London
020 7792 9090
www.theledbury.com
*Pigeon Tea with Warm
Game Canapés*
page 94

BRIAN TURNER
www.brianturner.co.uk
*Roast Rack of English Veal, Butter
Braised Carrots and Parsley Potatoes*
page 256

BRUCE POOLE
Chez Bruce
London
020 8672 0114
www.chezbruce.co.uk
Deep Fried Turbot with Tartare Sauce
page 168

CHRIS GALVIN
Galvin La Chapelle
London
020 7299 0400
www.galvinrestaurants.com
*Assiette of Pyrenean Lamb with
Pommes Boulanger, Braised Fennel
and a Dried Fruit Condiment*
page 224

CHRISTIAN OLSSON
Vassa Eggen
Stockholm
00 468 216 169
www.vassaeggen.com
*Seafood Escabeche, Scallop, Lobster,
Octopus, Garlic Parsley Foam*
page 230

CLAIRE CLARK
*Amedei Toscano Nut Brown and Mandarin
Chocolate and Praline Mille-feuille*
page 32

CLAUDE BOSI
Hibiscus
London
020 7629 2999
www.hibiscusrestaurant.co.uk
*Meadowsweet Panna Cotta, Golden
Delicious Purée amd Shortbread*
page 156

DANIEL CLIFFORD
Midsummer House
Cambridge
01223 369299
www.midsummerhouse.co.uk
*Amuse Bouche, Cep,
Pumpkin and Mushroom*
page 88

DANYEL COUET
Fredsgatan 12
Stockholm
00 46 8 24 8052
www.fredsgatan12.com
*Bruschetta "Gourmande",
Black Truffle and Figs*
page 258

DARINA ALLEN
Ballymaloe Cookery School
Ireland
00 353 21 464 6785
www.cookingisfun.ie
Potato, Chorizo and Flat Parsley Soup
page 210

DAVID THOMPSON
Nahm
London
020 7333 1000
www.halkin.como.bz
Red Curry of Duck with Santol
page 158

DIETER KOSCHINA
Vila Joya
Portugal
00 351 289 591 795
www.vilajoya.de
Medallion of Lobster with Mashed
Potatoes and Ceps
page 186

ERIC CHAVOT
Formerly of The Capital
Gianduja and Orange Crumble
with Nougat
page 182

FERGUS HENDERSON
St John Bar & Restaurant
London
020 7553 9842
www.stjohnrestaurant.co.uk
Roast Bone Marrow and Parsley Salad
page 160

GERMAIN SCHWAB
Formerly of Winteringham Fields
Quasis Rump of Venison with Chestnut,
Mushrooms and Red Cabbage
Compote, Gnocchi and
Sauce Grand Veneur
page 248

GIORGIO LOCATELLI
Locanda Locatelli
London
020 7486 9271
www.locandalocatelli.com
Oxtail Ravioli
page 214

GLYNN PURNELL
Purnell's
Birmingham
0121 212 9799
www.purnellsrestaurant.com
Poached Egg Yolk, Smoked Haddock
Milk Foam, Cornflakes, Curry Oil
page 92

HESTON BLUMENTHAL
The Fat Duck
Bray-on-Thames
01628 580333
www.fatduck.co.uk
Snail Porridge, Jabugo Ham
page 234

HUGH FEARNLEY-WHITTINGSTALL
River Cottage
Axminster
www.rivercottage.net
Tasty Fish Soup with Chilli Rouille
page 30

JACOB JAN BOERMA
Restaurant De Leest
Netherlands
00 31 578 571 382
www.restaurantdeleest.nl
Lightly Grilled Turbot with Butternut
Squash, Two Preparations of Scallops,
Winter Truffle, Purslane and Jus of Truffle
and Olive Oil
page 74

JAMES MARTIN
The Leeds Kitchen
Leeds
0113 341 3202
www.theleedskitchen.co.uk/
www.jamesmartinchef.co.uk
Trio of Lissara Duck
page 38

JASON ATHERTON
Pollen Street Social
London
020 7290 7600
www.jasonatherton.co.uk
Sweetcorn Vanilla Panna Cotta
page 102

JEFF GALVIN
Galvin La Chapelle
London
020 7299 0400
www.galvinrestaurants.com
Smoked Quail Consommé,
Pithiver of Quail page
228

JOHN CAMPBELL
Coworth Park
Ascot
01344 876600
www.coworthpark.com
"Mandarin" Parfait, E'spuma, Granita
page 204

KEN HOM
Maison Chin
Bangkok
+66 (0) 2266 0505
www.maisonchin.com/www.kenhom.com
Spicy Hot and Sour Soup
page 62

KENNY ATKINSON
Kenny Atkinson at the Orangery, Rockliffe
Hall
Darlington
01325 729999
www.rockliffehall.com
North East Line Caught Mackerel,
Gooseberries, Lemon and Mustard
page 20

LISA ALLEN
Northcote
Lancashire
01254 240555
www.northcote.com
Valrhona Chocolate Cylinder,
Smoked Nuts, Salted Organic
Sheep's Milk Ice Cream
page 66

West Coast Scallops, Lime and Ginger
Infused, Salsify and Apple
page 36

MARK EDWARDS
Nobu
London
020 7290 9222
www.noburestaurants.com
Black Cod with Sweet Miso
page 116

OBSESSION RECIPES /
CHEFS' RESTAURANTS INDEX

MARK HIX
Hix Oyster and Chop House
London
020 7017 1930
www.hixoysterandchophouse.co.uk
Baked Razor Clams with Chorizo and Wild Garlic
page 166

MARTIN BURGE
The Dining Room, Whatley Manor
Malmesbury
01666 822888
www.whatleymanor.com
Chicory Mousse Layered with Bitter Coffee, Mascarpone Cream and Chocolate Leaves
page 22

MARTIN WISHART
Restaurant Martin Wishart
Edinburgh
0131 553 3557
www.martin-wishart.co.uk
Halibut Ceviche
page 26

**MATTHEW FORT &
TOM PARKER BOWLES**
*Petto D'Anatra con Orzotto E Zucca
(Duck Breast with Barley Risotto and Pumpkin)*
page 58

MICHAEL CAINES
Gidleigh Park
Devon
01647 432367
www.gidleigh.com
Pan Fried Scallops with Celeriac Purée, Truffle Vinaigrette and Tomato Lamb Jus
page 144

MICHEL ROUX JR
Le Gavroche
London
020 7408 0881
www.le-gavroche.co.uk
Bitter Chocolate and Pear Tart, White Chocolate Ice Cream
page 140

NATHAN OUTLAW
Restaurant Nathan Outlaw
Cornwall
www.nathan-outlaw.com
Wreckfish, Mussels and Saffron with Red Pepper and Black Olives
page 70

NEIL WIGGLESWORTH
Formerly of Twin Farms
USA
Heather-Fed Bowland Lamb, Morecambe Bay Shrimp, Dry-Cured Ham and Herb Polenta
page 238

NICK NAIRN
Nick Nairn Cook School
Scotland
01877 389900
www.nicknairncookschool.com
Warm Salad of Wood Pigeon, Stornoway Black Pudding, Fifeshire Bacon and Cumberland Sauce Topped with Crispy Parsnips
page 278

NIGEL HAWORTH
Northcote
Lancashire
01254 240555
www.northcote.com
"Hindle Wakes" Goosnargh Chicken Broth Flavoured with Dried Plums, Brown Rice, Streaky Bacon and Basil
page 240
Apple Crumble Soufflé, Lancashire Cheese Ice Cream
page 260
Confit Shoulder of Lamb Studded with Rosemary and Garlic, Poached Plum Tomatoes, French Beans, Purée Potatoes
page 270
Free-Range Chicken 'Indian Game', Black Peas, Bacon, Medjool Dates, Game Chips
page 44
Goosnargh Cornfed Duckling Breast, Duck Straws, Spicy Red Cabbage, Mead
page 194

Local Game Baked in Butter Puff Pastry, Celeriac Purée
page 128
Seared Dexter Beef, Wild Herb and Salsify Salad, Lime Caramel, Roast Marrowbone
page 174
Tiny Melting Valrhona Chocolate Desserts
page 106
Treacle Salmon, Scallops, Pickled Ginger
page 218
Venison Carpaccio, Mushroom Pâté, Pickled Damsons, Hazelnuts
page 78
Warm Loin of Herdwick Mutton, Jerusalem Artichokes, Honey and Mint Dressing
page 150

PAUL CUNNINGHAM
The Paul
Copenhagen
00 45 3375 0775
www.thepaul.dk
Local Rabbit Grilled with Langoustines from Læsø
page 142

PAUL HEATHCOTE
Heathcotes
Preston
01772 200232
www.heathcotes.co.uk
Heathcote's Bread and Butter Pudding, Apricot Compote, Clotted Cream
page 104

PETER GORDON
The Providores and Tapas Room
London
020 7935 6175
www.theprovidores.co.uk
Chocolate Cake with Salted Almond Cream and Cranberry Rosewater Compote
page 202

PHIL HOWARD
The Square
London
020 7495 7100
www.squarerestaurant.org
*Banana Soufflé with
Chocolate Ice Cream*
page 232

*Braised Veal Cheek with a Fricassee
of Hand Rolled Macaroni, Cauliflower
and Truffle*
page 146

*Escabeche of Red Mullet with Sardine
Chantilly and Anchovies*
page 190

*Field Mushroom Velouté,
English Breakfast Garnish*
page 124

*Glazed Chicken Wings with Parmesan
Gnocchi, Field Mushroom Purée
and Black Truffle Jelly*
page 170

Kedgeree
page 96

*Mille-Feuille of Red Mullet and
Aubergines with a Vinaigrette of
Sardines and Wild Rocket*
page 252

*Sauté of Tiger Prawns with a Tarte
Fine of Onion and Thyme*
page 212

*Terrine of Dover Sole with Smoked
Eel and Oysters*
page 72

Tortellini of Crab with Herbs
page 274

PIERRE KOFFMANN
Koffmann's, The Berkeley
London
020 7235 1010
www.the-berkeley.co.uk
Pistachio Soufflé
page 118

RAYMOND BLANC
Le Manoir Aux Quat' Saisons
Oxfordshire
01844 278881
www.manoir.com
*Poached Fillet of Turbot, Oyster;
Cucumber and Wasabi Jus*
page 138

RICHARD CORRIGAN
Bentley's Oyster Bar and Grill
London
www.bentleys.org
0207 734 4756
*Crubeens, Jubuga Ham with
Woodland Sorrel, Beetroot and
Horseradish Remoulade*
page 192

ROBBIE MILLAR
*Seared Scallops with a Purée of Carrot
and Ginger, Crispy Carrots, Chinese
Five Spice*
page 254

ROWLEY LEIGH
Le Café Anglais
London
020 7221 1415
www.lecafeanglais.co.uk
*Partridge with Pigs' Trotters
and Lentils*
page 208

ROY BRETT
Ondine Restaurant
Edinburgh
www.ondinerestaurant.co.uk
*Fish and Shellfish Soup with Rouille
and Parmesan*
page 188

SAT BAINS
Restaurant Sat Bains
Nottingham
0115 986 6566
www.restaurantsatbains.com
*Dry Aged Scotch Beef,
"Textures" of the Onion Family*
page 184

Mutton with Beer, Shallots and Herbs
page 40

SHANE OSBORN
Pied à Terre
London
020 7636 1178
www.pied-de-terre.co.uk
*Venison with Celeriac and
Chanterelles*
page 126

SHAUN RANKIN
Bohemia Bar and Restaurant
Jersey
01534 880 588
www.bohemiajersey.com
*Lightly Poached Royal Bay Oysters
with Sevruga Caviar, Saffron Noodles
and Lemon Butter*
page 90

SIMON ROGAN
L'Enclume, Cartmel
Cumbria
01539 536362
www.lenclume.co.uk
*Jerusalem Artichokes, Flesh and Skin,
Soft Malt, Goat's Cheese, Calamint,
Howbarrow Shoots*
page 28

TERRY LAYBOURNE
Café 21
Newcastle upon Tyne
0191 222 0755
www.cafetwentyone.co.uk
*Coconut Panna Cotta with
Tropical Fruits*
page 268

THEO RANDALL
The Intercontinental
London
020 7409 3131
www.intercontinental.com
*Pan Fried Scallops with Chilli, Sage,
Capers and Anchovies*
page 60

TOM KITCHIN
The Kitchin
Edinburgh
0131 555 1755
www.thekitchin.com
Razor Clams
page 56

VIVEK SINGH
The Cinnamon Club
London
020 7222 2555
www.cinnamonclub.com
*Tandoori Breast of Squab Pigeon, Smoked
Paprika Raita*
page 42

SPONSORS

ASHE PARK FINE WATERS

ASHLEIGH SIGNS LTD

BAKER BOOTHMAN & EDY LTD

BARCLAYS COMMERCIAL BANK

BAXTER STOREY

BEGBIES TRAYNOR GROUP

BELL TRAILER RENTAL LTD

BLACKBURN ROVERS FOOTBALL CLUB

BMI HEALTHCARE

BOOTHS SUPERMARKETS

BOWKER BMW

CARDBOARD BOX COMPANY LTD

C N G FOOD SERVICE EQUIPMENT LTD

DUNBIA

EBLEX

EPS LTD

FARMHOUSE FARE LTD

HALLIWELLS COMMERCIAL LAW FIRM

H GREAVES & SON (MEAT PRODUCTS) LTD

H G STEPHENSON LTD

INSHORE FISHERIES LTD

J R TAYLOR ST ANNES

KING HENRY VI SPRING WATER

LANCASHIRE AND BLACKPOOL TOURIST BOARD

LOUIS ROEDERER CHAMPAGNE

MAUREEN COOKSON LTD

M N H PLATINUM LTD

NEALES WASTE MANAGEMENT LTD

NORTH WEST FINE FOODS

PRESTON AUDI & BLACKBURN AUDI

RIBBLE VALLEY JOINERY AND BUILDING

RICHARD WELLOCKS & SON

RICKETT MITCHELL AND PARTNERS LTD

RILEYHOLMES LTD

SHARROCKS FRESH PRODUCE LTD

ST JOHN'S COLLEGE CATERING & CONFERENCE CENTRE

SYNEXUS CLINICAL RESEARCH LTD

TASTE LANCASHIRE

TASTE TRADITION LTD

THE BEARDWOOD HOSPITAL

THE LIVESEY GROUP

THE MALL BLACKBURN

THE WRIGHT WINE COMPANY LTD

THWAITES BREWERY

TOTAL FOOD SERVICE SOLUTIONS LTD

VILLEROY & BOCH

WAVERLEY TBS

WELLGATE FISHERIES

ZEUS GROUP